CHARLIE

C·H·A·R·L·I·E

The improbable life and times of
CHARLES MacARTHUR

by Ben Hecht

ILLUSTRATED

 HARPER & BROTHERS

Publishers, New York

To HELEN HAYES MAC ARTHUR

Contents

A section of illustrations follows page 84.

My Charlie

ONCE I asked Edward Sheldon to describe Ellen Terry, the actress, on stage. He was silent for a while, carefully summoning the exact descriptive words—then he said, "She was like a shaft of light in a dim room." That was all. Ardent neophyte of the theatre that I was, I pressed for details. How did she look, how did she speak, walk—what did she do to make the magic? It was no use, he told me; the brightness of the light she shed bedazzled the critical faculties, obliterated detail.

I have thought of that conversation often as I have tried to talk about Charlie with Ben—or as I have watched Ben struggle with the problem of translating a shaft of light into words. Light affects everything it touches differently. It makes beauty more beautiful, the shabby more shabby; the invisible to take on substance, the dull to glow a little, the brilliant to send out sparkles in all the colors there are.

Charlie was a different man to everyone he touched. The only thing that everyone seems to agree on is that he was special. All of us who knew him had our own private personal Charlie created after our own needs. Gay people thought him the gayest, people in trouble had a way of calling him "poor Charlie" and dumping their troubles into his lap—"to help him forget" his own. Timid people, afraid to project themselves with others, felt at ease with him and tried to help him over his shyness. Pompous people whom he had an irresistible urge to deflate usually adopted him—since they figured they alone really understood him. Rascals recognized a kindred spirit—a partner in mischief. Good people felt especially close to him. The minister of our church in Nyack called him a true man of God.

Ben must have had quite a time with the avalanche of "Charlies" that swept down on him when it became known he was writing this book. So many wanted their "Charlie" to be understood: "This story I want to tell Ben about Charlie and me brings out a wholly different side of the man that would amaze you. . . ." I had long since got over being amazed at the "wholly different sides" of Charlie. The one thing left to amaze me is that for all our possessiveness, our pursuit, our searching, Charlie eluded us to the end. He remained his secret self.

Brave, wise Ben, to hold fast to his own Charlie . . . his Roman candle of a man.

My Charlie would not have been spectacular enough to be a book. He was my gentle lover, my understanding husband, my gay companion, the sympathetic father of our children. How could you make a book out of that? But it made a lovely life.

I hail Ben's Charlie with gratitude and delight.

HELEN HAYES MACARTHUR

Mexico, 1957

Youth
and
Chicago

Charlie

I HAVE in my keeping the memory of a unique man, Charles MacArthur.

He was a newspaperman, a playwright, a soldier, a story writer, a worker in the Hollywood jute mills and a traveler as nimble and mysterious as Prester John.

He married Helen Hayes, who was to become the theatre's "first lady."

His gay and macabre antics as a newspaperman are part of a "legendary" Chicago still talked about in its saloons and pressrooms. His first book, *A Bug's Eye View of the War*, was a shout of laughter such as had never come from any battlefield. His playwriting in *Lulu Belle*, *The Front Page*, *Twentieth Century* added a lustiness to the theatre. His movie writing was equally arresting—*Rasputin*, *The Sin of Madelon Claudet*, *Rip Tide*, *Gunga Din*, *Barbary Coast*, *Crime Without Passion*, *Wuthering Heights*, *The Scoundrel*. We collaborated on some of these entertainments but I'll not deny him praise out of co-author modesty.

His soldiering began in his teens in Mexico and continued through the First and Second World Wars. (An ulcer kept him out of Korea.) The rank under which he attended the last excitement—lieutenant colonel—embarrassed him slightly. He was always, in his mind, a soldier without authority, out to frolic amid danger.

But if I wrote of each of these activities in full I'd miss the man by a mile. The main thing about MacArthur was his attractiveness.

He had a remarkable allure for every human who came across him. There may have been some self-sunk, carping sidewalk stander who, meeting MacArthur, let him pass with-

3

out notice. You can always bank on a blind man or two lining the curbstones.

To the rest of us MacArthur was as definite an attraction as a hit play on Broadway. Men and women fell in love with him all over the place—on boats, planes, deserts, mountains and a score of foreign climes where he functioned without language.

This last was a considerable lessening, for MacArthur's talk was festive and acrobatic. He was of those wastrel geniuses who find the pencil a gag, and paper a gunnysack. Relieved of these trade tools, MacArthur was a shelfful of minnesingers.

Yet this nabob of words was equally effective without them. With his vocabulary locked in his wallet, his spirit went traveling. In France, China, Italy and Mexico he moved amid cronies like a dumb-show Cyrano. He seldom laughed, never boasted, and lolled in an alien barroom as relaxed as a beauty in her bath. Corsairs, panhandlers and hyperthyroids came pantomiming to his table. In the grin that slightly turned the edges of his lips, and in the foggy look of his eyes, there lurked always the promise of "lively doings."

This was a pet phrase of his. He treasured a postal card sent him by Hilda, cook for the MacArthur household, who had returned in 1938 to her home base in Berlin.

"Dear Mr. MacArthur," wrote the effervescent Teuton, "I am happy to be home. Adolf Hitler is a fine boss and there's lots of lively doings."

The understatement of tragedy and disaster was part of MacArthur's style. Like Cyrano, he would defend a cause with his life, but he would speak of it mockingly, if at all.

Some Last Words

I'LL write something here about my friend's spirit before going on to the tale of his lively doings. Were he collaborating on this I'm sure MacArthur would say, "To hell with psychology. Let the story tell it."

My friend had a snake's cunning for psychology and could spot inner quirks quicker than an analyst from Vienna. But he was not one for voicing the science. Like most men in hiding, he was opposed to discoursing on addresses.

As a result, this teller of exuberant anecdote who could talk the night away left behind chiefly a memory of reticence. None of the thousand friends, including the women who loved him—except one—knew him deeply. Of our forty years of friendship I can remember hundreds of things he did, but nothing he felt. He never told me.

Since we are not collaborating, at least not in the way we used to, I'll veto the MacArthur advice and run on about his spirit. But I'll skip those matters of which psychiatrists write —the gaudy frets and guilts that set us all to banging our heads against walls. My friend was a Roman holiday of wry urges, but they had as little to do with his spirit as the paint on an altar has to do with its holiness.

By spirit I mean the shield and sword with which a man meets existence. MacArthur's spirit was the product of awareness of death. He was born without the illusion of permanence. He knew, at the beginning, the road's end.

The philosophers say that the concern with death makes a man either poet or saint. My friend was neither, openly. And he may turn in his grave at my hinting at such news. For he was a man of much modesty. He disliked overstatement as most people dislike arson or purse-snatching. But I have made the hint and I'll let it stand.

5

From the day I first met him at nineteen till the day he died at sixty, my friend had his eye on mortality. He did not brood on his dying, even when its hour came near. But he lived with it. It was the dream under his hat.

Last hours were a minor hobby for my friend. A flash of wit from a death cell or a guillotine received his homage. His favorite was that of the French marquis who, listening to the pompous death warrant sentencing him to the Robespierre guillotine, interrupted irritably with the phrase: "Tut, tut—the style of Diderot."

When the time came, MacArthur had his own line of wit for tragedy. Recovering consciousness before dying, he looked at the conclave of white-coated medicos around him in the hospital room and inquired, "What the hell is this—a block party?" A few minutes later he managed another utterance: "If you sawbones will cease your attentions and vamoose I promise to put a feather in the cap of medicine. I'll walk out of here on my own two legs."

His wife, Helen, sat close to him and said softly to his silent face, "I love you." Opening his eyes for a last time, he answered brightly, "You should," and died.

Tale of the Young Sleuth

HE was all his life a man with a light of amusement in his eyes. He created laughter and diversion as other men create steel industries and department stores. Yet it was death he held hands with all the while.

His first writings were of hangmen, morgues, death cells and funeral parlors. He wrote gaily of them. They had for him the merriment which familiarity brings into the mind.

Of the hundreds of tales about MacArthur I pick the Carl Wanderer story as an opener. Like most of Charlie's early adventures. death was in it, and a Dickensian grin at its details.

The story was a murder classic in Chicago's twenties—when the Windy City led the world in the matter of riddled corpses.

On his way home from the movies one summer night with his young wife, World War I hero Lieutenant Carl Wanderer was confronted by a seedy-looking figure in the hallway of his apartment building. The seedy one with drawn gun demanded his money or his life. Trained to combat, the lieutenant whipped out his own weapon and shot it out with the highwayman. Wanderer brought him down with two slugs in the belly, and then jumped on him and banged the dying man's head on the ground until it cracked. But he was too late. The thug had already shot Mrs. Wanderer, killing her instantly.

This was Wanderer's story, backed up by his war medals. The police, with the American Legion whooping over the bereaved veteran's valor, were moved to believe it. But there was something about Wanderer that didn't go down with fellow-veteran MacArthur, reporter for the *Examiner*. The lieutenant had a smugness in his talk and a pair of bragging eyes that started the young Hearst reporter off on a trail. The trail was the checking of the gun in the dead man's hand.

I, too, was on the story for the *Daily News*; and I, too, had my suspicions. It was during these days that our friendship took on the dimension of collaboration.

Charlie's suspicions resulted from a compassion for the dead man, whom he titled in print "the Ragged Stranger." The starveling look of the corpse gave Charlie a hunch that no such puny fellow would prowl the streets with an army pistol in his pockets—with wrist muscles hardly strong enough to point the weapon.

"He's the kind of man who mutters at you on the corner for a cup of coffee," said Charlie.

My suspicions came out of an interview with Wanderer the morning after the battle in the vestibule. Wanderer was in his shorts, freshly shaved, pressing his pants and whistling "It's a Long Way to Tipperary."

His face was too pink and he seemed too happy for a man

whose wife had been shot to death a few hours before. I had read in a book by Dr. Stekel, an early Freudian robin, that homosexuals grew much disturbed when their wives became pregnant. Faced with such proof of their unwanted manhood, they sometimes became violent. My lectures on the subject to homicide chief Norton puckered his brow. He summoned the war hero for a second grilling, and learned his wife had been pregnant.

In the meantime Charlie was busy on two trails—the Ragged Stranger's gun, and the Ragged Stranger himself. No one had come forward to identify the dead man. A bartender named Andy put in a bid for the corpse. He laid it in state on the end of the bar, and doubled his business. Hundreds passed through the saloon to see if the Ragged Stranger was known to them, and paused to shake their heads over a beer.

A curious occurrence in the City Morgue a while back had made possible this barroom display. The event had brought about the partial embalming of all accident and murder victims just as soon as they arrived in their baskets. Charlie had covered that story and added a man of fascination to his days. He was Denis McCarthy, keeper of the City Morgue and known as First Search McCarthy to his friends. Denis was the first to shake out the pockets of his cold arrivals. Denis McCarthy's assistant was a powerful-looking Negro named Walter. Wallie was a modest, sober and attentive washer of the dead. When the mystery gripped the morgue, Wallie was the last one First Search suspected. The mystery was a matter of corpse mutilation. Every week or so some animal gnawed off part of a cadaver.

Wallie turned out to be the culprit. He suffered from periodic throwbacks to cannibalism. He had tackled an undertaker's reject, and a dose of embalming fluid had put an end to him. After this matter was cleared up by coroner's physician Joe Springer, the rule of half embalming the morgue bodies went into effect.

Some weeks after the Ragged Stranger was killed, Charlie ran down the real murderer of Mrs. Wanderer, and put a noose around his neck. It was the man he had suspected on first sight, the war-hero husband.

The gun in the hand of the dead man in the vestibule was a Colt, serial number 2282. The Colt factory said 2282 was part of a shipment to Van Lengerke & Antoine, a Chicago store. The store's records showed it had been purchased by John Hoffman in 1913.

Charlie interviewed Hoffman.

"I gave the gun to a friend of mine," Hoffman said, "a fella named Fred."

"Fred who?" Charlie asked.

"Fred Wanderer," said Hoffman.

An hour later Charlie asked Fred Wanderer, "Did you lend a gun to your cousin Carl? A Colt, serial number 2282?"

Fred Wanderer fainted dead away.

Carl was brought to Homicide again. After sixteen tall tales about 2282, Wanderer confessed. It was his gun. The Ragged Stranger had been unarmed.

When he finished killing his young wife, and the bum he had hired "to pull a little gag," Wanderer had wiped the 2282 barrel clean and stuck it in the dying man's hand.

"This is how it was," said Wanderer in his confession. "I picked up the bum in a saloon. I told him I had a lot of money that I didn't want my wife to get her hands on. His job was to pretend to hold me up and pretend he took the money from me. I told him I'd meet him afterward, and give him twenty-five bucks for being a pal."

The Wanderer objective was the murder of his missus. War-hero Wanderer was a pansy and his psyche was in trouble because his wife was pregnant.

"Yes, I murdered my wife," Wanderer told Captain Norton, "because I hated married life. . . . I think the thought of becoming a father must have driven me mad."

Oddly, Charlie and I, who had collaborated on putting Wanderer's neck in the noose, were much admired by the lieutenant marking time before the gallows. We were the only two reporters with whom he would play rummy in his death cell, "for cash." It was the one time I ever saw MacArthur win at cards. He held a hand of cards in his large fingers as if they were bandages, and he played them with equal misunderstanding.

A day before the hanging, MacArthur came to the death cell with a favor to ask of our Carl, who had run out of funds the night before and owed us some ten dollars.

"We'll call it off," said Charlie. Carl thanked him. "What I'd like to know," continued Charlie, "is if you have anything in mind for your last words."

"Nothing in particular," the doomed man replied.

"Good," said MacArthur, "because I've written a speech that I'd like you to recite—before the event. It's only a half page long."

"I'm not good at memorizing," our Carl said, "especially now."

"How about just reading it?" MacArthur said.

"Let's hear it first," Carl said. "I don't want to say anything up there that might be against the grain."

"Fair enough," MacArthur conceded.

He read the speech out loud. It was a spicy attack on the character of the *Examiner's* city editor, Frank Carson.

Wanderer chuckled and said it was just the thing.

I asked MacArthur if I could add a few lines to it. My friend magnanimously agreed. I wrote several sentences exposing the habits of James Gilruth. Mr. Gilruth was my city editor on the *News*.

"That will teach them not to point," said MacArthur.

Our plot went agley. In the lust of authorship we had forgotten that the first thing that happened to a man on a gallows was that his arms were strapped to his sides.

"Have you anything you wanna say?" Warden Jacobi asked of the man with the rope around his neck.

"Yes," our Carl answered loyally.

His eyes strained toward the sheet of typewritten paper three feet away in his tethered hand. Then, with an apologetic look at the two authors out front, the war hero threw back his head and started singing, "Dear Old Pal o' Mine."

The drop banged and the song ended. Our first venture in collaboration died unheard on the gallows air.

"Down the River Bank with Spring"

I'LL save the stories about MacArthur as a newspaperman for a further page. I am still busy with the MacArthur basic fact, the odd attractiveness. Among the iron-plated egos of that newspaper world, MacArthur was as much the charmer as he was ever to be in flossier circles. There was neither push nor drive in him. He was going nowhere, with no favors to confer. Nor was his voice loud, nor his wit running wild. He was, in fact, more silent than is usual in youth. Yet we sat around him as if awaiting something.

Saki writes in his droll tragedy *The Unbearable Bassington* of two schoolmasters discussing the pawky youths in their charge. Says one of the masters, "We must always remember they are Nature's raw material." Says the other master, with a cautious glance at Bassington, "There are some boys who are Nature's finished product."

Alexander Woollcott, the sprightly outcast who devoted his life to making a family of his betters, wrote of MacArthur, one of his favorite "relatives": "It is sometimes easiest to convey an impression of such difficult portrait subjects by trying to visualize them in the costume of whatever century seems their natural background. You may picture MacArthur, if you will, in Lincoln green and pointed cap. He clearly belongs in the early thirteenth century, astray, as like as not, from Robin Hood's band, and vaguely headed for the Holy Land, but (with all his worldly goods done up in a handkerchief) sitting, for the nonce, outside an English inn and willing to delay his pilgrimage indefinitely in swapping yarns and a mug of ale with any passing friar."

Woollcott was not only a master of punctuation, as the foregoing reveals, but a man of perception where his friends were concerned. He perceived in MacArthur, on whom he doted to the end of his own life, a man far away. But the road on which Woollcott saw him squatting in his pointed cap with his mug of ale (a drink Charlie hated) was no point in history. It was the road of youth from which, though his hair whitened and his belly thickened, my friend would never venture. He was a finished product and his wisdom told him there was no better place.

I remember him at the beginning. Muscled arms and heavy fists, a lean, longish face, untelltale eyes, gypsy hair with a widow's peak, a pointed nose with an oversensitive tip, a mouth clown-turned at the edges, the neckline of a hungry man, slow moving and as full of graceful posture as an artist's model, unable to dance, sing or pay long attention to anything, smiling when others laughed, still drinking when comas took his companions, uttering brief lines from Rossetti, Swinburne, Matthew, Luke, Mark and Job, and as detached from world problems as a man basking on a pier—this was our young friend, fresh from the mint and beckoning like a gold piece.

This MacArthur allure extended even into the badlands of our town. (We called them badlands in print but poked around in them as happily as if they were our grandmother's attic.) Not only the drinking scribes and fancy hostesses were after Charles, but gangsters and killers were keen for his society.

The sawed-off-shotgun menace Deanie O'Bannion was a chum of MacArthur's. O'Bannion ran a flower shop on the near North Side and practiced murder after store hours. He was a dimple-cheeked Irishman with a soft voice, and a first-rate flower salesman. He was finally shot to death in the window of his shop, expiring in a bank of Easter lilies on display.

It was believed by the police, who were always vague about such events, that O'Bannion had been paid off for participation in the St. Valentine's Day Massacre. On that occasion, a dozen or so gangsters had been lined up, faces to a brick garage wall, and murdered "by parties unknown."

O'Bannion's fondness for MacArthur included free posies from his flower shop, thus enabling my friend to shine beyond his salary as a Don Juan. It included also automobile rides in the Chicago dawn.

O'Bannion would arrive at the Stillson or Quincy Number 9 saloon, pluck MacArthur from Howey's side and be off with him for a canter in the O'Bannion flivver as the sun was coming up over Grant Park (our downtown lake front). The route was always the same. Turning into Michigan Avenue at Randolph Street, O'Bannion would scorn the highway and urge his car up on the broad sidewalk. Scooting along the sidewalk, O'Bannion would continue to Twelfth Street in what he called his daily bullfight. His flivver was the bull, and pedestrians and policemen were *toreros* and matadors. There were no casualties. Everyone abroad at this hour knew it was O'Bannion and gave gangway to the flivver.

"You're not going with that low, dirty, murdering bastard," said Editor Howey to his ace reporter one dawn in Quincy 9. "You're going home and go to bed."

"I'll sleep better if I relax first," said MacArthur, with a smile for O'Bannion. "Deanie is my sandman."

Out of this untroubled time, I recall another sportive incident full of psychology. It was MacArthur's first bid to the ballrooms of fashion. He was due at the Dudley mansion on the Gold Coast at nine for dinner and black-tie small talk.

Dressed in a borrowed tuxedo, known among us then as a "wedding suit," MacArthur walked moodily eastward through a night of falling snow. At Dearborn Street he paused and addressed himself to two taxi drivers parked in front of a saloon, awaiting fares.

The two drivers sat listening with some surprise to a flow of insults coming from the fashionable-looking man in the snow. Stung finally into movement, both leaped from their cabs and closed in on their detractor. They were husky fellows and the fight lasted five minutes. At its finish MacArthur was minus two teeth, and the drivers lay dormant in the snow. Said MacArthur, who was to attend a thousand glittering parties, "I hoped they might stop me."

Comedy Cannon

IN that pre-World War I time, we still had our war veterans with tales to tell of Cuba, China, the Transvaal and the Philippines. The youngest of these veterans was MacArthur. He had interrupted his cub days to march off to Mexico with the Illinois militia under Colonel Milton Foreman.

It was a cavalry outfit, and every saddle and saber in it was the apple of Colonel Foreman's eye. Black Jack Pershing, in charge of the hostilities, dubbed it "Colonel Foreman's Dog and Pony Show."

Our patriotic objective in that time was the overthrow of Pancho Villa and his *insurrectos*. That Pancho turned out to be the beloved liberator of Mexico and the permanent scourge of its tyrants was an error that interested MacArthur neither then nor later.

"War is war," he said, "and politicians are politicians."

About MacArthur in Mexico, hell-bent after Pancho, I recall that my friend and another young warrior named Jed Kiley ran a regimental journal intended to celebrate the cunning and valor of Colonel Foreman. And that during the heroic campaign, wherever MacArthur and Kiley trod, rivers flowed uphill, señoritas stormed the tents, rum poured out of the palm trees, and commanding officers were torn between suicide and desertion.

In another decade MacArthur and his bride Helen were New Year's Eve guests at the Tavern Club in Chicago.

"I want you to meet my first colonel," said Charles, and brought his Helen to a table where sat the Pancho Villa chaser, Colonel Milton Foreman. After introducing his bride, Charles added, "I was with you in Mexico, Colonel."

"Any man who fought with me is always welcome at my side," the colonel beamed. "Please, sit down."

MacArthur sat down, and a proud Helen with him.

"What did you say your name was?" the colonel added.

"Charles MacArthur," the battle buddy answered.

Helen told me the incident.

"The colonel's face turned slowly purple," she said, "and his eyes seemed to go out of focus. Then, without saying a word, he stood up and stalked away. Charlie was pretty young to have been a soldier, and I guess he must have given Colonel Foreman some trouble."

It was on his return from his Mexican activities that I first saw MacArthur. I was covering the parade of Colonel Foreman's militia heroes, home from the war. Some hundred thousand citizens filled the sidewalks from Madison Street to Congress Street waiting impatiently for a first sight of the sunburned militia and its victorious banners.

Pancho Villa had not been captured or suppressed, but adventure had been served. And who asked for more in that merry time?

A roar went up from the sidewalks. The parade was finally coming. The two hundred policemen pushed the jubilant crowds sternly back on the curbings.

We saw a single battered automobile moving oddly down the empty street. It zigzagged from curb to curb. A uniformed soldier sat at the wheel, steering with one hand and waving a topheavy American flag with the other. He was Private Charles MacArthur. Never a good driver, in this hour of triumph MacArthur careened from sidewalk to sidewalk, waving his flag and shouting strange battle cries. "Down with Colonel Foreman!" "Down with Tin-pants Milton!"

The crowd, albeit a bit let down by so small a military display, cheered loyally. Five minutes later the regimental bands sounded in the distance. And a red-faced, glowering Colonel Foreman appeared on horseback leading his Illinois Uhlans down the avenue.

MacArthur was placed under military arrest that evening and removed to the militia headquarters at Fort Sheridan. Here for two days he moved around the grounds of the fort picking up pieces of paper with the end of a stick and dropping them into a disposal bag hanging from his shoulder. He was dressed in a prisoner suit of blue overall denim.

On the second day, a Sunday, Colonel Foreman, presiding at a lawn fete in front of the North Shore Fortress, was startled by a cry from a friendly dowager beside him: "Milton, what is that general doing?"

The "general" was MacArthur. He had improved his prisoner's suit with gold radiator paint, adding epaulets and many other decorations. And he was picking up bits of paper with a sword and dropping them into a bag painted with two crossed American flags. His bearing befitted his splendor. He marched stiffly up to each bit of paper, saluted, stabbed it with his sword and deposited it in his bag.

Colonel Foreman ordered the "general" removed at once from the lawn fete. That evening, dismissing MacArthur indignantly from the army, the colonel said:

"I don't know what the hell's going to become of you. But I'm sure of one thing. You're never going to make a soldier."

It was among the more idiotic of military prophecies. Soldiering was to be one of MacArthur's chief callings. He was to be in all the wars that followed, of his own volition, always a strain on discipline but a delight to all good men at arms.

Happy Warriors

WAR was one of MacArthur's homelands, and he brought to it an unwavering standard. He was a gay soldier. His book recounting his artillery service in World War I is the only witty story of battle and death that I have read. In it a mysterious joke sounds above the bloodiest cannon barrages. The pursuit of laughter continues amid exploding shells as if they were the *décor* of some carnival.

The book is funny on the subject of men fighting and dying. Nor was it written with attitudes invented in retrospect. It was written immediately after the shooting ended. MacArthur's infatuated war buddies insisted, before they were demobilized, that he write an account of the "fun" they had all had together. They chipped in and paid for the book's publication. The title page reads:

A BUG'S EYE VIEW OF THE WAR

In which the Various Deeds performed
by a Battery of Field Artillery in
Foreign Lands during the years 1917
and 1918 are Set Down in the Hope
they may recall to Doddering Old
Age the Scenes of Our Warrior Days—
when they are Long Since gone.

Privately printed by members of
Battery F, One Hundred and Forty
Ninth United States Field Artillery.

I know of no other such document in either military or literary annals. Dead and wounded pile up around Battery F at Cantigny, Château-Thierry and the Argonne. Blood flows. Bodies are shattered. Exhaustion and death ring iron bells.

They are given a grudging phrase here and there. "There were tears." "He was dead."

Mirth, however, remains the soul of the book. And in the presence of death always the smile of Cyrano.

I have seen MacArthur fight with his fists. At such times his lips turned up and amusement stayed in his eyes. I imagine the same expression stood beside his seventy-five at Cantigny. And singlehanded the Lone Musketeer seems to have infected the whole of Battery F. Its survivors considered his antic, hooligan tale to be a true account of battles as seen and felt by the soldiers who had fought them. Salutay—Buck Bristol, Pryor, Yacullo, Daugherty, MacFarland, "late of Senn High School," Pappy de Prohon, Red Lawrence, Chuck Bull, Ross Braun, Harry Kaulocouris, Bud Huling, Karl Geisendorfer, Herb Mooney, Dick Patton, Andy Gartner, all you who laughed in battle with a young MacArthur.

The same Pied Piper who had trailed through Chicago evidently helped load the guns in the Argonne.

Two Battle Tidbits

For a time after 1918, MacArthur specialized in war anecdotes. To retell anecdotes of a witty man is like staging a play without scenery or footlights. And the wrong cast. A man dies and his anecdotes hang in the air like lessening echoes. It is like watching a soul vanish.

When my friend told them they were listened to with delight because they were unlike any war tales coming from the two million other returned doughboys. Apparently the A.E.F. and the MacArthur had fought on two different fronts.

"Our battery," said MacArthur at a famed dinner table, "got a little bored with saluting its officers as was demanded by the rules of war. So we cooked up a plan to improve our own social standing without disturbing this army caste system.

Every morning at breakfast, if there was a breakfast, we elected a caliph from our lowly midst. Only privates, in fact, were eligible for this supreme honor.

"And for the rest of the day every private addressing his caliph had to bow low two times and begin each conversation with the august words, 'O Commander of the Faithful, is it true that, etc.'

"It made our officers seem small potatoes when you saw us privates constantly salaaming to a fellow private and using only high-flown language."

There was another story MacArthur never tired of telling, unmindful of how often I had heard it.

"It was on the way to Cantigny," went this tale. "Our battery was enfiladed by enemy fire on a railroad embankment. The Heinies had drawn a bead on us and were peppering us with big shells. We'd been ordered to halt, and stand by our half-witted artillery horses. I stood watching the goddamn shells explode, each a few inches nearer my toes. Finally our officer came out of his siesta and gave the order to take cover. I let go my nag and dived off the embankment. I landed head first in an abandoned German latrine. Smothered by enemy crap, and with shells blasting all around, I got an optimistic feeling. I said to myself, 'MacArthur, this is the lowest point in your life. From here on everything has got to be an improvement.' "

I remember the indignation one night at the swanky home of Samuel Chotzinoff, the music critic. He gave a party at which piano virtuosi and international baritones were to perform. Most of the tuxedoed and tiaraed music lovers of the town were on hand.

Mr. Chotzinoff was miffed because nothing could pry those same music aficionados out of the kitchen, where MacArthur stood talking the night away.

With his anecdotes he brought back a little repertoire of songs. He sang them shyly and a bit off tune. And he learned to play them on the clarinet and the harmonica. One of his lyrical favorites ran:

She's gone, let her go, God bless her!
For she never belo-onged to me.
She can lard-ass her way through the A.E.F.,
    buddy,
But she'll never find a sucker like me.

A mournful sort of tune went with the other pet song of his—"Poor Boy."

My mother called me to her dyin' bedside,
And these were the words that she said,
"You'll be in trouble before you're dead,
    poor boy,
You'll be in trouble before you're dead."

The Mysterious Suitcase

IN MacArthur's odd response to war there was nothing callous. Nor was there bellicosity or avid patriotism in his penchant for battlefields.

He was lured to them as the poet is lured to sunset and moonlight. His dark friend, the ever-beckoning One, was there. Standing near to death, MacArthur relaxed as he used to in O'Bannion's flivver.

Remembering him over forty years, I see the most potent factor of his charm. It was his detachment. One man with a secret is more interesting than a stageful of people without secrets.

The secret? I think—the worm of mortality was the philosopher in my friend. It put a vagueness in his competitiveness and touched his opinions with grace. He was the poet with death and a summer's day balanced before his eyes. And God, Whom he saluted in no church, was always a-buzz in the air and peering out of the night. God made things come to light and grow. The other one, Death, was God's janitor.

He wrote me once, "I don't think God is interested in us after puberty. He is interested only in our births, for this requires His magic. Our dying requires only His indifference."

His philosophy sharpened also his disdains. He saw the world's strut and vainglory always with a hole in its pants—and its mortality showing.

To sum up these generalities, I remember MacArthur from the first week I knew him as seeming to be a visitor with a suitcase, smiling at an absurd and impermanent land.

Only now do I know the contents of this suitcase at the jaunty traveler's side. It contained his cerements.

When he was dead it could be said of him, more than of any other man I have known, that the world had enjoyed him.

Around a Ghostly Table

I sit with Charlie's widow, Helen, in her Nyack home, talking. Outside an autumn cold thins the garden that rolls to the Hudson. We are here to remember MacArthur for this book. But data evade us. When a man dies it is as if a painting fell out of a frame, and you are left staring at an incredible bit of unoccupied space.

This is the house in which Charlie lived for some twenty-five years. The walls, chairs and doorways stare at us on this morning like empty frames.

The round table at which we sit is piled with letters written by Charlie to Helen during their thirty years together. Helen reads sentences aloud, and Cyrano and Abelard sound in Nyack.

"Your letter this morning gives me an ecstasy so fresh and thrilling that everything in life seems suddenly worthwhile. You said you'd been living with only half yourself. So have I."

"You may have these," says Helen, "after I finish reading them again."

She reads on in silence and adds, "He was so wonderful."

The voice that speaks is one of the most moving voices in the world. It has spoken from hundreds of stages, fetched tears, loosed laughter and thrilled a myriad of bosoms.

There is a Helen Hayes Theatre in New York, an honor few living actresses have attained. Newspaper and magazine files and books hold the sparkling tale of her fame from the days when Charlie first loved her as the blue-eyed enchantress of the Nile in Shaw's *Caesar and Cleopatra*.

But there is no fame in this Nyack room.

Shakespeare describes it: "Grief fills the room up."

A few years ago, Helen's mother, who lived here, died. Charlie used to call her "Brownie." And in the days when Charlie was courting her daughter, Mrs. Brown used to call him, sinisterly, "that satire!" She meant satyr.

A few years ago, also, the MacArthur daughter, Mary, the adored one, died. And now bonny Charlie has made his exit. No first lady of the theatre sits here, but a little tree without leaves.

"We evidently had a quarrel," says Helen, looking up from a faded letter in her hand. She smiles. "For the life of me, I can't remember what it was about."

She hands me a page which begins: "This feeling I have for you my young, thoughtless darling vibrates like a harp all day long."

Helen says, "It was that way all the time."

Eyes, thirty years older, look longingly at this empty frame of a room.

Another pile of letters covers the couch behind Helen.

"These," she says, "came after Charlie's death."

I read them. They are from what the reporters call "every walk of life." Statesmen, moochers, generals, fashion models, theatre and movie stars, ex-bootleggers, literary lions, stage hands, studio carpenters, aristocrats, bar flies from vanished barrooms, war buddies, travel buddies and nobodies—all write the same letter, all echo William Butler Yeats' cry in "Oedipus": "Even in your absence our love shall follow you."

A Child vs. Eternal Damnation

I'LL stop pretending to myself that I am writing a biography. What I am writing is obviously a letter about a friend who died. My communication may have in it chiefly the moonings of one left on empty battlements. This admission cheers me. What might well have seemed an insufficient biography will, I hope, be full enough as a letter. To whom? To Battery F, and all the rest who knew him.

What I know of his family and childhood he told me long ago when we were young and the world was a new pack of cards. Twilight was an hour of promise, and dinnertime a period of hilarity.

The youth of a man is as hard to describe as the bright dream remembered on awakening. We look—a young face rebukes us, a gay voice and gesture mock us, an orphan whistles and turns his back on us.

Thus the MacArthur who talked of his childhood peers rebukingly out of a mist. He was young, and he spoke a great deal of his parents, who had not receded, as parents must, into the wings.

These happily told tales of parents are usually the end of the spell they cast over their young. This spell never ended for my friend.

MacArthur's father was one of his favorite themes. The old gentleman's activities, that continued till his death, at eighty odd, always fascinated Charlie.

William Telfer MacArthur was an evangelist. He had heard "the call" while watching his threshing machine go up in flames on his Pennsylvania farm, ordained himself on the spot as a minister, and gone forth to recruit souls for the Lord.

His four sons, Alfred, Telfer, John and Charles, saw to it in later years that he was never shy of traveling expenses, a fine coat and good vittles as he roamed the earth.

"He specializes in doting old ladies," said Charles, "and brings the word of God to them in their far-flung parlors, from Glasgow to Hong Kong."

Charlie seemed pleased and diverted by his father's revivalist gallivanting. He referred to him as the "Old Pollywog" and liked to describe him standing tall in a parlor and roaring at old ladies about the evils of the world and the splendors of the hereafter. It was, obviously, a picture the son envied though he had in him neither dogma nor the remotest instinct for intrusion. And he could no more deliver a speech than float out of a window.

When Reverend MacArthur came to New York, Charlie would whisk him off to some gaudy night club. I think it was not temptation the son offered but proof to himself that his Bible-spouting parent was mysteriously immune to the flesh-pots. Charlie sat, a vicarious monk, at virtue's side.

"I took the Old Pollywog to the opening of Gil Boag's night club," Charlie said with a proud chuckle, "and wangled a front-row table. Gilda Gray came out dressed in a few beads and wiggled like mad for ten minutes within groping distance. 'How'd you like that?' I asked the Reverend. He took a moody sip of his lemonade and answered, 'First nice pair of legs I've seen since your mother died.' "

Preacher MacArthur was born in Cherry Valley, New York. His parents had come from Aberdeen, Scotland.

The lady with the nice legs he had married was Georgiana Welstead, one of nineteen children of an English remittance man. He had served as an officer in the East Indian Army, a fact of which Georgiana boasted gently during a life of vicissitude. She was a handsome and witty girl with a grin for hardships and for the unbending man of God who brought them down on her like a ton of bricks.

For, with seven children achieved—there were two daughters, and a son who was to die—the "call hearer" MacArthur turned his talents to serving the Lord.

And what a hell-fighting shambles of a life came on all the MacArthurs! With all normal income cut off, the self-ordained Reverend stood on crossroads under naphtha lights and invaded skimpy meeting halls, calling tirelessly for sinners to repent and come to God.

"We lived in various houses in New York and Pennsylvania," said Charles. "The houses began to fill up with missionaries and disciples. They came tagging home with his nibs around suppertime.

"There was no food to feed them; hardly enough for ourselves. My mother would stretch a cabbage to cover twenty plates and water down the lemonade until it tasted like yesterday's dishwater. The only thing big enough in which to mix such wholesale libation was the chamber pot. She used it. There was never enough bread to go around, but hallelujahs a-plenty.

"Finally some of the more devoted disciples took to bivouacking in our house. Mother tried to starve them out by cutting off their vittles behind the Reverend's back, although he was too busy plucking souls from the burning to notice who was eating or not.

"But starving them out didn't work. Mother was amazed to see a cluster of deacons sticking in the house, and thriving and praying without a morsel of food passing their lips. The Reverend, when it was called to his attention, considered this a minor miracle brought on by his holy work. But Mother finally solved it. She uncovered rolls of salami and other goodies hidden under the pillows of the Deacon Elijahs, and after that we had a little elbow room in the house."

Reverend MacArthur's pursuit of sinners was not confined to meeting halls and crossroads. The pursuit began at home, at dawn. It was the Reverend's conviction that his own off-spring were in Satan's hands.

"The Old Pollywog roared at us from morning to night," said MacArthur. "He was constantly uncovering some new streak of wickedness in us. He would line us up at night, all still hungry as wolves, beseech God in a firm voice to forgive us, uncover our backs and whale the hell out of us. He kept a strap soaked in vinegar to make it a finer instrument of the Lord."

At the age of seven, God afflicted young Charles for his sins in a fashion that shook the Reverend to the soles of his boots. A boil appeared on the boy's neck and swelled up as big as a gourd. Charles' mother, busy with cooking, sewing, cleaning, washing for a family of nine and an ever-present gallery of admiring deacons, seized the sullen, neck-bulging Charles and started for a doctor's office. The Reverend caught her in time.

"This is no case for medical attention," he said. "Our son has been afflicted for his sins. I will gather our people to pray for him tonight."

That night, and every night for a week, the young sinner found himself and his ballooning neck on a platform under naphtha flares. Around and below him men and women prayed, imploring God to forgive the sinner for his sins and to remove the carbuncular mark of His disfavor.

The miracle happened. Young Charles, sweating under the naphtha lights, suddenly felt warm matter oozing down his side. The prayers had been answered. God had punctured the abscess and taken His wrath from the boy's neck. The rejoicing continued for hours. At midnight young Charles was brought home in triumph, a proof of the Lord's forgiveness and medical ability.

A thin pucker marred the MacArthur neck for the rest of his years. He grinned at it whenever he shaved.

The poverty and hullabaloo of an evangelist's life filled the various MacArthur manses. The good preacher fished for sinners as far west as Chicago and then packed his flock east again—this time to a tabernacle-studded hill in Nyack.

At thirteen, in Nyack, Charles read the forbidden books of Sir Walter Scott and Charles Dickens, locking himself away for these sinful studies in the only MacArthur room privileged with a key. This was the bathroom, called by the family "the house of refuge." On the toilet seat, safe from the voice of God, Charles bent over the tabooed pages of literature.

At fourteen, Charles transferred his seat of learning to the Wilson Memorial Academy. Father MacArthur was certain the Devil was barred from its halls. His deacons taught there.

The Wilson Academy in those days was a Nyack school devoted to turning its hundred adolescents into ministers or missionaries to the heathen. Prayer, Bible study and denunciation of sin were its routine. Men who glowered at evil as grimly as his father, and were after it like baying hounds, were Charlie's teachers. And around him were ninety-nine boys and girls who bemoaned daily the fact that they were full of original sin, and promised their Maker daily to rise above the Devil's lures. Dancing, movie-going, "promiscuous" reading, mingling with the citizenry of Nyack, Piermont, Snedden's Landing, Blauvelt and Haverstraw—these were part of the Academy taboos. Contact with the world beyond the Wilson Memorial Academy was flirting with Gomorrah.

Charlie (he was called Chick then) sat for three years under the same moral bludgeoning he had received from infancy in his home. The world, he learned, was dark with sin. Pleasure and curiosity were Satan's inventions. And whosoever yielded to their temptations would burn eternally in the fires of hell. This philosophy entered the pores of student Charles, and wrapped itself around his solar plexus.

His spirit, however, balked at monkhood. I have it from a schoolmate during these years, James Nalbud, that "Chick" was a believer, that he bowed his head, and affirmed daily that he was a sinner in need of the rod. But a sinner he stayed. He risked hellfire in daily misdeeds. He wandered off to mingle with the unanointed of Blauvelt and Haverstraw. He investigated slyly the sin of dancing and movie-going. To set himself apart from his ninety-nine schoolmates, he wore a black derby, a headpiece bewildering to the pious.

And, like Galileo, he created a scandal. There was a discussion in his class of the evils of liquor. Each of the students offered evidence of its vileness. Recited one of the students ringingly from the gospel, "Wine is a mocker, strong drink is raging: and whosoever is deceived thereby is not wise."

A gangly, boy-cheeked MacArthur took his turn in the discussion. He recited from a book not in the curriculum of the deacons—the *Rubáiyát of Omar Khayyám of* Naishápúr.

> Come, fill the Cup, and in the fire of Spring
> Your Winter-garment of Repentance fling. . . .
> . . . .
> Drink! for you know not whence you came, nor why:
> Drink! for you know not why you go, nor where.

Young Chick was not expelled. Authorities removed from the school's library all copies of the *Rubáiyát* that the Devil's hand had placed there; and the prayer hours were stepped up.

James Nalbud, resident of Brooklyn, writes me a letter of these days.

"Charlie's antics were not always pranks," he says. "One day he passed the hat around the students 'for a good cause.' He raised ten dollars, and was off to town. We all thought the 'good cause' was Charles MacArthur, and there was murmuring against his slick ways. A few days later I ran across an item in the Nyack 'Journal' of the eviction of a poor family on the outskirts of the town, and how some unknown youthful benefactor had secured new quarters for them by a down-payment of rent. I showed Charlie the story about the eviction. He grinned and said, 'Shut up, Dubie.' "

Letter-writer Dubie continues:

"Charlie was versatile. He could do most anything. He was vice president of our Literary Society. He was also an artist. The 1913 Year Book of the Academy is filled with pen and ink drawings signed 'Chas. MacArthur.'

"The oddest thing in this book called 'Criterion' is a blank space. After each picture is printed the school record of the original. Most of the pictures contain six to eight lines, listing their 'distinctions.' Beside Charlie's picture the white space is conspicuous.

"Years later Charlie came to a reunion of Wilson students in New York. A copy of the 1913 'Criterion' was shown him, and he was asked to list his distinctions of which the world was now aware. He wrote on the white space—'Pres. Late Sleepers' Club; Trustee: Bar Companions (a Pub); Editor: Who's Who (a Humor Sheet).' "

James Nalbud's letter concludes:

"At Charlie's funeral, when the minister began the intonation of the scriptures, I picked up my raincoat and went out into the murky day. I strolled around until the services were over. There I took a position at the side entrance of the funeral church to pay my last respects. As the rose-laden coffin was brought out and placed on the hearse to be taken to Nyack for burial, I wafted a kiss to Charlie and with tears in my eyes, 'Goodbye, Charlie. You've wandered through many countries and your footprints will be sought out and examined. Right now they're returning to the scene of your early youth. Rest in Peace.' "

Reverend William Telfer MacArthur's middle years were disturbed by a thing he had long suspected and tried sturdily to correct in his children. They had not turned to God and would never follow the road he had shown them. Not even his most gifted, Charles, from whose poet's tongue he had hoped to hear great hosannas. Alfred, the tallest, was already off dickering with the money changers. Telfer had gone to kick up his heels in distant ventures. A shotgun accident half blew off the head of his youngest, Roderick. The mother, holding the dying boy in her apron, carried him into the house. As she wept beside him, the mother heard a disturbance on the front steps. A group of disciples were bringing the Reverend home on a shutter. He had broken his leg.

Winter was coming in Nyack and Charles watched his father weather the storms, and his flock increase. The house rocked with hymns and prayers, louder than ever.

But the mother had gone her course. No strength was left in the lady who had toiled without end since the threshing machine had gone up in flames. Georgiana Welstead MacArthur was unable now to wash, cook, clean and sew—and prepare the feasts for the vineyard workers. The faithful came from the Tabernacle to help out the Reverend's ailing wife at her tasks.

As the winter began, the mother took on a new and alien chore. She started planting tulip bulbs. When the tulip bulbs were all in the ground, the mother went to bed, sick and spent.

"The flowers will be up in the spring," she said to Charles, her most loved. "I'd like to see them."

She died before the tulips bloomed.

And Charles was off into the world.

Up and Down on Calvary

In New York City a dozen years later, Charlie MacArthur sat in Tony's speakeasy on Fifty-second Street. It was 1 A.M., December.

With him were three musketeer friends, Bob Benchley, Dotty Parker and Scott Fitzgerald.

Benchley, already Satire Champion of the U.S.A., was laughing. His laugh was a sort of buoy warning. It signaled his presence on the high seas.

Miss Parker was also laughing. The poetess and Banderilla Girl of the Eastern Seaboard had the mousy laugh of a wall-flower. After midnight she practiced it on bus boys, policemen—and MacArthur.

The boyish-faced Scotty, Prince of American Letters,

chortled and called for four more slugs all around. The Christmas season with its ruthless clichés was almost upon them, and liquor was the only bastion.

A mood was on MacArthur and he laughed not. The mood was one only a young lover could understand. It was a disdain for love, accompanied by a thrashing of the spirit like unto a caribou with its foot in an Eskimo trap.

While his friends lassoed the night with their laughter, MacArthur sat silent and oddly occupied. He was drawing on the tablecloth with a pencil.

It was a picture of Jesus Christ, bearded, nailed and crowned with thorns. To these traditional items Charlie had added a pair of missionary's cuffs around the ankles and a ring through the nose.

Done with this cannibal chieftain of a Saviour, Charlie swayed to his feet and followed his chums into the winter night.

What parties to go to now? What Green Room to invade or soirees to tip over? Where were Woollcott, Broun, Mankiewicz, Ross, Kaufman and Bob Sherwood?

"Picking the lint out of their cloth heads," said MacArthur.

"Naughty darling," said Miss Parker. "Mustn't use words that rhyme with Alfred Lunt."

"You're stealing my stuff, Charlie," said Fitzgerald. "I have the *Weltschmerz* rights for Fifty-second Street."

Benchley tooted his New Year's horn of a laugh and took wing in the snow.

MacArthur went home to the Madison Avenue roost he shared with laugh-fountain Bob and put himself to bed. This was an early Charlie talent. However hull down with alcohol he was, Charlie retired always in perfect order, removing neatly all his clothes, including his socks and shoes, and extinguishing all the cigarette stubs. He moved at such times as unerringly as a guided missile.

An hour later Charlie opened his eyes. Outside the window was a heavily falling snow. It was 3 A.M.

He sat up and dressed as carefully as he had undressed.

31

Other youths might signal their defiance of Prohibition by a sock off or a lapel twisted. But not Charlie. His clothes were always sober.

The falling snow was thick enough to hit with a baseball bat. Charlie walked the white-latticed night back to Fifty-second Street. Outside of Tony's darkened speakeasy he set up a sudden halloo.

The speakeasy door opened. Tony, noble heart, had heard the cries in the night. A still swaying MacArthur entered the darkened oasis. He made his way by matchlight to the table at which he had sat with his chums. Here he sat down again.

Removing an eraser from his pocket, he erased line by line the caricature of Jesus he had drawn on the tablecloth.

Solo for Kettle Drums

It's a fine thing to be a reporter. And young, and working in Chicago—1915. Other towns have newspapers and fine saloons. But they're far away. St. Louis, Kansas City, Omaha, New York, New Orleans—they are places you go to hide.

In Chicago you're out in the open with the eyes of great men on you—J. God Keeley, Joe Patterson, Teddy Beck of the *Tribune*, Walter Howey, Andy Lawrence of the *Examiner*, H. Justin Smith of the *Daily News*, Dick Finnegan of the *Journal*, Joe Sheehan of the *Post*.

And scores of notable prime ministers beside them— Floyd Gibbons, Ashton Stevens, Sherman Duffy, James Pegler, Jo Swerling, Jack Lait, Junius Wood, Lloyd Lewis, Percy Hammond, Ring Lardner, Carl Sandburg, James Whittaker, Dan MacGregor, Harry Hochstader, Jess Kruger, Robert Casey, Charlie Dryden, Richard Henry Little, Wallace Smith, Jimmy Murphy, Drury Underwood, William Chenery, Walter Royce, Roy Benzinger, Kent Sykes, Frank Honeywell, Harry Reitlinger, Mary Synon, Warren O'Malley, George Wharton, J. P. McEvoy, Morrow Krum, Walter Noble Burns, Bert L. Taylor, Harry Hansen, Llewellyn Jones, Webb Miller, Burton Rascoe, Spike Hennessey, Greg Dillon, Guy Core, Chester Faust, Tom Kennedy, Paul Newman, Charlie Starrett, Ben Pratt, Fanny Butcher, George Briggs, John B. Kennedy, Ronald Millar, Lowell Thomas, Tom Ballyntine, Tony Czarnecki, Jack Malloy, Ray Quisno, Meyer Levin, Clarence Bradley, Woody Kentuck, Leolla Allard, Charles McGurk, Hildy Johnson—I pull these names out of a hat and leave it still full.

I write them down for a reason. With these names looking at me, 97 per cent of them through coffin lids, I'll write more carefully. These gentlemen (including Mary and Fanny and Leolla) were not only truth sticklers, but they sneered at obscurantism and bridled at bird calls. They were for lucidity and laughter, when sober. Lit up, they wrote their names across the sky in crane wings—meaning they were high and noisy and as full of combinations as a swarm of sorcerers.

This is the town to which MacArthur came shortly after the Nyack tulips bloomed that spring. And these were the palace guards among whom he raised his curly head, minus the longer curls his mother used to iron into tubes on an ironing board so he might look more cherubic at the Reverend's prayer meetings.

Frank Lloyd Wright, Edna Ferber, Floyd Dell, Lou Sarrett, Carl Van Vechten, Professors Breasted, Linn, Herrick and Harper walked the byways of this town. Sherwood Anderson, Harriet Monroe, Keith Preston, Arthur Davidson Ficke, Benny Goodman, Ernest Hemingway, John Gunther, Alfred Kreymborg, Jane Addams, Maxwell Bodenheim, Frisco, Bix Beiderbecke, Sam Insull, Packy McFarland, Drs. Fishbein, Murphy, Billings and Richter, Fritz Leiber, Marshall Field, Leo Dietrichstein, Ogden Armour, Bennie Leonard, Julius Tannen, John Hertz, Richard Carle, Opie Read, George Ade, Henry B. Fuller, Lorado Taft, Maurice Browne, Walter Eckersall, Charles E. Erbstein, Clarence Darrow, Jack Johnson were in our streets.

If my memory were less will-o'-the-wisp, I could put down a catalogue of greatness that would make a New York columnist's eyes bug out with envy. On the other hand, what profit to play host for a line of tombstones—with an entrance arch reading "My Contemporaries"?

But about Chicago in 1915 there is something you can say about no other town. First, everybody is alive, and next—you don't need press notices for renown. You can get famous just standing in a barroom, heisting a beer. Jap, the laconic barkeep, will study your slow consumption of the beer and growl, "Never mind paying it this week. I'll put it on the bill." And you're famous. Or let me write it this way—you'll never feel more famous than in that hour.

There's music in the town. Skipping Mr. Stock's symphony boys at Orchestra Hall and Signor Campanini's operatic troupes in the pit of the Auditorium, and the Flonzaley Quartet a-grapple with Mozart; and other quartets, piano bangers, fiddlers and singers—dePachman, Schelling, Godowsky, Paderewski, Eddy Brown, the Heifetz boy, Kreisler, Spalding, Tetrazzini, Raisa, Mary Garden, Galli-Curci, Ruffo, Muratore—skipping all these Vesuvian music-makers we come to the two orchestras playing nightly at Sunset Number One, a café. When one orchestra stops to get its wind, the other one vaults into the breach so that the dancing won't be interrupted.

This is music more favored by reportorial ears. And there are events here of interest. In addition to stabbings and shootings, in Sunset Number One everyone dances—even reporters, who are usually above such frippery. A blue light is on the dance floor. You can hardly see your partner's nose, especially when it's dark-skinned. (In Sunset Number One the name Crow exists only on a liquor bottle.) Dancing in this blue-shadowed ballroom, as thick with terpsichoreans as the Elysian revels under Tartullean, you don't have to glide around or hop-skip. The customers cover small ground, content to sway and take a step now and then out of courtesy to the sweating drummers. This is the dance that saves room rent.

Jim Colosimo's, Buxbaum's, Freiburg's, Mangler's, Mike Fritzl's, The Bucket of Blood, Ike Bloom's, Roy Jones', the Three Deuces, Kelly's Stables, and various drops and cul-de-sacs whose names I forget—these are also full of music, but less dancing.

And if you want fine piano playing without the discomfort of dressing up and sitting cramped in a theatre seat, there are the cat houses. Here the professors, with cigarettes dangling from the corners of hungry mouths, tinkle out the first sound-ings of Jazz. The advance guard for Gershwin, Arlen, Berlin, Porter is in the Chicago honkytonks.

The town is full of them, although an eager beaver named Merriam works fiercely to get himself elected mayor and clean up our lava beds. He doesn't get elected. "Honest Bill" Thompson remains mayor and continues to loot the till and beam on corruption, as is the Will of the Voters.

So on a summer evening the "Bunny Hug," the "Oceana Roll" and the "Turkey Trot" float out of pink-lit windows, which are also full of pretty girls with their tits out, whis-tling. Not in all the streets, although the way Mr. Merriam carries on you'd think there were more whores than cobble-stones in the town. This is political buncombe. A half hour in any direction lies respectability. Beyond the near North Side and the near South Side stand Evanston and Hyde Park and similar pious precincts into which journalists vanish after they get married, and buy bedroom suites on installments.

The saloons in which our young hero trains are fine, too: Vogelsang's, Stillson's, Metzger's, Kuh's, Schlogl's, the Con-gress Bar, the Colonel's Bar, Pete Gentleman's, De Jongh's Wine Cellar, Quincy Number 9, The Workingman's Ex-change, and a new rendezvous, probably the most spectacular in the world, called the College Inn. Its creator, Ernest By-field, owner of the Sherman Hotel and Charles' first million-aire friend, is a thwarted scholar barred by early poverty from the ivied walls. Therefore the scholastic title on the Randolph Street marquee. The College Inn, as devoid of college folk as the Drainage Canal of goldfish, introduces the club sandwich and Maxfield Parrish to the town. His painting over the long bar of King Cole and his four and twenty blackbirds soothes the eye with muted blues and convinces the bar flies that they are not wasting time on drink alone but also looking at high art.

Our inn introduces, too, a new type of restaurateur—Mr. Byfield, a hail-fellow who operates without bouncers and without a sideline of "souls for sale" (nice-smelling girls in long black stockings).

Mr. Byfield adds a new proprietor etiquette to his domain. He will get drunk with his customers beginning at 9 P.M. and, thereafter, pick up everybody's tab and pay for everybody's drink. This is a greater boon to journalism than the birth of the Newspaper Guild, which came much later. Homely Ernie, with his pink and swarthy face, his expectant grin, his head on the side, his Indian beak (if there were Jewish Indians), salute! I can hear you and Charlie foregathered in some nook in space cursing me out for omitting your favorite tales from this chronicle. But what the hell, boys— lucky with all the world's racket around me and my waning metabolism that I remember as much as I do.

And salute our young hero's famed friend, Charles Erbstein, legal idol of the town's crooks and murderers. We'll match Erbstein against Fallon of New York and Rogers of San Francisco, and give fifty pounds away.

Who was Charlie Erbstein? You might as well ask who were Bob Cantwell, Clarence Darrow, Pat O'Donnell, Ropes O'Brien. They were lawyers, and Mr. Erbstein was their better—a man beloved by porch climbers, embezzlers, rapists, wife slayers, love-nest killers, con men and bandits; a man who could drive policemen into apoplexy, make monkeys out of the state's attorneys, set a jury to sobbing and outwit justice as nimbly as Houdini could get out of a potato sack.

He was indicted for jury bribing, and won acquittal by the

testimony of a Catholic priest who stated that the defendant had been sitting in his rectory at the very moment the jurors in question were allegedly being bribed fifteen miles away. The Father remembered the time because Mr. Erbstein, during the night, had called his attention to the clock on the mantelpiece. Grateful for this assist, Erbstein joined the Catholic Church the following week and later donated a stained-glass window to the Father's house of worship. The window depicted a Biblical scene. The caption at its bottom read: "Christ Stripped of His Clothes." The donor's name was below in smaller letters: "by Charles E. Erbstein."

Bob Cantwell, rival barrister and a Catholic of longer standing, paused on his way to Mass and studied the stained-glass window for the first time.

"By God," said lawyer Cantwell, "and he's the sonofabitch who could do it."

I am going at MacArthur's background with a leisurely pencil because it was part of MacArthur, and if you knew him thirty years later you met this background. Also, I like it. I was there.

And, again, I have just reread Gene Fowler's fine book, *The Great Mouthpiece*, and noted his powerful array of details. And about where? New York. A town we hardly knew existed.

I write in this fashion (a little naïvely) hoping to bring out the mood of innocence in that day. For innocent is what we were; not in our doings but in our point of view.

We looked on the hopheads, crooks and gunsels and on their bawdy ladies as members of a family among whom we were privileged to move. The reporter's hello was the same for the psycho-killer as for the obliging waitress in King's restaurant. There was no caste system, moral or social, in our manners. We trotted, coach-dog fashion, at the heels of the human race, our tails a-wag.

Variations on a Dead Magdalene

I HAVE here the story of an unhappy bawd told me years ago by my friend. I'll ramble through it, as he used to do, for he never told one story without two more warming up in the bull pen. And a tale he might start about Akron, Ohio, might well take in the arrival of the new Lama in Lhasa. This was not because he liked to keep everybody else from talking—a charge which I made against him frequently—but because he loved to remember out loud. Life lived for him vividly when he spoke of it.

So to the whorehouse tale. But a few vital curlicues, before. MacArthur knew less about whores and whorehouses than was par for the roving newspaper pack. It may have been that his Scotch blood curdled at the price of the ladies—five to ten dollars, almost half a week's salary. Or his ego may have shied at buying his way into a bedroom. The good marksman turns his back on sitting ducks. Or a fear of germs may have kept him out of the busy saddles. This last was a large moral force in the days before penicillin.

But I think there were other forces working with Mac-Arthur. He was a youth who was more likely to be fetched into the hay by a woman's wit than by her what-you-may-call-it. He looked for talent, charm and clean fingernails in his ladies, and for the dash of personality that makes a girl glitter when turning a street corner. These were bargains not especially featured in the cat houses, although a little patience and faith could find you a woman who . . . But this is not my story.

There was also the problem of sin with MacArthur, a problem that was never to leave his soul for all his days. Just why he considered sex sinful is his own secret. The voice of God and its vinegar-soaked strap may have been involved. And, too, there's a sense of sin that rises out of a misuse of oneself, or of somebody else. My friend gave off evidences of that. Not that nervousness about sin was actually a curb with MacArthur. It served, mainly, to make him more selective. If he was going to hell he liked to pick a worth-while traveling companion.

MacArthur's first trip to a whorehouse (and his last for twenty years) was under the aegis of his managing editor on the Chicago *Tribune*, James Keeley, called J. God Keeley— who will now take over for a spell.

Mr. Keeley was a newspaper throwback even in those days. He considered his local room a trireme, and his staff a parcel of Carthaginians chained to the McCormick oars.

Mr. Keeley fancied himself a great editor, which in many ways he was. He exacted a fourteen-hour day from his oarsmen, disbelieved in their alibis and expense accounts, and considered the Chicago *Tribune* a more important institution than Heaven or Hell. He was a bulldog-faced man with a glower that could whiten a reporter's hair. But, like all tyrants, when he was pleased he was mightily pleased.

On Saturday nights, after the last edition had been put to bed, Mr. Keeley would unbend socially. This was a dreaded weekly event for the slaves singled out for democratic contact. Mr. Keeley would lead his little band to the back room of a saloon and play poker with them until he had won all their money. He was a cunning poker player with a fat bank roll to back him up in "freeze-out." There was no getting the best of him with thirty dollars in your pocket, and the fear of two days' hunger in your draw.

With all the reportorial loose clash clipped to his roll, Mr. Keeley would dismiss the bankrupts with a brief talk on the ins and outs of good gambling.

Among the things that mightily pleased Mr. Keeley was the

Tribune's new Mr. MacArthur. It was a young one with a foggy smile, and an aloof, neat air about it—but Mr. Keeley had heard things to offset this gentlemanly exterior.

Birth of a Journalist

THE young MacArthur had an unusually brief journalistic past for the high post of a Keeley minion. He had worked on a semi-bucolic publication, *Oak Leaves*. Here his first assignment as a news gatherer had revealed him a reportorial finished product. Editor Otto McFeeley assigned him to spend a freezing winter's night in a Chicago flophouse, disguised as a bum, and to write up his findings.

Young Charles, who had never put words together before, wrote a professional and seductive tale for *Oak Leaves*. As a result, however, a feud had developed between Mr. McFeeley's fledgling and Chicago's roaring Chief of Police, Mr. Sweeney.

Young MacArthur refused to state the indignity that had been done him. "I'll get even with that lard-head Sweeney," was his only utterance.

Identifying himself as the editor-in-chief of the Chicago *Tribune* (next to the President of the United States, the most puissant title in Chicago), Charlie spoke to Chief Sweeney on the phone.

"You are holding under arrest an innocent man," he said, "who is a close personal friend of the *Tribune*. What's more, he's a distinguished citizen whom the *Tribune* can vouch for as incapable of rape. He's a hermaphrodite, sir!"

Chief Sweeney blanched at all these misfortunate details.

"What's the gentleman's name?" Sweeney asked.

"Henry Wadsworth Longfellow," the indignant "editor-in-chief" replied.

(The name of the New England poet had fascinated

Charlie since his childhood, and was to figure often in his life. Why this was, I don't know. My friend responded oddly to names. Any Russian name would stir a grin in him. German names with z's in them, or any name with an "ooh" sound, titillated him. He once introduced a new character into a script we were writing named Joe Mooglia. He had seen the name signed to a "Voice of the People" letter in the *News*. When I asked why the new character, Charlie answered, "We can't miss with that name.")

"I'm giving you one hour to release Henry Wadsworth Longfellow," concluded the "editor-in-chief," "before the *Tribune* starts blasting. And, Mr. Sweeney, I don't need to tell you what that means."

Charlie hung up, and then checked with the sergeants in various police stations. He was satisfied with what he learned. Chief Sweeney and all the staff were busy phoning every station house in the city, demanding to know if they were holding a hermaphrodite named Henry Wadsworth Longfellow and, if so, to release him at once. Search in the bull pens and dungeons of the town for Mr. Longfellow tied up the police department for the afternoon.

Having tasted the magic powers of the word *Tribune*, MacArthur set his heart on it as his new homeland. He did a short hitch first in the City Press—which was like being an understudy in the theatre. Except that you worked like a devil. City Press editors Brown and Hubka ran you ragged and paid you in nickels. But the worst part was you were a busy sailor without a ship.

The deed that earned MacArthur the *Tribune* police card —"All courtesies extended the bearer will be appreciated by Thomas Sweeney, Chief of Police"—is lost in the mists. This card was once a magic open-sesame, although I remember an occasion when it didn't suffice. Ring Lardner and MacArthur were sent to cover a heavyweight prize fight in some Indiana town. Their police cards were scorned by truculent gate-keepers who feared a police raid, and the journalists were twice booted out while trying to trickle in. They turned their backs on the event and headed for the railroad depot. Here they refreshed themselves and entered the lavatory. Their keen eyes noted a new type of can. Instead of chain or lever for flushing, there was a large button on the toilet back. It was marked, in black letters, "Press."

The journalists dismantled the toilets, removing their plungers, and stuck the buttons reading "Press" in their lapels. Heads high, they walked into the fight arena, with the gatekeepers nodding courteously at their insignia.

A Wounded Spaniard

I HAVE a story about the day when Mr. Keeley first pricked up his ears at the name MacArthur. Word swept the local room that the new boy, MacArthur, had exchanged blows with Lionel Moisse in Mangler's saloon for five minutes without being rushed to the emergency ward of Passavant Hospital; that the new *Tribune* boy had, in fact, concluded the fracas still on his feet and with his opponent leaning thoughtfully against the bar, bleeding from the nose.

We sidle off here into the topic Moisse. Moisse had worked for Mr. Keeley a year before and had been considered by him a good reporter but lacking in discipline. He was a tall, sandy-haired, rawboned and poetical import from the Kansas City *Star*. A good writer, a sensitive and witty citizen, but a bad-man in his cups. He was known to knock out from one to five colleagues of an evening as a result of crap-game debates. He was also touchy on literary matters and had broken several jaws in behalf of George Moore, whom he admired over Robert Louis Stevenson.

After leaving the *Tribune*, Moisse had found a footing on the *Evening Post*, where he had terrorized himself into the slot of assistant city editor. Some argument resulted in Moisse throwing the *Post* city editor and two copy readers down a flight of stairs. He was turning his attention to Mr. Shaffer, the publisher, when the police arrived and cut short his services on the *Post*.

Moisse (pronounced Moe-eese, with accent on the second syllable) was, until this night in Mangler's, the bully boy of our pack. It was believed that no one could take him, with the exception possibly of Henry Hochstader of the *Journal's* sports department—over whom I must pronounce a few words while in this ghost land.

Harry was a pale, sleepy-eyed young man who, like the poet Maxwell Bodenheim, was the son of a popular South Side butcher. He had started drinking and dissipating at the age of fourteen. Fifteen years later, he had yet to get a night's sleep or draw a sober breath after sundown. Despite this lack of proper training, Harry had matured into a great battler. He had heavy fists and a keg of dynamite for a heart.

Nobody, least of all Mr. Keeley, who knew the sparrow's fall, would have been surprised if Harry had poleaxed Moisse and hung him up to dry. But news that an underweight unknown had slugged it out successfully with this Kansas littérateur sent a buzz down Dearborn Street.

And Mr. Keeley's ears pricked up. He liked champions at the galley oars. When, a few days later, J. God discovered that he had not only a Packy McFarland on his staff but—in the same package—a Mark Twain, his boss's heart shed an inch of its armor plate.

This fame had resulted from a casual assignment of reporter MacArthur to interview a literary foreigner named Blasco-Ibáñez. Señor Ibáñez had written *Blood and Sand* and some other novels about the peculiarities of Spaniards. *Blood and Sand* was currently being turned into a movie in a Western village with a Pollyanna name—Hollywood. This last fact added no importance to our Spaniard as a news source.

Looked at from the vantage of the *Tribune* city desk in that day (possibly in this one, too), Hollywood and its moviemaking were a cut above the activities of Professor Humboldt, in South State Street, who presided over a combination flea circus and tattoo parlor.

A year later the cinema hero of *Blood and Sand*—Rudolph Valentino—was to read a *Tribune* editorial deriding him as a sissy for wearing a wrist watch, and to come valiantly alone into the *Tribune* local room offering to battle any member of the staff with sword, fist or pistol. There being no MacArthur or Moisse on the payroll, Valentino was to walk out with his challenge untaken, and a victory by default in his belt.

When reporter MacArthur started out for an eight-o'clock appointment with the Señor at the Blackstone Hotel, he knew well that nothing more was expected than a few lame paragraphs on what Spain's leading novelist thought of Chicago's Loop and stockyards, and how did the local women compare with those of Madrid and Seville.

Three hours later, when he had covered the half mile to the hotel, he found the Spanish novelist in bed, wearing a nightgown and pouting.

MacArthur apologized for his tardiness, blaming it on a traffic tie-up, and sat down deferentially, as before genius. No questions were required. The Señor was a self-starter. Assisted by an interpreter with sideburns, he embarked on a bitter critique of American culture, politics, women and bad elevator service. The reporter from the *Tribune* sat in motionless attention. It was one of my friend's many social accomplishments. He could appear spellbound when he was in the land of nod.

MacArthur's interview with Blasco-Ibáñez was carried on the front page by the *Tribune*—a rare spot for literary items. It tickled the town. MacArthur had written a thousand words, chiefly on the shape, size and activity of the Ibáñez toes, which had been sticking out from under the bedclothes while the great man tiraded.

Chicago chuckled at this deft riposte to the author's fulminations, which had been given accurate but lesser space.

Spanish honor tied up the *Tribune* phones demanding apologies. But there was one thing about the *Tribune* under Keeley, Beck and Joe Patterson. It was as easy to frighten as King Kong.

There being no United Nations to take up the matter in plenary session, no international relations snapped.

Señor Ibáñez and his culture moved into the gold fields of Hollywood, and Chicago was left smiling at his scorn. There was in those days small sale for superior foreign attitudes in our town.

Brothel Sermon

I AM almost at the whorehouse. Mr. Keeley's Saturday-night unbendings had failed to fetch the new reporter to his side. Invitations to join the boss in the back room and spend a relaxing night at poker were nimbly sidestepped by Mac-Arthur. Our young hero was never a gambler and, in an odd way, he was a frugal man. He had heard about the poker sessions from smarting scribes. He would as soon have thought of joining one as of lying down on a railroad track.

But my friend was cunning at evasions. He had even then a genius for not doing what people wanted of him without losing their faith or admiration. He did this by confusing the issue with promises and deceits, and a magician's gift for misdirection—so that you would think he was going north when he was headed south.

Thus it befell that, deprived of MacArthur as a poker victim, Mr. Keeley set his cap for him as a purely social companion. He invited him out on the town.

That a renowned editor should single out a cub, with the fuzz of adolescence still on him, to go sporting with was a thing for some curbstone questions. Just as it made talk among some of the bilious, years later, when folk of great estate found a chum in MacArthur. The talk said it was MacArthur who went fishing greedily after titles and nabobs, and that he was more bounder than friend in his waltz across the world.

My friend was no ninny. He was willing to use any attention he attracted, if need be, as a social steppingstone. But it was the folk of great estate who were the bounders—as they usually are toward artists and works of art. My friend qualified in the open market as both. These are the words of Scott Fitzgerald to Charlie's bride, Helen, on the subject: "Some men do not have to create something to prove they are artists. They have only to exist. Charlie is one of them."

As the mighty Mr. Keeley did on this night, so the high and fancy folk of the world were to do for another four decades —make bids to a man who asked for none.

Madam Farrington's whorehouse was perhaps the most elite of such trysting places in the town. It occupied the second and third floors of the "Michigan View Hotel" at Twelfth Street and Michigan Boulevard. The girls wore petticoats and underpants, refrained from profanity and gauche advances, and were all under twenty-five.

MacArthur told the story of his debut:

"Madam Farrington greeted Keeley as if he were King Solomon," he said. "She ordered up three bottles of wine and said two of her fairest would be on deck in a few minutes. Keeley sat down and started banging a piano and moaning out a song. The song was 'Little Boy Blue,' a Gene Field poem. It was about a toy tin soldier that had belonged to a little boy. One night the little boy stood the tin soldier in the corner of his nursery, and never woke up. After the little boy was buried, the tin soldier remained standing, loyally, in the nursery corner—waiting.

"A door adjoining the parlor flung open and a naked girl appeared screaming, with her hair down.

" 'Stop that song!' she yelled. 'For Christ's sake, don't sing that song.'

"Well, Keeley was not a man for taking orders. He went on singing it twice as loud as the first time around. The girl —her name was Vera—ducked back into the bedroom and slammed the door. Keeley was still warbling about Little Boy

Blue and his sturdy and staunch tin soldier when Vera's door popped open again. This time a bald-headed gent in long underwear came bouncing out with a piece of news that electrified the company. Vera, he said, had drunk the antiseptic.

"Madam led the way into the bedroom. The girl was writhing on the floor. She died in the Passavant Hospital an hour later.

"Miss Farrington explained to Keeley, who was sore as hell about the whole thing, that Vera had been a little eccentric since her three-year-old kid died last summer. Keeley accepted the apology but said, 'Let's get the hell out of this abattoir.' Which was fine with me."

Pardon Me, Charlie

I SEE something curious in Charlie's story—told me long ago in Chicago. Neither of us attached any meaning to it then, more than a tale that went with drinking. But I do, now.

Approaching age, a man begins to look for such meanings, possibly because there is little else for him to look for. Usually he looks into the future for the secrets of life. Our friend Fowler threw himself headfirst into the arms of Catholicism. Pressed for explanation, he answered, "I didn't think it could do any harm."

Among the things MacArthur and I had in common was that we were of the tribe who, sitting lonely around the last campfires, search the past. We look to no heaven for signs, but we begin to make tea-leaf readings of our youth, and to see mystic points in it that escaped our attention when life was popping around us. Though Dickens began us, Kafka rewrites us (and there's a bore for you).

The heaven-lookers see a little more than we do. We have to settle for a few psychiatric findings that boil down to the fact that we were riding on tracks when we thought we were capering over the landscape. And that parents clamped a bit in our mouths, et cetera.

But there's another matter that beckons out of Madam Farrington's vanished parlor—a coincidence. In his first trip to a house of ill fame, MacArthur beheld death strike down a naked Jezebel. The wrath of God smote the abomination, and ghostly hallelujahs echoed in this Satan's lair.

Dismissing the possibility that God was personally after Charlie, I'm left with a little wonder about the word coincidence. So much for Kafka.

But a salute to J. God Keeley before he and his baritone bow out of these pages. It was in Mr. Keeley's local room that Chicago's greatest newspaperman was hatched and trained. He was Walter Howey.

The Cockeyed World
of Howey

THE newspapers in Chicago of 1915 were grudgingly giving up some space to foreign news. A world war (so called) was going on. And some local reporters had been sent over to cover it. Floyd Gibbons, Harry Hansen, Paul Scott Mowrer and even our best dramatic critic—Percy Hammond.

Casualties were high, the fighting fierce, victory fluctuating. Such things could not be denied white space. But our papers stuck their nose in slowly. We were set against foreign news. And we had a cold shoulder for national politics. A Washington date line on a story was like an admonition—"Don't read me." As it still is, to me.

The only good copy in politics was the great nominating convention that broke out every fourth year, usually in Chicago. So was the candidate's sprint to election, with job holders and would-be job holders yipping on the side lines. But the winner, once he got his nose "in the public trough," as we described it, had to beat up his mother or jump out of a window to get his name in our papers.

Today the city desks are as global-minded as an oil company, and they respond to political incantations like Holy Rollers. But not then.

Our editors winked when they sent us to interview a politician. They expected us to come back with a comic valentine.

A bear hibernating in a hollow log was an amateur isolationist alongside our editors. They considered life as something that was happening in Chicago, and hardly anyplace else. Our news sources were the plot turns of passion and skullduggery.

This was one of the reasons why one reporter out of four in that day turned into a novelist, poet or dramatist. It was as natural for a police reporter to start writing a novel or a play as it was for an ant to climb a grass blade.

The king cobra life-chaser of our local rooms was Walter Howey. Back from his duties with Battery F, MacArthur enrolled under him on the *Examiner*.

We wrote the Damon and Pythias love affair of Howey and MacArthur in *The Front Page*. But we watered it down. The Howey and MacArthur of the *Examiner* office in 1919 would have made too eerie a tale for any theatre.

I'll try to put Walter down on paper again, but without Charlie handy to call the shots it will be an insufficient piece. There is, however, Charlie's last published writing to help out. It appeared after Howey's death under the title "Mister Front Page."

Howey looked like a small-town merchant. He cooed like a dove, smiled like a wide-eyed sightseer in from the sticks. He wore a polka-dot bow tie, neat linen and a pressed suit. His shoes were shined like any bank teller's. His blondish hair was always politely combed. Outside the fact that his left eye was disabled (the gossips had it he had fallen into a drunken stupor while sitting at his desk and impaled the eye on a copy spike)—outside this unfunctioning optic you couldn't have imagined a less fierce-looking character than Howey. He even smelled of cologne.

Yes, Mr. Howey, God rest his wild bones, had a soft, benevolent look and air, voice and manner. But the Assyrians menacing Sinai were casual folk beside him. He could plot like Caesar Borgia and strike like Genghis Khan. On top of which he was a dreamer. He could moon like Keats. The hearts of people were his nightingales. I have saved his basic characteristic for the last: he could foretell the future. There's an editor for you.

It's impossible for me, even at this distant day, to write with true affection of Howey, as MacArthur could. MacArthur was his cohort. I was on the other side, bedeviled for thirteen years by the existence of an unscrupulous master mind on a rival paper.

I would see the man purring in a barroom and feel the hair on the back of my neck rise. And I would enter the state offices in quest of legitimate information on an upcoming murder trial and learn that the whole staff were speaking to nobody—except Mr. Howey's representative, usually MacArthur.

This was because Mr. Howey had a high state official's resignation in his *Examiner* desk, ready to publish at the moment the official disobeyed him. He had caught him red-handed in some foul business and blackmailed the resignation out of him. Thereafter, this powerful public official was a Howey pawn.

Mr. Howey had a half dozen other such resignations in his desk. In more bitter moments I used to look on nearly every cop and office holder as Howey myrmidons held in thrall by his basilisk eye.

Go love a man like that—on the other side.

Sang the Nightingale

OF the hundred fabled deeds performed by MacArthur under the goad of this Martian, I'll tell only one—the one my friend was fond of repeating.

"A little girl with golden curls has disappeared from her home near Moline," Walter said wistfully to his favorite wazir (Charlie), "and I have it on good authority that she's locked away in the railroad safe in the Moline station. It's a big safe, five feet high. The stationmaster closed it without noticing the child had stepped inside. I've just been talking to him on the phone. He was in bed with hysterics."

"Was he sober?" MacArthur inquired.

"The soberest man I ever talked to," said Walter dreamily. "There's just enough air in that safe to allow the little tot to stay alive till midnight."

"Why the hell doesn't that gazumping stationmaster open it, if he's so sober?" asked MacArthur, sensing the night's travail that lay ahead.

"It's a beautiful story," said Howey. "It's an old safe and hasn't been used for ten years. It's been kept open till tonight. Now that it's locked, there's nobody alive knows the combination. Dynamiting is out of the question," he added quickly. "It would only blow the little one to hell and gone. Our object is to get her out of that safe alive."

MacArthur sighed.

"It's only seven o'clock," said Howey. "The *Examiner* has exactly five hours to save a human life. I had the stationmaster give me the dimensions of the safe and have just been informed by Doc Springer how long a human being of that size can last with that many cubic feet of air. We're working on an exact schedule. Twelve o'clock is the deadline for the little girl, and also for our home edition. I've arranged for the

Chicago and Alton to shoot a special train to Joliet in fifteen minutes. You'd better move fast."

MacArthur needed no further briefing about why Joliet. The state prison was in Joliet. It was full of burglars and expert safe crackers. His first duties would be to take three or four of the best safe crackers out of their cells, and hustle them to the safe in Moline as fast as hell. From his desk, full of resignations, Editor Howey would arrange it with numerous high officials to let a bevy of Jimmy Valentines loose from prison for this great humanitarian chore.

"The prison was coming apart with excitement when I got there," said MacArthur. "Every goddamn yegg and footpad in the place claimed to be a wizard at opening safes with sandpapered fingers. They were all bragging to the warden of the big jobs they had pulled off that the police had never heard of yet. Finally, we picked two with bona fide records. Getting to Moline in a hurry looked like a problem. But Howey solved it at the other end. He tracked down the railroad president in a Springfield hospital where he was fighting pneumonia and got him to put on a special flyer from Joliet to Moline. It was almost ten o'clock. Walter screamed at me on the phone to move faster. He had rushed two of Chicago's leading doctors and their nurses to Moline, where they were standing by outside the safe, ready with first aid.

"'And remember above all else,' Walter purred on the phone, 'we've got to keep the story locked up till that little baby is restored to her mother's arms. I've got the mother and several other members of the family under close watch, and photographers standing by waiting for that steel door of doom to open. So move fast.'"

Accompanied by the two safe-cracking experts, three prison guards, the warden and assistant warden, and with a box of sandpaper sheets in his lap, MacArthur had ridden the flyer to Moline.

"There were about a hundred people milling around in front of the safe in the depot," said MacArthur, "all pulled out of their beds and parlors by Howey. Doctors, nurses, railroad officials. And two vice-presidents ready to do their all.

"A cheer went up as my safe crackers appeared, still in their prison suits. Everybody wanted to wring their hands. You never saw two such giddy heroes. I had already promised them a governor's pardon, knowing that Howey would expect it of me.

"We quieted the demonstration and my two boys fell to work, sandpapering their fingers and cleaning out their ears. We kept a big light on them and the photographers kept shooting pictures of their every move.

"At exactly ten minutes to midnight the two sweating convicts turned to the warden with the thrilling words, 'The door is open, Chief.'

"The vice-presidents pulled the heavy door open, with the cameras clicking. I was half ready for the denouement. There was no little girl with golden curls in the safe. There were only a lot of old suitcases and a pile of old ledgers.

"Everybody was sore as hell, including the two yeggs, who started howling for their governor's pardon and had to be taken back to Joliet at rifle's point.

"I was pretty sore myself and was happy to break the news to Walter about what a horse's ass he had made out of half of Illinois, including the Chicago *Examiner*. The little girl, I told him for a clincher, was home in bed. She had hidden in the attic after supper because she was miffed with her grandmother for getting drunk in front of her schoolmates."

At this point in the story MacArthur would pause and the nearest thing to idolatry I ever saw in him would touch his eyes.

"Without a pause that daffy bastard Howey crackled right back at me: 'It's a terrific story. I'll get you a rewrite man. Give him every detail you've got. Everything all those wonderful people said. How everybody from the lowest to the highest rode to the rescue of that little girl.'

"I thought he'd gone crazy. I yelled at him: 'I told you! There *wasn't* any little girl!'

"He kept right on in a kind of chant, 'It's not a story about a little girl. It's a story about humanity. The goodness in people's hearts. The safe blowers, vice-presidents, doctors, nurses, the warden, the governor, the fellow with pneumonia and everybody who answered a cry of human distress.'

"'I got you,' I said. I dictated for an hour. The story in the morning covered half the front page. The seven-column head above it read: IT'S A WONDERFUL WORLD.

Walter Crawford Howey died in a Boston hospital in 1955. I'll let Charlie write his obit, as it appeared in *Saga* magazine.

"I went to work for the Captain of Space Cadets on my return from the First World War," the MacArthur tribute begins. And it concludes:

"In 1928, Ben Hecht and I wrote 'The Front Page,' a play about newspaper life in which the principal character was an editor who stopped at nothing to get a story. In the last act he gave his star reporter a watch inscribed: 'To the best news-paperman I know,' and then had him arrested for stealing it.

"This was not a double-cross so much as the desperate act of Damon refusing to part with Pythias.

"So when Howey was hit by an automobile a few months ago and lay in a Boston hospital with a broken back and ten fractured ribs, near dying, I took him a watch bearing the same inscription.

"Ill winds had blown over his heart. His young wife had died of shock a few days before, while he was still in a coma. There seemed nothing left to live for. But he was as scrappy as a cougar in his plaster cast, and his face seemed younger than ever. Already telephone linemen were getting a direct connection through to his paper. [He had been running the Boston *American*.] He talked all afternoon of his future plans. But his adored wife must have whispered something to him in his sleep—for in the morning he was gone.

"All I know is: journalism will never see his like again."

54

Lazarus Loses His Head

THE next tale is more of a MacArthur solo deed, for which reason he told it less frequently than many lesser ones. He was no good at a story in which he played the hero. His wit would ebb, his details go lame, and he was likely to forget the climax. There was modesty and also another reason for this. In his anecdotes, Charlie preferred the role of onlooker, or, at best, assistant participant. However heels up and head down he had been involved in the doing, he was seldom more than a shadowy figure in the telling. It was others who were the world.

Yet it was in his echo of events that their real magic sounded. Life was less in the streets than in his vocabulary. When he told his skyrocket tales, our detached and brooding spectator was about as contemplative as the chute-the-chutes. His words entered a room like a troupe of Armenian tumblers. And his spirit was kin to the boyo of whom the ballad sang:

> If you wanted a man
> To encourage the van
> Or harass the foe from the rear
> Or storm a redoubt
> You had only to shout
> For Abdul Ábulbul Amir.

The story of Charlie's Lazarus was born in an interview with Dr. Murphy, one of the superior surgeons of our town. He had invented a viscera clamp called the "Murphy Button" which swept the operating rooms of the world.

During the interview, Dr. Murphy had put in a good word for a new drug named adrenalin. It was being pumped successfully, he said, into people who had died, but only temporarily, as it turned out.

MacArthur inquired casually if the new drug could revive a man who had been hanged. Dr. Murphy answered it was no good for mending broken necks.

"If the neck isn't broken," persisted MacArthur, "and say a man dies by just choking to death in the noose, how about that?"

Dr. Murphy answered that a man seemingly choked to death might be revived if the adrenalin was shot into him quickly enough. And the great Frank Piano resurrection was on.

Frank Piano was an Italian youth occupying a death cell in the county jail—across from the Kinzie Street bridge. He was waiting to be hanged for stabbing somebody to death. Reprieve had been denied. The drop would bang down on a Friday morning two weeks hence.

Ah, that old county jail with its shabby Roman façade, its rows of cells full of talkative felons, its wily warden, Mr. Jacobi, its cheery buzz of graft and corruption. Tommy O'Connor walked out of his death cell the day before he was due for hanging and nobody could ever find him again. Madam Lil Hamilton's ten-dollar Jezebels were permitted visiting hours. Madam Minnie Sheema, duenna of the House of All Nations, protested the monopoly to our mayor—and justice was done. A stream of Mongolian and Latin young-lady visitors trickled in and out of the cell blocks thereafter. And in this busy place the journalist, however tottering or unshaven, was treated always with fine courtesy.

Other institutions might frown on the news gatherer, and there were public officials enow ready to kick him down the stairs. (Lionel Moisse, with the aid of flying cuspidors, once held his own against the Board of Education for half an hour.) But this unswept, latrine-smelling edifice of the barred windows and the gallows chamber was a place of hospitality for him.

The warden offered free liquor and free telephones and

card games which he and his staff took turns losing. All they asked in return was that we overlook any news items short of a jail break or a fatal stabbing. We were happy to turn our backs on such minor matters as dope smuggling, sodomy, bribery, the trollops in the cells and the occasional night off allowed a prosperous prisoner.

Warden Jacobi listened wide eyed to MacArthur's proposition.

"It's all legal and above board," Charlie explained. "You hang him Friday morning per schedule. The doctor puts the stethoscope on him after he's gone limp and pronounces him dead. All I'm asking is that you put the noose knot near his windpipe instead of the side of his neck. You've done it in the last three hangings by mistake. It took Teddy Webb and Blackie Weed fourteen minutes apiece to choke to death, if you'll recall. So nobody's going to be surprised if you bungle it again."

"That's true," said the warden thoughtfully, "but what the hell good is it going to do? I mean, what do I get out of it?"

"What do you get out of it!" MacArthur repeated indignantly. "That's a pretty rotten attitude when I tell you I'm going to bring a man back to life. The only hanged man in the history of our whole country ever to resume life again as if nothing had happened. Besides," MacArthur pointed out, "the name Jacobi will go down in science as well as hit the headlines all over the world."

"For doing what?" asked the warden cautiously.

"For doing nothing!" MacArthur answered. "It's the best way to get famous I ever heard of. No kickbacks. No investigations. Good, clean fame."

The warden nodded and the deal was consummated with a bottle.

For the next ten days MacArthur was as busy a member as the Fourth Estate had ever known. He spent hours with the doomed man, advising him how to behave after he went through the drop.

"Don't fight it," he told him. "When the rope starts chok-

57

ing you, let it. Just pretend you're going under an anesthetic. The quicker you choke to death the easier it'll be for the doctor to get you back on your feet."

The doomed man nodded. The certainty and high spirits of his adviser lifted the fear out of him. You would think, listening to this young reporter, that it was he who was going to be pulled back from the dead, so enthusiastic was he about the project.

MacArthur's enthusiasm for the macabre project was this time heightened by a need for cash. Romance had come into Charlie's life, with its usual strain on the pocketbook. The infatuated young journalist had figured out a lone-wolf financial operation. It involved a slight betrayal of Mr. Howey. But love—and its unpaid bills—will lead a man into dark ways.

With the connivance of the head telegraph operator of the *Examiner*, MacArthur had sent out secret queries to a score of far-off editors inquiring how much they were willing to pay for a story of a hanged man brought back to life again. The replies added up to over five hundred dollars. With this bonanza in the wind, the insolvent swain would be able to square accounts with Mandel Bros. and Jo Swerling, the jewelry store and the local-room Samaritan.

MacArthur also spent some time with Frank Piano's family in Galt Court, the main street of Chicago's "Little Italy." It was ticklish going here, and all the young journalist's winning ways were needed.

The thirty or forty relatives of the doomed man were in bitter rebellion against the press and the law for having collaborated on their Frankie's downfall. After a noisy first hour they had fallen silent, however, and listened to their visitor's information.

"Frankie will be home Friday for lunch," MacArthur declared. "It would be a nice idea if you would prepare a big homecoming feast for him, with music and dancing. But the whole thing has to be kept a secret. If a word of it gets out, good-by Frankie. I'm bringing him home myself in the ambulance, as good as new."

There would be a feast. There would be accordions, singing and dancing. And all would be arranged secretly. No human being beyond Galt Court would know of the great Friday Festa.

A doctor, a syringe full of adrenalin, an ambulance with its motor running in the alley outside the gallows chamber door, a couple of huskies to help carry the sheeted Frankie out—these problems were all resolved when the execution morning dawned.

I can tell the rest of the story at first hand, for I was on deck for the hanging. A dozen young men, with pencils and whiskey pints ready, sat in the front row of the thirty picnic benches. The rest of the seating space was occupied by influential sightseers.

It was a long, slotlike room with a high ceiling. A steel balcony, fifteen feet above the floor, ran along one wall. A small door opened on the balcony. Through this door the death march would come and move to the gallows platform at the end of this vault of a room.

From a crossbeam above the platform hung a bright new Manila rope with a noose on its end the size of a man's head. A half dozen electric bulbs in wire cages lighted the gallows.

Behind the gallows was a wall with a small circular window in it. The face of the hangman was shadowy behind it. A hand with a handkerchief kept polishing the circular glass. At a signal from the warden, the polisher would go to his real work.

I sat beside Wallace Smith from the Chicago *American*. Wallie was young, tall, black haired and well tailored and with the disdain of the expert always on his good-looking face. He was an expert at noticing things, and seeing through people. I would like to say we were formidable opponents at this game.

He noticed MacArthur. Our *Examiner* pal had not joined us on the picnic benches. He was popping in and out of a door in the rear of the room that opened on the alley. We knew Charlie, whatever the event, as a relaxed performer. He was, this dawn, in an odd state of flutters.

"I wonder what the bastard is up to," Wallie muttered as we watched Charlie's peculiar comings and goings preceding the death march.

When Frankie, surrounded by priests, warden and jail guards, came through the door on the steel balcony and started toward the dangling rope we forgot about the antics of our *Examiner* rival. Frankie seemed in a novel mood.

We had more or less ignored him in the death cell, for he was a youth of little color, and the murder he had done was equally uninteresting. But this Frankie who took his place on the gallows platform was a fellow of downright appeal. He was smiling as if he had arrived on the scaffold to attend some high-school exercises. Who could imagine that he was dreaming of ravioli- and antipasto-heaped tables in his mother's home, with Chianti flowing and "Ciribiribin" ringing clear?

When the guards started strapping his arms and draping the white robe on him, Frankie flashed them a preoccupied smile. Wallie, who was always mysteriously indigant toward men about to be hanged, whispered to me: "He's gone nuts. Look at the silly sonofabitch. He doesn't know where he is. Well, he'll soon find out."

The hanging went off per schedule. Frankie shot through the drop, the tautened rope started whining, the white-sheeted figure started puffing as it spun. Doc Springer, the coroner's physician, stood by with stethoscope ready. No sound came from the picnic benches for a long time.

The body went limp. Doc Springer stepped up to it and put his receiver on the white sheet.

"I pronounce him dead," he said. "The time is nine minutes."

MacArthur and two husky newcomers appeared from the alley door. Warden Jacobi was sawing away at the rope with a large jackknife. But MacArthur and his two guests never reached the dangling Frankie.

A red-faced, gray-haired man stood up from the spectator

benches. Two plain-clothes cops stood up with him. We recognized Sheriff Pete Bartzen.

Sheriff Bartzen and his two aides stepped quickly to the space under the gallows.

"In the name of Cook County, I hereby claim the body," said the sheriff. His voice sounded angry. MacArthur had made a single miscalculation. He had forgotten to declare the sheriff in on the big secret, which had been brought to that official by a stool pigeon. Stung by the prospect of an underling, Warden Jacobi, hogging all the publicity, Sheriff Bartzen acted swiftly.

The body was cut down and carried off by the two cops into the alley. Here MacArthur made a stand against the proceedings. His wild protests were ignored. The thwarted miracle worker had to watch his Frankie, due for lunch at the Galt Court Festa, hoisted into the sheriff's morgue truck. The truck rattled off.

A half hour later Frankie Piano was placed on a dissecting table in the Cook County Hospital. A house physician cut his head off.

Hearts and Flowers

CHARLIE married when he was twenty-two. His bride was the new "Little Girl Reporter" on the *Examiner*, named Carol Frink. Howey had added her to his staff. Her duties were to add an antic note to the news columns.

The Little Girl Reporter was another Howey success. She spent the night alone on a skyscraper roof and reported her musings. She dressed up as a Western Union messenger boy and delivered telegrams. A recital of similar quaint adventures appeared daily in the *Examiner*.

Ashton Stevens took the new girl journalist under his wing.

I pause for an Ashton aria. He was Charlie's first theatre signpost.

Ashton was our leading dramatic critic. He loomed in the *Examiner* like an oasis of wit and sophistication. He was a devotee of the stage and the most avid devourer of books in town. We considered him twice as smart as anybody in New York or Boston.

And he was no pompous savant, either. He was our leading man-about-town. You couldn't tell by looking at him that he had ever been near a book. He concealed his great erudition by wearing a wing collar, a blue polka-dot tie, English-cut tweeds and spats. He toted a cane, and his bell-shaped, kimono-sleeved overcoat was as near to an Inverness as a Chicagoan dared go.

His talk was the printed word on the loose. It was casual but always edited and often brilliant. We had many talkers.

George Wharton, the bitter and hilarious one; Wallace Smith, the sardonic one; Jo Swerling, the humanity lover; James Pegler, the epithetician; Richard Henry Little, the apostle of the ludicrous; Carl Sandburg, of the hurdy-gurdy metaphors; Lloyd Lewis, a-crackle with satire; brother Alfred MacArthur, the Kipling of La Salle Street—these and a score of barroom bombinators and local-room moonshooters were around MacArthur like a Sorbonne faculty. Of them all, Ashton Stevens pointed the direction of his future.

Charlie was fascinated by his theatre excitements and his getup.

"You'd never think he was a critic," he said. "He looks more like a breach-of-promise defendant, an Airedale fancier or a native of Monte Carlo."

You couldn't be under Ashton's wing, as was the Little Girl Reporter, without hatching into something highfalutin. Carol emerged as something of a giddy celebrity. She was a pretty girl with a small waistline and an elfin air. Her blond hair was cut like an Ivanhoe page boy's. She had a moody smile and was full of unexpected answers. Her head was full, also, of all the books Ashton had read, and all the scintillant things he had said about them.

Charlie, exposed to her presence in the local room, considered her a genius. This was one of the reasons for the marriage. There were others.

"I Hight Sir Launcelot du Lane, the Child"

Most of the reporters of that day in Chicago married young, myself included. It is likely we had the same inspiration.

One of the problems of youth in that time was sex. Not what it was about, but where. It's hard to believe in today's pleasant promiscuity that only a few decades ago fornication was as difficult an achievement as political office.

There were trollops galore—young, painted, mascara-eyed, in shining gowns, scorning girdles and ready to divert the solvent stranger. There was also a less gaudy pushover type called "fly girls." These were a little advanced in years, usually over twenty-seven. They were to be found in honorable surroundings but, having missed the marriage boat, were willing to try a dishonorable bed, if (as we used to say) properly approached.

But youth has a secret aversion for tarts and obliging elderly ladies. The young male stirrings of sex are accompanied by a sort of fiddle music. It is amour and its gallant dreams that youth craves, as much as a lifted dress. I mean, it wants them all.

There were thousands of good girls to be seen by a reporter with half an eye. The restaurants, department stores and streetcars were full of them. But they might as well have been quartered in Tibet.

For one thing, reporters spent nearly all their time with each other, huddled in saloons, over crap games or talk fests. Newspaper work was much like a love affair. You drank, ate, cursed, fought and slept with it. There was little time left over for work on the opposite sex—if it required much more than undressing.

There was, also, a money factor. None of us could afford to take a girl to dinner and a show, or a concert, or a trip across Lake Michigan—or other costly preliminaries of romance. The best we could offer was an afternoon in a roller-skating rink (which was like luring Isolde into a boiler factory); a dark movie theatre, a walk in Lincoln Park, or merely a long private palaver in some unfrequented hallway.

Almost the only girls we met socially, outside the painted ladies in shiny gowns, were those we ran into on news stories. But young women involved in love-shootings, rapes and disappearances were not of whom we dreamed.

We dreamed of the meeting of souls and the first passion of a pure girl, exclusively offered. As my friend Sherman Duffy used to say, "He was the first that ever burst into that silent sea." We sighed for Juliet, unsullied until we climbed the balcony.

In that day the price was marriage. We paid it, some eagerly, some sourly. There were a few cynics among us who poohpoohed the sanctity of virginity. But most of us subscribed to its status as a pearl of great price. The Victorian era was dead as a dodo but we didn't know it. Or, being young, we preferred not to know it . . . and continued aping its moony gallantries. If you tampered with a good girl you had to marry her, or else her life was blighted. You had deprived her forever of wedlock and motherhood—for who would marry a girl tarnished by illegal passion?

Needless to say, many did. How the devil could a young man, reciting Ernest Dowson and Dante Gabriel Rossetti, and composing madrigals of his own, how could he play sleuth

64

on a girl's virginity? It was only necessary for a girl to lay claim to that high status and we were all ready to spread Sir Walter's cloak for her innocent feet.

Thus, we young bridegrooms were, to an extent, all victims of our times. We were immoral as Panurge, and virile and ruthless to boot. But we kowtowed to virginity. Willy-nilly, we married our first love.

And Repent at Leisure

MacArthur's bridal night turned into a hare-and-hounds affair. Reporters had tacked a large painted sign over his desk, proclaiming:

Welcome Bridegroom!
Hotsy Totsy

But the bridegroom cameth not to his desk. Word spread that he had fled the city. A dozen Hearst men, including Editor Howey and Ashton Stevens, hunted vainly in the saloons for several days. The bridegroom was finally run down in a Turkish bath, comatose in a cloud of steam.

I have no memory of where the newlyweds lived or how they lived. I saw them occasionally, walking down Madison Street, holding hands—surprisingly unjournalistic manners. I met them once on a story in the Morrison Hotel mezzanine. It was Carol's story. A beekeepers' convention was in session and the Little Girl Reporter was cooking up something droll.

They sat buzzing together in a corner. Carol's eyes were shining. There was no handsomer mustang in town than this one on a snaffle beside her.

Of this meeting and several others, I can remember nothing MacArthur said. I see him attentive and amiable. Carol talks. She is planning a novel. She also plans a comedy for the theatre. She is at work on a short story, too. And Charlie is a wonderful help. A perfect critic to have right in your own home. A vibrant girl with a page boy's haircut and a small waistline chatters away half daft with love and dreams of fame—this is as much as I remember of the newlyweds.

There is one climactic piece of business. On an autumn afternoon a few months later Charlie came to see me at the *Daily News*. He sat down nervously at my desk. I noted an oddity about my friend. He didn't seem well turned out. Charlie caught the noticing.

"I'm working two jobs," he explained, "and haven't had a chance even to get to a barbershop. Carol's taken a couple of months off and gone to Michigan, where it's quiet, to write a novel. It's going to be something fine. I think Carol's a genius. She needed a new typewriter and a raccoon coat, on account of it's cold in Michigan. So I'm working part-time for Telfer on his *Oak Leaves*. Fifteen bucks a week, board and keep. All for literature."

He grinned.

"What I thought," said Charlie, "is that you might help me get Carol started."

It was my turn to look nervous. This was a MacArthur bewilderingly out of character. I felt a bit less depressed about my own confused home fires.

"You write for *The Smart Set*," Charlie went on, "and you know H. L. Mencken. I thought it might be a good thing if you sent one of Carol's stories to him. Providing you liked it."

He handed me a manuscript.

I called at the *Examiner* the next day and sat beside Charlie's desk. I told him I didn't like Carol's story and gave him back the manuscript.

"How about you?" I said. "Lloyd Lewis tells me you've written some kind of short story."

Charlie answered, "Lloyd's a goddamn snitch."

"You got it handy?"

Charlie took a manuscript out of a drawer. It was typed on copy paper, and full of corrections in his cobwebby handwriting. The story was titled "Rope."

I read it while he conferred with Howey on his night's assignment. It was one of the best short stories I'd ever read. Nikolai Gogol might have written it if he had known our county jail and its half-idiotic officials. It was a story about the hangman and his love troubles. Money was at the root of them. His was piecework. He got paid only per hanging. The governor had reprieved two doomed men and thus robbed the hero of the money his girl insisted he must have before she gave herself to him in wedlock. After an afternoon of innumerable frustrations, the hangman sought cheer by lighting the big cigar the warden had given him as a wedding present. It was a trick cigar. It blew up in his face.

I sent the story to Mencken, who gleefully printed it.

"MacArthur's a big find," Mencken wrote me. "Lock him in a cage and keep him writing."

Charlie sent the fifty-dollar check from Mencken to the toiling genius in Michigan. He continued to talk about her "forthcoming novel." He wrote Mencken a letter, hoping to whet the sage's appetite for it.

There is a letter from Charlie to Carol on faded *Examiner* copy paper. It was written at his newspaper desk. It reads, in part:

"As you know, I do not want you to work at anything that is distasteful to you. I hesitate in telling you this. But the only real work you will ever do will be the result of driving. I hope the driving comes from within.

"I know I am right in this. You have a letter from the editor of the Red Book that is almost two years old. That was an opportunity never capitalized. I stand ready to provide whatever facilities and environment are necessary for the development of your genius. . . ."

There is a basic MacArthurism in the letter. He could write circles around Carol. His newspaper copy, as well as short stories, had the leap of fine writing in them. But his own work is not mentioned in this letter. The world is others'—other people's dreams.

I sit with my eyes on the past, filching these small items out of it. And I grow confused. Was there actually such a past, such a Charlie, and such a me? I see parts of streets and hear parts of sentences. A picture half torn away comes to my eyes, and names echo like the mournful cry of birds in the mist. These I can complete and fit easily into copy. But that other matter—the illusion that age was no kin of ours, that youth was endless. Was that how we felt?

I see us there as a permanent cast of young men and women, living in a forever of adolescence. Except that Charlie did detach himself from this vision. Even in this beginning he had the secretive look of a man who has had his fortune told. Not endless horizons, but a handful of hours, said the fortune-teller.

There is another quality that marks Charlie in these squandering days. It will mark him to the end. Under the serenity of MacArthur there is a violence. At whom it is aimed, or why, is not to be seen. I recall that one night, in Mangler's saloon, I said to a smiling MacArthur with his seventh drink in hand, "You brood like Hamlet."

Long Live Art

I WAS running a weekly newspaper (barred from all the Midwestern campuses) when I received a letter with an enclosure from the *émigré* MacArthur.

"This is a lousy town. Avoid it if you can. The enclosed is from a pal, Sadie, whom I once met on a pier. It explains why New York is a lousy town and why Art will never get further east than Benton Harbor, Michigan. Sadie is still a-bloom in N. Dearborn Street. Bert Weber, the poet involved, is a pal of mine. He differs from the poets of New York who all live in penthouses and are served breakfast in bed by their butlers. What a town—Chicago. Please print Sadie's communiqué in that windy sheet of yours."

The enclosure (printed in the newspaper) read:

DEAR FRIEND,

A grand rally and picnic of the Chicago Intelligentsia has been billed for Thursday, May 1st, at Bughouse Square, Chicago. The proceeds from this monster feast of reason and brawn will go towards paying off the $600 fine imposed on Bertram Lestram Weber, the poet who had the misfortune to break in a plate glass window in endeavoring to silence a public nuisance last Sabbath day.

After frantic phoning to the police to end the ringing of an alarm bell that had wakened him at 2 A.M. poet Weber sallied forth himself, tracked down the peace disturbing gong. He found it to be a police box on a stone wall. Taking aim with an inkwell which had accompanied him as a weapon, the poet let fly. He missed the alarm box and sailed his ink pot through the 11-by-8 foot window of a nearby second-hand book store. As usual, when art is in error, two bulls were on hand. Weber was hoosegowed. The next day the judge gave our poet until May 5th to pay for the damaged window. He might as well have saddled him with the German War debt. Hence the monster demonstration.

The May Day Ceremonies will start by an assembly in Tooker Alley. Trip Hammer Johnson and his Dill Pickle Symphony orchestra will lead the march. Next in line will be Jack Jones and his Doodle Opera Troupe, followed in turn by Vincent Nogi and his House of Correction extortion squad, Jack Ryan and his hoodelizers, and others.

Tickets may be had from Jerry the Junkman at his book store near the Clark Street Bridge.

SADIE

We were all fools to have left Chicago. It was a town to play in; a town where you could stay yourself, and where the hoots of the critics couldn't frighten your style or drain your soul. Charlie preserved it in his heart. Our friendship was based, largely, on the nostalgia we shared for this stockyard Athens. We both knew that the world would turn up nothing better for us than the frowsy streets and hooligan towers of Chicago.

New York

Hello New York

Now that I have brought Charlie to New York, by jettisoning most of his Chicago history, I am inclined to wistfulness. To write of a friend who has died is to stick a leg into your own grave. To write of a friend's youth is even more pensive work. For beside his youth is your own—both hell and gone forever.

Since lament for the snows of yesteryear was my friend's theme song, consider these lines as much his as mine. There's a mystery about Time no poet or scientist has solved (to my satisfaction)—the fact that it doesn't exist. It is a pit into which everything falls, and there's no bottom to it. A day is a hole, a year is a bigger one. Make the mistake of thinking a day exists, and you'll pay with a tear drop.

In the poet's eye Time is a circus always packing up and moving away. And he asks us to remember how happy its music made us. When? What happiness? Where is it? What music? Yesterday's happiness is as missing from the soul as yesterday's food from the stomach. It was never ours to keep. Try putting on an old thrill, an old sigh, and you'll know. It doesn't fit. Old dreams, old raptures hang ludicrously on us. It was someone else who wore them once.

It is the writer's task to soften the calamity of Time. The scientist can do no more than make a clock to tick a constant farewell. But writers, being liars and infants, can pretend it never went away, and that it exists as if it were a monument instead of a nowhere-hole. What's so dreadful about the atom bomb? Time is a bigger one. Go find youth in its rubble. I'll now put my zither away.

It was there for Charlie—this young time in New York. There are chiefly corpses for witnesses. But I have also memories and documents that so testify.

It flourished in the Brevoort and LaFayette Hotels; in Morrill Goddard's Hearst headquarters, where stories about the end of the world, and the accomplishments of fleas, and Caligula's orgies were concocted; in speakeasies, taxicabs, hotel lobbies, back stages, drawing rooms and bedrooms; on street corners and sometimes in mid-air.

How revive this youth on paper—especially with an autumn vocabulary?

Turgenev threw a memorable line to it: "How red, how red were the roses . . ."

Youth was Charlie's religion. He kept youth going by walking backward through life, genuflecting at its distant altars. Watching Charlie as he aged, you were aware chiefly of the fact that he was staying young. It is the same trick of faith that keeps afflicted people believing in the benevolence of God.

In a speakeasy, once, a college boy jumped on top of the upright piano. His foot went through the top into the strings. Waving his free foot in the air, the college boy cried, "Look, I've lost my other galosha!"

Charlie sighed at a nearby table: "That word galosha wouldn't have occurred to me any more. He's younger than I am."

Weather Change

IT was a different Charlie in New York than Chicago had known. The smiling Abednego who had walked through fiery furnaces without getting singed began to lose a little of his immunity.

The change was due to the sprouting of talent in him.

Talent's a thing to throw a man into the meat chopper, however detached his eye. A man who writes takes his skin off. Where cannon shells exploding in his ears couldn't make our hero blink, critics' spitballs could send him scampering for cover. And there is only one refuge from critics: you quit writing.

Before this happened—and it never happened entirely—Charlie wooed his muse with a loud skirl of his bagpipes. He stole hours from revelry and wrote. His three companions of that time—Jimmy Whittaker, Gene Fowler and Jo Swerling—wag their heads doubtfully today at this news.

Said Mr. Whittaker, still at the Hearst oars: "My dear sir, impossible. I recall clearly his many activities. They included neither raffia weaving nor writing."

But the proof survives. Piles of yellowed pages, with cobwebby pencil emendations, are in front of me. There is one story, of a drunken partygoer who was swindled by a woman and prematurely embalmed by an overzealous undertaker's assistant, that is as good literature as I have ever read. Charlie put a whole world he knew into its thirty macabre pages.

Unbeknownst to his intimates, Charlie wrote. Manuscripts piled up between hangovers. Short stories and play scripts (with an act or two missing) took up as much drawer space as his new tuxedo and its appurtenances.

Come to this great cake-walking city on the Hudson, Charlie was not alone. More and more there appeared around him the familiar, human faces of Chicago—for an exodus was on from the Windy City. Its young landmarks were drifting eastward on the New York Central and the Nickel Plate. What emptied Chicago within two years of most of its bright lads and celebrities-to-be is hard to say. My memory is that, being all more or less of the same age, they got involved with women—either fighting like Cossacks to leave them, or chasing like lunatics after them. Either way, it seems to me, looking back, that it was the girls who gutted Chicago's literary renaissance. There were some lads who drifted off with no yonic disturbances, like Jimmy Butts, who was offered twenty dollars more a week on the Shanghai *Sun*; and John Gunther, who couldn't get himself hired as a local reporter and went off looking for copy he might peddle at space rates; and Ernest Hemingway, who was a born sight-seer.

For the Chicago-haunted MacArthur, the citizenry of his new town consisted mainly of Jimmy Whittaker, Gene Fowler and Jo Swerling. There were a few other home folks—Burton Rascoe, Gene Markey, Carl Sandburg, J. P. McEvoy, and Jap, the Stillson bartender, resplendent in a tuxedo and king of a basement speakeasy in Manhattan. And another one was sitting walleyed at the helm of the newly founded *Morning Mirror*. This was Walter Howey.

Walter believed in his Chicago lucky pieces. He had sent for two of them, Swerling and Whittaker, to join his new staff. They had answered his Lorelei summons. MacArthur, at work a hundred feet away in the Hearst Rider Haggard department, had resisted the sorcery. Let Howey yodel his brains out, Charlie announced he would stick in the ramshackle loft on Gold Street, whose windows looked on Brooklyn Bridge and whose chief was more concerned with the craters of the moon than the highways of Gotham.

"I'd like to work for you, Walter," said Charlie. "You know that. But I don't want to be a reporter in this goddamn town."

"Why not?" purred Walter. "There's a lot of stuff going on."

"Because it's a phony, smart-aleck, fat-headed town," said Charlie. "It's for press agents, not newspapermen."

There were two equally strong impulses prodding the Mac-Arthur id. One was an itch to write plays and thus outwit the economic system. This phony town to which he had come was the headwaters of theatre fame. Broadway was full of jackpots.

The other was a more moody thing. It was a loyalty to Chicago—and to a memory of perfect existence. Quincy Number 9, Keeley and the *Trib*, Howey and the *Examiner*, Deanie O'Bannion, the Criminal Courts building pressroom, Stillson's, Sunset Number One—glee and corruption around you, and the heart undaunted, and the world loving you because you grinned in a barroom (and nothing more was required for fame); go find another place like that. Chicago was the highlands to which Charlie's heart cleaved. New York was alien ground and would so remain all his life. Success, love and a thousand friendships were to mute his disdain for this peacock of a town, but never remove it.

"You've got to love a town to be a reporter in it," MacArthur said to the persistent Howey, "and, baby, I don't love."

"For God's sake," said Howey. "Do you want to go back to Chicago?"

"No," said MacArthur. "That's over. But there's noplace else."

Recalling his time of weaning, Jimmy Whittaker said, "He was like some captive in the tents of Pompey. The minute he got lit, he'd start off for a subway entrance. He'd stand there till he spotted a husky fellow heading underground. And he'd accost the fellow angrily with some such remark as, 'Hey, you lousy New Yorker, where do you think you're going?'

"Jo and I would say, 'Come on, Charlie. This gentleman is doing no harm!' And Charlie would answer, 'Don't tell me! He's a goddamn New Yorker.' He'd stick his face close to the husky and yell, 'Deny it! Deny you're a lousy New Yorker!' The confused husky usually lost his temper and took a poke at his heckler. And the fight would be on. Hardly a week passed, but Charlie had a new black eye or cut lip."

Charlie's one-man commando raid on Gotham petered out after a year.

His First Musketeers

CHARLIE had met Gene Fowler in Chicago. It's part of Gene's story and he's busy writing it, so I'll put down only a blueprint. The tall, Chesterfieldian Westerner, thin faced and with a Wyatt Earp drawl, was making his first pilgrimage to the East. He was on his way from the local rooms of Denver to Mr. Hearst's *American* in New York. As a means of saving railroad fare, the young traveler had offered himself to a Denver undertaker as chaperon for a New York-bound corpse. A live monitor was required by law for such transport.

The remains Fowler was baby-sitting with across the country were those of a Denver Jezebel. Fowler draped the casket in French flags and promoted its occupant to a captain of French chasseurs who had given his life heading off the Kaiser and his hordes from Paris.

A desire to see the native land of which he had read so much urged Fowler to pursue a zigzag route eastward, with many stopovers. At these pausing places there were often reception committees eager to pay homage to the casketed hero, and to provide its gallant guardian with free liquor.

"I have no particular hero worship myself," said Fowler, "but I knew even then the little I know now about people. They always care more for anybody who buys renown by shedding his blood than for him who, without dying, wins praise. That's from Martial, the Roman Walter Winchell."

What the devil a French chasseur was doing in Denver, dead or alive, I don't know. But this is the story Charlie, much moved, told me over the phone in Chicago.

"He's right now in the Harrison Street bull pen under arrest," said Charlie. "According to all I can get, he entered the lobby of the Morrison Hotel around ten A.M. You know that big American flag made out of electric lights in the lobby? It roused our visitor's anger. He said it was an insult to George Washington. And he picked up one of the big goldfish globes beside it and tossed it at the offensive ensign.

"No," Charlie answered a query, "he's not a pro-German. He's just against electric lights. I think we ought to go meet him." We did.

Charlie met the Denver Charon again some months later in the town of Mt. Clemens, Michigan. Here, in the local courthouse, automobile manufacturer Henry Ford was suing the Chicago *Tribune*, demanding libel damages for having been called an ignoramus. Fowler was there for the Hearst press. MacArthur went as a reporter from the embattled *Tribune*.

Tales of the doings of MacArthur and Fowler in Mt. Clemens took precedence in Chicago over the progress of the trial. The one that made the Ford-*Tribune* libel case memorable for years to come was the MacArthur stealing of the streetcar. It is the MacArthur version I'll tell, it being the least gaudy of the reports brought back. Charlie was standing on a corner waiting patiently for a streetcar—Mt. Clemens was a summer-resort town with a vague Traction Company—when one came down the pike. Despite the correspondent's signaling, it refused to stop and take him to the courthouse. The correspondent gave chase.

Charlie overtook the streetcar after three blocks and boarded it. He tossed the inattentive motorman into the street and took his place at the controls.

"There will be no extra fare," Charlie called to the passengers. "Just hold tight. We're going for a spin through Mt. Clemens."

With heel banging the loud floor bell, Charlie opened her up. In no time at all the leaping, swaying streetcar arrived safely at the city limits—and the end of the tracks. Charlie changed car ends.

The return trip offered added excitement. A fire engine and two automobiles filled with policemen appeared off the port bow and gave chase. Vacationers cheered the spectacle from the sidewalks. Charlie held the throttle down and his streetcar, clanging triumphantly, left the chasers in the lurch. Arrived at the hilly avenue that led to his hotel headquarters, Charlie put on the brakes, jumped to the street and started up the hill. A dozen police- and firemen, still lagging by a block, started after him.

At the top of the hill stood a Civil War monument—a Union soldier on a stone base. At each side of the base was a pyramid of cannon balls, four feet high.

Winded by his climb, Charlie paused beside the monument.

The police and fire departments of Mt. Clemens were scaling the steep hill on foot, intent on his capture. Charlie went into battle. One by one he removed the cannon balls and rolled them down the hill at the oncoming enemy. Correspondents watched and cheered from the hotel windows as police and fire departments sought cover. The artillerist who was to stand at Château-Thierry stood on Mt. Clemens till the battle was won. He retired victorious to his base in the hotel bar-room.

"It was a stirring sight," said Fowler, "and we toasted our Davy Crockett until the *Tribune* legal battery, luckily on the scene, made peace with the city fathers of Mt. Clemens. Then we toasted the *Tribune* barristers, and then, also, the city fathers. There were no hard feelings."

Musketeer Whittaker was an odd one for a local room. He was well built, cherubic faced and with the kind of blond mane usually worn by concert pianists. Whittaker was entitled to the eruption of hair because he was, in truth, a concert pianist. He had been cooed out of his career by Howey.

At fourteen Jimmy had left Chicago to study piano playing in Leipzig and Paris. At twenty he had followed the concert trail blazed by Paderewski, banging out Liszt, Chopin, Brahms, Franck and Beethoven in all the capitals of Europe. He then exchanged the concert stage for the 4th Field Artillery of the U.S. Army's 32nd Division, and covered much the same ground as MacArthur's Battery F. Like MacArthur, Whittaker faced the Krauts at Château-Thierry and the Argonne. Whittaker's battery had the distinction of being the only German-speaking outfit on the Allied side. It was made up of Wisconsin draftees, mostly from Milwaukee.

"It was an odd war for me," said Jimmy. "We spoke German, sang German songs, told German stories—and our battle cry was 'Down with the Germans.'"

The confused artillerist returned to Chicago and landed on the Hearst payroll as music critic for the *Examiner*. It was his plan to keep eating while he restored his fingers to their prewar agility. But Howey intruded. No Paderewski haircut could hide a good newspaperman from Walter.

"Why do you want to waste your life," said Walter, "making those peewee sounds on a piano like a whorehouse professor? I have work for you."

Jimmy joined the staff, but remained true to the arts by marrying into them. His bride was the actress Ina Claire, a wit, a star and a dancing odalisque.

Of Jo Swerling, the third MacArthur musketeer, I can report, chiefly, that he was an infatuated do-gooder. Jo's deepest pleasures lay in lending money to friends and cadgers alike, bringing solace to the afflicted, and speaking well of all his fellows. There was a streak of this Lady Bountifulism in the young MacArthur and Fowler, both. They, too, went about rescuing strays and bringing pint bottles to the suffering. But they were only part-time Samaritans.

Jo was the first of the Chicago crew to sail off into fame. Long before our literary renaissance was officially underway, Jo's play, written with Jack Lait, *The Kibitzer*, saw the footlights.

One of his more recent compositions was the musical show *Guys and Dolls*.

These three were Charlie's friends in the time of his fretful debut in New York. They drank together, played penny ante together—a protective measure, for they were card players whom a blind man could have taken to the cleaner's. They roamed the streets and peeked into hideaways like four young Haroun al-Rashids looking for truth and diversion.

There was another familiar face for MacArthur to contemplate in that time. His young wife arrived on money he had carefully saved for a ménage in New York. The money went quickly. Carol, touched by the glamour of the great metropolis, insisted on the bridal suite in the Ritz Hotel and a daily salute of orchids as proof of her husband's devotion. She was, in fact, as Charlie viewed it, full of painful whims. The love idyll of the *Examiner* local room evolved into a tug of war that left both contestants with rope burns.

A distaste for marriage now bedeviled MacArthur. The urge for freedom added a quart of Scotch to his nights.

But the Little Girl Reporter was to fight his efforts to divorce her for seven years. I know of no other wife in the U.S. in that time who put up so fierce a battle to remain mated. After years of separation and lost legal set-tos, Carol still fought on.

A hint of the long Laocoön struggle ahead came to Charlie on his first footling breaks for liberty. He was a young man of considerable stamina. But, roar, buck, kick and leap into the air, there was no out for Charlie.

Charlie's Gold Rush

HEARST paid a hundred and fifty a week. Mencken was good for no more than sixty dollars a short story, maximum. There were several plays on the fire, but not ready for producer hands. An act or two was missing in each. As for a shot at the big magazines that paid thousand-dollar bills for fiction, that was a target at which Charlie never looked. The kind of stories he wrote would give a popular-magazine editor the fantods. He could write no other way.

The expenses of an unhappy marriage are usually larger than those of a happy one. Both parties need solacing. Trial separation trips and reconciliation wardrobes run into money. Bankruptcy breathed on Charlie and he turned to the business world for help.

Charlie's two tries in the Rotary Club realm are the only ones of which I know. They show, however, a flair for industry that might have ended him as a tycoon, had he kept to it.

The first venture was a sort of warm-up. Charlie went into partnership with an ex-Peruna peddler named Oscar, met in a speakeasy one night.

After several all-night conferences, Oscar and Charlie cooked up a new product for the public. It was a rejuvenating cream—much like a cold cream, except that it contained a youth-restoring ingredient distilled from the sex organs of a certain South American snake. The product restored the full bloom of youth—and preserved it. They gave it the name "Miriko."

"Miriko is a cinch," said Oscar. "It'll go like a house afire, if we can get an advertising campaign behind it. But for that we need a suitcase full of money."

"How would a double-page spread in the Hearst *Sunday Supplement* do?" asked Oscar's partner. Oscar said terrific.

"My boss, Morrill Goddard," said Charlie, "has a deep love for the bizarre. We printed a story last week about the possibility of there being spies from Mars in our midst, sizing up the planet as a first step in its conquest. We need something like that to hang Miriko on—and a million dollars in free advertising is ours."

Oscar was silent.

"What we'll do," said Charlie, "is get a couple of girls who'll say they've been kept young by using Miriko for seventy or eighty years. I know just where to get them—a pair of real beauties. Very sweet kids. They're sisters, real sisters, which will make it sound more authentic."

A week later Charlie was ready with his two lovely Miriko-using nonagenarians. He registered them at the Brevoort, where he had established a charge account, coached them and provided them with birth certificates, placing their natal days in the early 1830's.

Boss Goddard himself came to the Brevoort to interview the two examples of eternal youth flushed by his keen employee.

The first interview went off very well. Mr. Goddard was especially impressed by sister Bessie's detailed memory of the hanging of John Brown of Harpers Ferry. The second interview, however, ended the Miriko campaign. It is a painful scene, and I'll tell it briefly.

83

In the middle of the interview, as sister Emmaline was recalling the Indian wars that swept the Arizona territory in the 1850's, the hotel door opened. A handsome but indignant woman entered. She was in her late thirties but looked young for her age.

"So this is where I find you!" she cried at the nonagenarians. "In a hotel room with two men!"

"What have you to do with these two sweet old ladies?" Mr. Goddard demanded.

"What sweet old ladies?" the woman cried. "They are my daughters. I've been looking for them all week."

The next MacArthur venture into the business world was more successful. His eye, idling through the paper, had noted an announcement of a new cemetery, opened in New Jersey.

Charlie crossed the Hudson to offer his talents in the development of the new burial ground. It was a business field in which he felt at home and full of certainties.

"As I recall," said Whittaker, "Charlie made a couple of thousand dollars on the project. His first move caused quite a stir in the press as well as rival graveyard circles.

"Charlie went to Boston and arranged with some venal city official to have the remains of Henry Wadsworth Longfellow removed from their Boston resting place and replanted in New Jersey. In preparation for the poet's arrival, he had named a wing of the new cemetery the 'American Westminster Abbey.' "

(Longfellow's fascination for MacArthur had grown with the years. I haven't the faintest idea on what it was based.)

Continued Whittaker, "The spadework on Henry Wadsworth Longfellow was hardly begun when it attracted the attention of some Boston literary society. A cry went up against the great Boston bard being highjacked out of the state. Charlie fought this parochial attitude, contending that the great Henry Wadsworth belonged to all the nation. It was fitting, he argued, that the poet should be the first of a series of great corpses to be buried in the Westminster Abbey wing of the New Jersey cemetery.

Charlie bows in at thirteen. A natty Belmont collar, a seemingly indestructible mop of hair, and a glint of wisdom in his eyes. The wisdom stayed on.

Back from his debut as a warrior in pursuit of Pancho Villa in Mexico—Charlie hurried into a Rainbow Division suit for his first European battle tour.

Here's Charlie in his first years of playwright fame. The pho-
tographer arranged the double-pointed handkerchief and
draped the wicked left hook nonchalantly on the thigh. The
rest is authentic Charlie—including the overtones of Byron and
Pushkin. (*Nickolas Muray*)

We have here our hero caught in a moment of diversion with his pal Bob Benchley. Both lads are trying their best to look like Bowery flotsam—and succeeding rather well.

Here's Charlie's wedding picture with Helen. When I wrote this book this is the picture that looked at me. And a line from Turgenev hovered above it—"How red, how red were the roses."

Charlie had his fling as a camera bug in Nyack, equipped with darkroom and devoted personal model—Helen. From the thoughtful look in the artist's face it would seem he had bagged another nude. (*Clarence Sinclair Bull*)

One of Charlie's hobbies was circling the earth and saying hello to life everywhere. It's obvious that the camels recognize a friend.

Here is our gaiety salesman in his thirties. He rides on a boat, grins at the sea. No cloud is in the sky. Youth still pipes all hands on board.

This was one of those evenings in happy Hollywood when Cinderella was still the leading local product. The Cinderella here is the plump one, Marie Dressler. The other charmer is Lili Damita. A study of Charlie's tie reveals the fun he was having.

On a night of ermine and floodlights, Charlie pilots his movie star, Helen, and their friend Mary Pickford to a Hollywood première.

Helen and Charlie beamed on their daughter
Mary from the hour of her birth—

This was the homeland Charlie saw, looking out of his window in Nyack: the tended garden, the waiting pool, the Hudson River—and a thousand memories.

Young James MacArthur seems to have his right eye cocked against the pious counsel of his grandfather, Reverend William MacArthur.

It's a doting husband who'll stand for his wife's taking a yipping pooch along on a transcontinental journey. Charlie was that. (*Bernard Hoffman*)

A careful study of the books surrounding Charlie at his Nyack work desk reveals none that he copped from me.

In his last military suit, plastered with ribbons and symbols not quite clear to me, Colonel Charles MacArthur tackles World War II.

As happy an American family as ever basked in a vacation sun
—Charlie, Helen, Mary and Jim MacArthur. It was the last
picture of them together. (*Freddie Maura*)

Swifter than a guillotine ou[r]
camera moves on to a sick[?]
elderly gentleman on the *Per*[-]
son to Person television sho[w]
—with his wife sitting straigh[t]
enough for two.

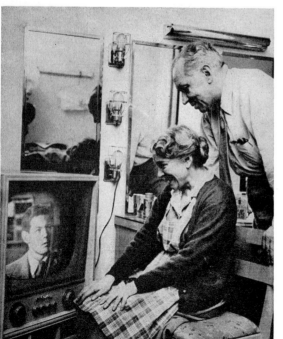

And here is Charlie's last lov[-]
ing look (in front of a cam[-]
era). He watches with Hele[n]
the successful television debu[t]
of their son, James.

"MacArthur returned to New York, certain of victory—so he confided in an interview. But there was no further news from Boston. Growing impatient at the delay in moving Longfellow to the new Westminster Abbey, Charlie wired his Boston contact: 'Roll them bones.'

"Longfellow was kept in Boston ground. But the ruckus stirred by MacArthur's raid was reported fully in the press. And the cemetery owners rewarded Charlie for his fine business vision."

As interesting as the attempted Longfellow kidnaping is the brochure Charlie wrote on the correct way to be a modern undertaker. It is a sly and mocking document.

In it Death is a sort of con man's assistant. The con man is the undertaker. On no other business did Charlie ever spend any sarcasm. The tycoons were too far away for his humor. But he chuckled at the mock pomp of the dollar-chasing mortician. Had he ever written a novel, its Babbitt hero would have been a master of the caskets.

"Long ere Rome Rang of Us,

They Had the Hang of Us—"

THE town MacArthur didn't like fell in love with him—not the whole five million, but that section of it that went to First Nights and Fancy Parties, that wrote books, plays, madrigals and the town's humor: its high-stepping critics, actors, and actresses, its speakeasy maîtres, its Russian *émigrés*, its slickest bootleggers and name-hunting hostesses, its anecdote-hungry columnists—young Winchell, Lyons, Sobel, Sullivan —its *bons vivants*, theatre producers, hotel clerks, Casanovas, and its Noah's Ark full of zanies. No such desired guest had been along for some time.

When I read of Byron's "day" in London, of Oscar Wilde's whirl through its drawing rooms, of Dumas père's capture of Paris, and Pushkin's fling in St. Petersburg, I think of the Charlie of the twenties. He shone as brightly.

"Please," said Prince Bibesco, his arm around MacArthur. "I have a suite at the Plaza. Four rooms. I am going away. Please use it. Give parties. Enjoy yourself. I return in a month. Good-by, my friend. You have made me very happy in New York."

"I am giving a party for seventy people," said the bellowing white-maned sculptor Bob Chanler, "all idiots. My society friends from Westchester will be there. God forgive me for being descended from those cliché-ridden nymphomaniacs. You must be at my party, Charlie, or I'll be sure to break a dozen skulls. You be there, Charlie, and drink with me, and I'll love everybody."

"Mr. MacArthur," said the hard-fisted Jack Kriendler, the dandy in charge of the town's new speakeasy, "21," "the place is yours. And if you get tired of the racket down here, you are welcome to my apartment upstairs. You can use it as a studio to write in or a place of refuge."

Nor was it an easy time in which to shine as is our present day, with the color drained out of nearly all of us and politics substituted, and a jabber about world affairs taking the place of wit and human sprightliness. In that other time this town was overrun with wags and spicy boys and girls. The cafés were like circus rings. The black-tie dinner tables were jousting fields for personality. Global thinking had not yet driven the mot to cover. It was a time when a man was judged by his own wits, and not by the editorials he espoused. And the women, I bow again. They needed more than a bowling-ball bosom and overmembranous lips to fetch attention.

Writing of my friend in those days, I look in my mind for basic facts. These always make writing easy—a man's ideas, beliefs, ideals, the causes he serves, and his battle out of defeat to success. Biography teems with such portraits. A face looks out of the past like the trade-mark for some achievement.

There were ideas and achievements in MacArthur. But, were I to tell you that my friend bloomed as a man of letters in the twenties, I'd be drawing him dimly. His attractiveness was still his special mark. The cocks of the walks of the twenties swarmed around him.

Most of them are dead. But they make a frame for Mac-Arthur, and they also seem MacArthur, too. Although he imitated none of them, Charlie was as much his friends as himself. This most detached and untouchable of egos (his) lived chiefly in other worlds than his own—as if he had none. As if—I said it before—he was the visitor enjoying someone else's party.

I am sure that there was a man full of self, and with a world all his own which he inhabited tenaciously. There are his writings and his dedication to one woman for thirty years to prove it. But Charlie kept this world to himself.

Whittaker, Charlie's intimate for fifteen years, said: "I only once got near to his spinal fluid. He came to my apartment late one night, sober, and his face without a smile. He walked up and down and said, 'I'm going to marry Helen. If I don't, I'll be lost and no good for the rest of my life. I've got to marry her. If I don't marry her my soul is doomed.' "

"Doomed to what?" I asked Whittaker.

"I don't know," said Whittaker. "He didn't say."

I go to Charlie's new friends, for a new look at him.

The Bed of Delphi

THE first and most important was a man who lay in a bed, unable to see or move. He was Edward Sheldon, a relative through Alfred MacArthur's marriage.

Sheldon had been a handsome, romantic man at the century's turn. He wrote a dozen plays, knew everybody, went everywhere, and glittered atop the theatre and social worlds of New York. Arthritis suddenly stiffened him into an invalid as motionless as a statue, and turned his eyes to stone.

Sheldon became a voice on a pillow. It was, seemingly, a serene voice. It had a kindly rumble and resonance. It spoke as if its owner were still in the midst of life, and stranger to all affliction.

The bedroom where Sheldon lay for twenty years, motionless and sightless, was one of the theatre's most popular Green Rooms. Stars, managers and playwrights came on visiting hours to discourse and gossip—and linger for advice. There were ex-stars, and ex-managers also, and a larger contingent of desperate souls than usually is found in a fashionable Green Room.

Ned Sheldon was their confessional. He was a man in whom all the impurities of the world seemed to have burned away. He was without malice or righteousness. He had an understanding of pain.

To MacArthur, Ned Sheldon was more than a friend. He was Charlie's good side that spoke from a pillow, a sort of external conscience that lay sightless in a blue-lighted room. Charlie also looked on Ned as a personification of the only two virtues to which he bowed—selflessness and gallantry.

There was an oddity in the relation. Charlie was the one visitor who brought few problems for Sheldon to solve or lighten. It was Sheldon who usually unloaded problems on

MacArthur. They were other people's problems that a blind, immobile man could not cope with. There was the ex-star, once a fine actress, at whose bed Sheldon sent Charlie to sit night after night as she screamed and sweated in a try to get the dope monkey off her back.

There was another star actress who died, leaving suicide evidence behind. Ned sent Charlie to find the suicide note before the police arrived, and tear it up; and to wangle an honorable death certificate out of some doctor. All this was done. The star was buried with her name untarnished and the legend of her proud ways intact.

For twenty years Charlie, usually as socially reliable as an amnesia victim, never failed his Ned on a single mission or appointment. There were scores of them—jobs for down-and-outers whom Sheldon had known in their fine hours; rooming-house castaways for Charlie to entertain for an evening with tales of the humming world; drunkards to nurse and help taper off; homicidal lovers to unwind; suicides to talk to sleep; and gifts to distribute.

MacArthur wrote his first successful play, *Lulu Belle*, with Sheldon. David Belasco produced it, and Charlie had another Sheldon assignment. It was to see that the "Guvnor" (Belasco) changed no line or plot turn of their joint work.

Charlie attended rehearsals and stymied Belasco, then lord of all Broadway, in his efforts to cut and rewrite. Despite the script-mugging that went on, Belasco delighted MacArthur. Belasco was the Land of the Theatre. He had a face borrowed from a thousand actors, mystic and foolish with sham importance that was not sham in the theatre. Charlie won most of the rehearsal debates. There were some he lost.

At one time Belasco cut a page of dialogue from Lenore Ulric's part. Miss Ulric was the star of *Lulu Belle*, and of the Guvnor's heart.

"I'm making the cut," said director Belasco in the metallic buzz produced by his antique dental plates, "so that you won't have to talk so fast on the stage, darling. It will enable you to get some sense and a little emotion into what you are trying to do, darling."

Miss Ulric screamed. Four other actors involved in the cut blanched. The Guvnor had cut out the best scene in the whole play, they cried out.

MacArthur protested vigorously.

"Quiet, you gray rat," Belasco responded in his dramatic gasp. "I am going to make you rich and famous with my genius."

"I'll tell you where you can stick your genius," the playwright retorted. And the stage, crowded with some forty white and Negro actors, exploded with mutiny.

The tumult bowed the Guvnor's silvered head. He listened in silence to the anger against him, and then raised a hand. Oddly, the stage quieted.

"Children," he spoke, "there will be a recess for ten minutes. I have an important decision to make. Please wait for my return."

"His pompous and mysterious remarks could always baffle any actress into silence," said MacArthur. "Lenore piped down and we all looked at him and wondered where the hell he had to go to all of a sudden. He had a weak bladder and used to make all kinds of impressive excuses to duck out to take a leak. But he didn't head for any can this time. He walked off the stage into the empty auditorium. Then he walked on to the back of the theatre.

"We watched him from the stage, pacing slowly and stopping, and nodding, and then he'd smack his forehead with his palm as if he'd discovered a new trade route. This silly performance went on for fifteen minutes, and he returned to the stage. 'I'm only sorry Ned isn't here to hear what I have to say,' he announced. 'Ned would understand it. He's a poet. I've just had a very interesting discussion about my proposed cut in the dialogue. I've been talking to Charles Frohman, the great producer who died so gallantly when the *Lusitania* went down. I told Mr. Frohman our problem, and how you and Ned feel about it, Charles, and you, Miss Ulric. He listened to both sides like a gentleman. And he told me I was right, and to go ahead and make the cut.' He glanced to the rear of the empty theatre and sort of moaned: 'I hope we don't disappoint Mr. Frohman. He's a very wise man and loves the theatre.'

"How," continued MacArthur, "could you argue with such a goddamn wonderful ham? I knew Ned would raise the roof, but I gave in."

When Charlie brought me to Sheldon for the first time, I was impressed to find all he had told about Ned to be true. There he lay, a black mask over his face, stiff as a Pharaoh in his box; and with no aura of pain or disablement about him. A bright voice spoke from the pillow. He told a story about the hanging of one of the men who had been in on the killing of Lincoln. The doomed man (or it may have been a woman) hung by the rope around his neck without any hint of giving up the ghost. The conspirator's neck muscles were too strong. An infuriated bailiff leaped from the gallows platform and landed on the figure dangling from the rope. His added weight did the job.

This tale, coming in salty phrases from this ghost of a man, impressed me. Sheldon was a fine high-wire act.

MacArthur also impressed me. I had never seen him toned down by anyone before. The MacArthur profanity was in an editor's hands.

The foggy smile went from his face. There was no abstracted pull at his fetlock. Charlie looked steadily and proudly at the sightless man, as if he were royalty.

Charlie and I were working in the Algonquin Hotel when Helen telephoned to tell him Ned Sheldon had just died. Charlie was silent for a moment, and then said quietly: "No—oh, no."

His Pal Pagliacci

On a summer's dawn in Fifth Avenue, Charlie walked with his new roommate, Bob Benchley. They shared an apartment on Madison Avenue, a sort of bachelor Cave of the Winds. Carol was in Cuba, trying out another separation. Benchley had left his conjugal fires in Long Island for the life of a littérateur in New York.

The sudden teaming up of Robert and Charles befell this way. MacArthur attended a stuffy social event. He was anchored at the punch bowl.

"What do you think of our hostess?" a guest struck up a conversation.

"Not very much," said MacArthur.

"A charming lady," said the loyal guest.

"She's too enthroned." MacArthur went at the punch bowl again.

A skittery-looking but lordly-mannered stranger stepped up to MacArthur.

"Very well put, sir," he said. "My name is Benchley. If you happen to be looking for a place to live, I have an apartment I'd be happy to share with you."

"I'm a late sleeper," said MacArthur.

"Delighted to hear it," said Benchley.

Explaining his sudden enthusiasm for MacArthur, that was never to diminish, Benchley said, "It was the first time I heard language at a Social Party."

At 5 A.M. on this Sunday morning, the roommates walking on Fifth Avenue were debating whether their Madison Avenue home was to the east or west. Charlie was burdened by a hundred-page edition of the Sunday *Times*. He was a great reader, even in those busy days.

The two friends were distracted by the appearance of a lone pedestrian in the empty, echoing avenue. They recognized young Colonel Teddy Roosevelt, L'Aiglon of the earth-shaking T.R.

Pleased to encounter friends in the morning wasteland, the Colonel stopped to chat.

"It's a little chilly for this time of year," he said.

"It is that," Benchley agreed.

MacArthur and the Sunday *Times* dropped behind the Colonel. While Benchley held the Roosevelt scion in bright social give and take, MacArthur crumpled several *Times* sections into a pile at the Colonel's heels. He put a match to it. The blaze leaped up in the chilly morning.

"It's getting a little warmer, I think," said Benchley.

"It is," said Colonel Roosevelt, and added a loud yell, "Holy jumping Judas, I'm on fire!"

Using their fedoras vigorously, the roommates put out their friend's smoldering rear. The damage was small, the jollity large.

This was the same Benchley who had arrived in Venice with Jock Whitney, carrying a suitcase full of horse manure. They had heard that no horse had ever been seen in Venice. In the wee hours, when the last gondola Caruso had hit the hay, Benchley and Whitney placed their imported horse droppings at proper intervals in the Piazza of St. Mark.

Charlie told the story proudly of his friend.

"The Venetians," he said, "considered the horse shit the only miracle of the twentieth century."

Charlie and Bob lived together for three years. Their work took them into opposite camps. Charlie wrote plays. Bob was a drama critic and a humorous essayist; more the latter. But there were never two men more at home with each other.

Benchley, unlike MacArthur, put a portion of his wit into print. Charlie wrote the beginnings of a few short stories, and a remarkable article about the inside moods and activities of the Campbell Funeral Parlors. It appeared in Harold Ross' new magazine, *The New Yorker*. But most of Charlie's efforts went into Morrill Goddard's Martian Supplement, and into

93

play writing. He worked on a play with Sidney Howard. It was called *Salvation*, and would appear on the stage under the banner of Arthur Hopkins, the pudgy, pink-faced dreamer of Better Theatre for Broadway. Pauline Lord would be its star.

MacArthur met Sidney Howard during an odd phase of that playwright's career. Howard was working for a new Hearst editor, Norman Hapgood, one of the leading *Weltanschauers* of the twenties. Hapgood had been coaxed onto the Hearst payroll by a promise of high-class activities. The promise was kept. Mr. Hapgood was given the task of suppressing the city's underworld. His first move was to put an end to its traffic in narcotics.

To assist him in this vital reform, Hapgood hired Howard, a writer of "think pieces" for the *New Republic*. Howard was a man of culture and important feelings about life. He was tall and always well barbered, and a moneyed citizen. He lived in the suburbs and was married to a famous actress, Clare Eames. The precision of his manners went into his play writing. He wrote out of a warm heart and with a cabinetmaker's attitude toward its contents.

Watching this man of taste giving chase to dope addicts and dope peddlers, MacArthur was moved to offer unofficial assistance.

Roommates Bob and Charlie remained unaware of each other's devotion to their Muses.

"Charlie's busy with something," Benchley said. "Possibly safe-cracking. He hasn't been to bed for several nights." (He was off in the suburbs working with Howard on *Salvation*.)

That Benchley's work appeared regularly in a number of magazines was an equal mystery to MacArthur. Benchley seemed to be a man devoted solely to drink and laughter, and the most unsuccessful of feminine entanglements. His addled love affairs were as comic as his prose. Girls he revered ended up in the arms of friends, whom he had allowed "the use of the apartment."

Chief among these Benchley poachers was Harpo Marx, the town's pet Harlequin. Literary lights from Bernard Shaw to

Woollcott boasted of friendship with this smiling and exhilarating Marx brother.

Harpo would wait for Benchley to fall in love, like a huntsman waiting for a bird dog to flush a pin-tailed snee.

The sound of Benchley's laughter, tooting like a tireless New Year's horn, seemed never to stop. Yet, in some difficult-to-imagine silence, Benchley put down his findings on the inadequacy of the human race. He had the gift, sought vainly by most humor writers, of putting clown faces on the commonplace. He seemed to do it as easily as he swallowed a highball. But this was illusion, as was much of the laughter that gurgled from him.

Writing was as great a torture to Benchley as it was to MacArthur. They dreamed of a place in the world of letters, but it was a tidy dream. Self-expression, as literature is called, seemed extraneous toil for these roommates, who felt themselves fully expressed when they put on their shoes at noon.

Though work was a pillory, almost every page Benchley managed to wring out of himself was full of easy wit. The reason for Benchley's success as a satirist was that he did not have to invent either the clown face or the commonplace. He wore them both like a pair of mismated socks. All the ineptitudes and foolish ignorances he needed as targets for his satire were right under his nose, in himself. Instead of considering them flaws to be hidden or lied about, he studied them as a prospector might a row of nuggets.

He, and not some alien inferior, was forever tripping over croquet wickets, being unable to attract the ear of a salesgirl, trembling before a bank teller or a crossing cop, boring people with rich anecdotes whose points had disappeared, missing trains and getting a spoon in his eye. Writing of his own deficiencies, he added a tolerance to the tale of human self-idiocy that made it seem lovable as well as comic.

MacArthur was as fascinated by Benchley's daily mishaps as by his waggery. But, most of all, Bob was a loyal traveler on the road Charlie called his own—the way of youth.

As Charlie's remark about the enthroned hostess endeared

him to the language-loving Benchley, so an old comment of Bob's forever pleased his roommate.

A friend was being buried from a third-floor walk-up flat. The pallbearers were carrying the coffin down the narrow, twisting stairway. They had to tilt it to get it around the landings.

Looking at the precariously tipped casket, turning the second floor, Benchley said, "Oh my, the change will fall out of his pocket."

Woollcott et al.

THIS was the Keeper of the Gate—the literary Cerberus of the town. He was drama critic on the New York *World*, the Parnassian daily run by Herbert Bayard Swope. There was a name in the twenties and thirties! And a newspaperman worthy of Chicago tradition. Swope had, moreover, a nose for literature as well as murder, and a passion for culture as deep as for scoops.

Alexander Woollcott wrote for Swope's fine newspaper. He wrote also for *The New Yorker*, and for other magazines. He was the first notable to take to the air and startle the radio admirers of "Amos and Andy" with elegant phrases.

Woollcott's writing was, in the main, a flourish of bonbons. He was at his best when he swooned over the talents and personalities of his friends. His friends were the bandwagon riders of the Broadway hour. Fine actors, actresses, composers and writers were among them. But their fineness was a secondary matter. The label he looked for was "success."

The gate that Alec kept opened wide for Charlie. Its keeper had not only an embrace for box-office artists; he was ready also with accolade for the successful personality—the citizen of bright heart and verve. But Alec was not solely a tuft hunter—or the tufts would have played skittish. Alec flirted with the underdog and his causes. There was an antenna in him for a cry of despair. His own divorce from womankind gave him a brotherly heart for all outcasts. He was a man of secret charities.

Woollcott lived on Forty-seventh Street near the Hudson, in a house shared by his war buddy and protégé Harold Ross. Ross was a newspaperman from San Francisco, of small experience but large gusto. He was seemingly Woollcott's opposite—a lean man with a hillbilly's face, bifurcated front teeth and a clipped pompadour. It gave his flat-nosed face a sort of burglar look. Ross was also a fellow given to unsocial guffaws and teamsterlike snorts at matters that displeased him. A bon mot was as foreign to Ross as a fez.

Yet these two opposites had an identical passion. They were born to beam on success, to be its happy baggage carriers. Success was the only proof of artistry, or even intelligence. If you failed you were a fool and a second-rater. You might fail like Keats with his *Endymion* torn to bits by its first critics; or like Flaubert with his *Madame Bovary* a flop in its first bookstores; or like Chekhov with his *Seagull* run out of Moscow in a week; or like Bizet with his *Carmen* booed off its first Paris stages. It made no difference. There was no recount on failure. No artistic halo lingered over any Broadway flop.

In Chicago we used to have a different kind of "leadership." There the party givers were keen for lost causes in the arts. They found swank in belonging to minorities, and they felt superior when defying the public taste.

But this doesn't mean they were an improvement on Woollcott and his co-Woollcotts. In Chicago there were no world beaters to collect for your parlor. If you wanted to loom as a ringmaster you had to offer your free liquor to novelists, playwrights, composers and painters as unknown as so many crossing cops.

In New York it was otherwise. Celebrities were as numerous as June bugs. It was not as "bad" as it is today. But it was the beginning of our present assembly-line crowns, plaques and blue ribbons. And it was very troublesome to the "sensitive artist."

Having occasionally been enrolled in this lodge myself, I know him only too well.

The "sensitive artist" is usually a fellow who prides himself on being above the heads of the crowd, and feels bitter about the way these same lowly heads ignore him. He sneers at the undeserved fame of talents less than his own. And he has a few sneers left over for the loud-mouth critics who lead the parade of mediocrity.

There's less complaint about this now than there used to be. The knifing of critics has died out as a literary sport. And it's almost impossible to be an "unknown" artist of any kind today. Sponsors, rating detectives and high-powered talent hunters from the advertising agencies are joined in a great man hunt for talent. Fame is as easy to achieve in New York as a head cold. The trouble is (there's always trouble about fame) that you can lose it as quickly and unreasonably as you got it. In the twenties and thirties the bay leaves were a bit more permanent, and they still came only in retail lots.

Young Woollcott set up shop, with Ross' aid, as the town's fame monitor. And so witty, bubbly, arrogant and attractive a fellow was he that the center of this fame seemed Alexander Woollcott himself.

Although he wrote like a taffy peddler and favored a sort of Fourth of July orator's style for his more ambitious works, Woollcott in conversation was a wildcat. A cliché would throw him into a fit. Crudity, boastfulness and, chiefly, dullness would set him snarling. Unlike Ross, he snarled in bons mots. He was a fine Elizabethan name caller. It was this bouncy ruthlessness more than his rounded hosannas in print that made him seem a fine critic. In truth, of all the sharp ones who came to hop-skip around the Woollcott Maypole, few were as bold of tongue and brave of opinion as the Master himself. Among the exceptions were MacArthur and roommate Benchley. And another one, Dorothy Parker—called, by the elect, Dotty.

Miss Parker was a poetess, a short-story and essay writer, and a critic. She was a cut above Woollcott in her tastes as well as output. She was among the first to conceive a passion for Hemingway. And a play by Eugene O'Neill or Sean O'Casey didn't drive her scowling into a speakeasy.

Her poems, while not as moody and witty as Edna Millay's, were civilized, and void of the hot girlishness that marked the rhyming of that day. Her prose wit was less than Benchley's, and her short stories fell below Lardner's. But these were two of the country's masters. Dorothy was a good runner-up.

Miss Parker's social side, however, had few peers in that day. She was a shapely, pleasant-faced brunette with a snowy skin. And with a fluttery, childlike manner that anyone was a fool to take seriously. Behind Miss Parker's helpless-seeming façade was a machine-gun nest capable of mowing a town down.

The meeting of Miss Parker and Mr. MacArthur was a Woollcott achievement. Himself a rabid but romantically helpless admirer of Miss Parker, Alec presented her, gallantly, to the young man he considered the most attractive male on tap in his circle.

Charlie's enthusiasm for women of genius was stirred anew by the poetess. She was not the literary gamine Carol Frink had been. However enchanted with life, Dotty would never turn cartwheels down Fifth Avenue, as Carol had done down Michigan Boulevard. But she could write far better. And, though she seldom smiled herself, she could keep others a-chuckle through a dozen highballs.

The Woollcottians followed the match, round by round. Dorothy seemed always ahead on points. But Charlie was a wary one. There was still a marriage hanging over his head, and its memory biting at him.

Toward the end Miss Parker wrote a sonnet which Charlie read without comment, other than a wince. It was a farewell to "his terrible porphyry eyes."

At a subsequent Halloween party, Miss Parker spoke one of her wryest sentences. Asked to join a group of merrymakers who were "ducking for apples," Dorothy said, "Change one letter in that phrase and you have my life story."

The Heroine

SHE enters here (November, 1924)—the girl with radiant blue eyes who is playing the lead in the Kaufman-Connelly hit *To the Ladies*. Her name, Helen Hayes, is known in the town but its bearer is as unknown as a ferryboat rider.

There was, possibly, no other leading lady such as Helen on that November afternoon. I'm not commenting on her talent, already off its springboard. Her picture was out front, her name in lights. Critics smiled in print, although there was one who had terrified her of the tribe for years to come. Franklin P. Adams had written of her performance in *The Wren* that she "suffered from fallen archness." But those were now words for critics to eat. A new star was rising—and audiences beamed and applauded. With all this, Helen was a sort of theatrical stowaway. The glitter and intrigue of Broadway—the parties, the celebrities, the gabby amours, the speakeasy carnivals— were as far removed from her as the corridors of Xanadu.

Innocence is a little odd in a pretty woman past twenty. In an actress it is possibly unique. Not that actresses are more erotic than other girls. It has to do with earning your own living. Young women who don't have to look to the male for support are not overly interested in his theories about chastity. Besides, a woman of talent feels she has something more important to offer than romance in semi-atrophy. But these were matters over our young Miss Hayes' head.

Helen's innocence on this November day of her entrance into MacArthur's life went further than amour inexperience. It included all the areas of the world except the six hundred square feet of it behind the footlights. Here, Helen was at home as a princess in her tower. But the rest of it was a hall bedroom shared with Mama Brown, or a tiny flat divided with another girl—and Mama Brown.

Actresses, however busy or guarded, can manage to find "life" without budging out of their dressing rooms. Helen was an exception. Since childhood she had found nothing but work. Her innocence of play was as complete as her innocence of sex. As a result, in this stronghearted girl there was a shyness toward humans you wouldn't expect in an actress who bowed so gracefully at curtain calls.

Miss Hayes, walking on Fifth Avenue this November afternoon, blinked with alarm when she heard her name called. What man knew her well enough to call out her first name in the street? It must be some fresh stranger.

The man came alongside. He was Marc Connelly, co-author of the hit in which she was playing at the Maxine Elliott Theatre. The mystery was explained.

He was shopping for a Christmas present to give the lady of his dreams, Margalo Gilmore, said Connelly. And would his lovely young star come along and help him select something beautiful? Helen blushed. To go look at a lot of exotic lingerie and other female pretties with a strange man at your side called for a little study. But Mr. Connelly was a writer and a gentleman, and he had a bald head and a sense of humor that was a little long-winded, but not vulgar.

"I'll be glad to come along," Helen said.

To Helen's surprise, Mr. Connelly walked by the lingerie markets and headed for a bookstore. Here Mr. Connelly bought his lady a Tenniel original of *Alice*. It was very expensive.

The shopping was over. It was time for Miss Hayes to go home to 15 Park Avenue and read the evening papers and wait for dinner. It was also time for a story to begin, called Charlie and Helen.

"Wherefore Art Thou——"

MR. CONNELLY walked his slim, ash-blonde companion to Fifty-seventh Street and Seventh Avenue, and up a flight of stairs. A door opened and Helen stood looking at a large room filled with people. It was an all-star cast. The town's leading geniuses, wags and seducers were jabbering away and taking turns laughing at witticisms. It was Neysa McMein's studio. People of sparkle or distinction considered Neysa's atelier a port of call between 4 and 7 P.M. Mr. Connelly entered with a funny story nobody had heard—and a companion equally unknown, except by name.

Helen sat in a corner and smiled and listened, cocked her head and chuckled, just as if she were on the stage—but without any lines. A young Irving Berlin with authentically inky hair was playing the piano. A young George Gershwin, pink cheeked and sad eyed, was talking to a pudgy, owl-faced young Alec Woollcott, already a-strut like a mandarin. A young Bob Benchley laughed and laughed as if nothing would ever shut him off. And a youngish Alice Duer Miller, with a straight back and Boston accent, was talking to a great idol of Helen's—Winifred Lenihan, the first to play Shaw's *Saint Joan*—quite as if that marvelous achievement didn't matter.

In fact, nothing in this large room seemed to matter but laughter. There were more people talking than listening. And the hostess acted as if no one were present at all. She sat in a smock, with rumpled hair, in front of an easel, and kept on painting. A runner from some corner of the room would bring to her side a newly minted epigram or freshly uncovered scandal. At this, Miss McMein would utter a semi-baritone laugh.

Miss McMein was Marjorie Moran from Chicago, where she had been the only solvent artist at work in the Fine Arts Building on Michigan Boulevard. She had made the luscious "My

Lady" drawings for the Palmolive soap ads. A numerologist had advised her to alter her name as an insurance of greater success. A triumph for this science, Neysa McMein came to New York and drew covers and illustrations for the nation's biggest magazines, and presided over one of the town's most popular celebrity water holes.

In her corner Helen continued her pantomime of listening and cocking her head charmingly, and being as ignored as a Salvation Army lassie in an opening-night foyer—when the following happened.

She tells it some thirty-two years later:

"A beautiful young man came up to me with a bag of peanuts in his hand and said, 'Want a peanut?'

"Somebody had spoken to me! I was amazed, but I answered correctly, 'Yes, thank you.' The young man poured several peanuts out of his bag into my hands. Then he smiled at me and said, 'I wish they were emeralds.' Then he asked to take me home. I forgot all about Mr. Connelly, and everything else."

Chariot Ride

THE afternoon sky was bright over Central Park and wide, lively Fifty-ninth Street. This is the part of New York that belongs to hotel guests, pigeon feeders and slow-motion pedestrians.

"I take the subway over there, I think," said Miss Hayes, pointing westward.

The young man steered her elbow eastward.

"It really isn't worthwhile taking a taxi, Mr. MacArthur," pursued Miss Hayes.

The young man smiled and kept them headed eastward toward the Plaza Hotel, in the vicinity of which New York looks like a foreign land. A half dozen open barouches lined the Park curbing. Their horses stood with heads down, like anchors. The drivers wore faded ulsters and clownish top hats. They looked like a row of red-nosed uncles taking a nap.

"My gracious," said Miss Hayes, "are we going in one of those carriages?"

Mr. MacArthur nodded and spoke to one of the uncles.

"Once around the park," he said, "and thence south on Fifth Avenue."

Miss Hayes entered the musty carriage. The red-nosed one clucked twice, and they were off.

A ride in Central Park on a sunny afternoon with a horse clop-clopping, and a nostalgic stable smell in the air; moving leisurely under autumn trees as colorful as barber poles; everyone whizzing by in taxicabs and you unhurried, as if you belonged to a more graceful, bygone time; and with the best-looking member of the all-star cast beside you—Helen sighed, smiled and trembled, lest all the excitement drive the Kaufman-Connelly lines out of her head for the evening performance. But that couldn't ever happen, no matter how close the peanut eater sat next to her. Anyway, he looked more like a gentleman than a seducer. His eyes were moody.

It was fine that the smiling young man preferred to ride in silence as if he wanted to share her enjoyment of the park scenery, which looked remarkably beautiful, surveyed from a barouche. He was probably a poet, for he seemed to understand the special look of the afternoon.

When the poet finally broke his moody silence, Miss Hayes was surprised by the subject that he selected—the urinating problems of the A.E.F. during the war with the Germans. It was a brand-new type of topic but, on the other hand, she had never been alone with a young man before. Brownie had always said they were peculiar. The subject was not without interest, the way he put it. His fellow soldiers in France, being Americans and used to the best plumbing, didn't like just plain holes in the ground. And they were unable to compete with the French soldiers, who were used to micturating openly, with a flourish. (One could only hope micturating was Number One and not Number Two. Somebody in the cast of *To the Ladies!* would know.) The Americans, he revealed to her, would have won the war sooner and saved thousands of lives if they hadn't spent half their vital energies building water closets. But Mr. MacArthur (now called Charlie) conceded they were wonderful soldiers, especially good as choral singers. One choral group, called the Battery F Castrati, had been rehearsed all through the war by Charlie himself. After the war was won, it marched through all the cheering French towns, leading the whole Rainbow Division in a song called "Jesus Wants Me for a Sunbeam."

They were out of the park, clop-clopping down Fifth Avenue, and Charlie took to bowing to the peasantry on the sidewalk and calling out in a royal voice, "Let them eat cake!" It was as funny as anything in a play. When they passed some men who were tearing up the street with noisy pneumatic drills, Charlie yelled at them, "Lost something?" It went on all the way to Thirty-fifth Street, and Helen hardly stopped laughing.

What a ride to end, to be over, never to clop-clop again!

Charlie helped her out of the barouche as if it were a queen's carriage. He bowed over her hand and asked, quietly, "What's your phone number?" Helen said, "I'm in the telephone book."

"Good," said Charlie. "I'll call you up."

He was back in the barouche, smiling mysteriously and riding away.

A Kiss for Cinderella

"It can't be because he's forgotten your name," said actress Jean Dixon, who shared the apartment with Helen and her mother. It was so modern you couldn't hang up pictures. The nail bent when you tried to hammer it into the wall. "Because," said Miss Dixon, "if he did forget your name he could have asked Mr. Connelly. And we can be sure of Mr. Connelly's memory."

"That's true," said Helen. "He probably called when nobody was home. We ought to have a maid."

The much-discussed call never came. Helen was left with a memory of a carriage moving under autumn trees, the urinating problems of the A.E.F., and a few other haunting matters.

Instead of Charlie MacArthur, another young man called. He was David Wallace, a theatrical press agent, but unusually famous. His name appeared every week in *The New Yorker*. There were items always beginning, "As David Wallace said," or "The final word on the subject was uttered by David Wallace."

Readers of *The New Yorker* hadn't the faintest notion who David Wallace was, but they smiled at what was obviously some private joke among the Inner Circle. Helen, however, was not up to such perspicacity.

The fact was that Wallace was a patsy for the Algonquin Round Table, where he lunched daily with "everybody," and that Ross and Woollcott were having fun pretending in print he was a deep one. Being a nice fellow, and a press agent, Wallace took the hazing amiably. He knew his position was solid. He enabled the Wits of the Round Table to shine by comparison.

On a Sunday evening in February, Helen, escorted by David, went to her first New York party. Hundreds of people gave parties in New York, but they weren't like Alec Woollcott's. You were just a guest, elsewhere. Under Alec's roof you became a member of a family—like the Plantagenets. Head of this Broadway royal family was, of course, Alec. And everybody agreed he was entitled to the position. He could snarl, pout, rage, insult everybody like a true monarch, and, withal, he was very lovable and could get your name in the paper and on the air.

The same thing happened to Helen in Mr. Woollcott's

house that happened in Miss McMein's studio—despite the new evening dress and the new slippers. She ended up in a corner and sat smiling, and cocking her head charmingly, and thanking the butler with all her soul when he offered the little sausages with toothpicks through them.

After a spell of silence and an unaccustomed Alexander cocktail, Helen, who was moving to a new apartment, remarked ingratiatingly to the company at large: "Anyone who wants my piano is willing to it."

Mr. Kaufman, near by, answered: "That's very seldom of you." After this brillig exchange, Helen was left to nibble on her little sausage—and watch.

Ah, what Helen saw from her corner that evening! A gloria mundi the like of which would never be again. The untormented yesterday without dictators, genocides, nuclear fission and television—when a party (particularly like Woollcott's) was more important than a headline; when a mot by George Kaufman took precedence over an utterance by President Coolidge.

I pause to describe Alec's party because, like the saloons, murder stories and scenery of Chicago, it was now Charlie MacArthur's world. He was no monarch in it like the Owl-faced One. But he was one of its Prince Charmings—possibly the only one who wore such title without seeming lessened by it.

The songsmiths Berlin and Gershwin were there. Irving, the ex-saloon piano banger, was making headlines with his wooing of society heiress Ellin Mackay. Kaufman and Connelly were present. The bored Kaufman face under its exclamatory pompadour was one of the success signposts of the hour. The comedies he wrote with Connelly and others brought a new Molière laughter to the town.

Producer Sam Harris, the soft-spoken, dish-faced charmer, looked on, hearing little of what was said, for he was half deaf, but beaming on it all. Producer Sam made deals by nodding or raising a finger. Nobody knew how a man who had been a prize-fight manager and who had never read anything could turn into a gentleman of taste and theatrical acumen—but there he was.

Jeanne Eagels came in, two champagne bottles under her arm—it was her only tipple—and trailing the most expensive fur pieces in town, the gift of an underworld chieftain.

The unpressed suit of Heywood Broun was in evidence. The tailor's loss was the *prolétaire's* gain. Heywood, one of Mr. Swope's leading philosophers on the *Morning World*, had taken to brooding on the sins of capitalism. The Russian-born Causes were beginning, and Broun was sounding one of the early tocsins. He had followers—recruited from the highest salon ranks. There were rewards for radicals that no longer obtain. You got into a minimum of trouble and achieved a maximum of publicity. You crucified yourself on billboards, and came down for bows. (At least, that's the way it looked to my Chicago eye.)

Boss Swope, a tall, rumbling-voiced chesspiece of a man— the Red Knight (the red was coloring, not ideology)—added distinction as well as noise to the Woollcott ensemble. Beside him, his trim, dark-haired Maggie stood like a police cordon, for the place teemed with "vampires." A husband in those days walked in danger.

There was present also the French lady Madeleine to protect her Irish savant husband, Ernest Boyd, the critical eagle grounded in the New York speakeasies. A young Ruth Gordon, coy and clamorous with talent, and her brilliant actor-husband, Gregory Kelly; a young Alfred Lunt, with his Finnish accent not yet perfected; a younger Jascha Heifetz, flying from his fiddle and pleading for the music to stop and people to make jokes; Myra Hampton, darling of the Round Table, her eggshell beauty swathed in pale chiffons; Madge Kennedy, the early pin-up lady from W. C. Fields' happy cast of *Poppy*—these were there for the smiling Helen to watch and overhear.

I feel like a society reporter untrue to the guest list if I stop here, and will, therefore, continue. The Dublin heller, J. M. Kerrigan, was poised at the piano, ready to offer his repertoire of song—"Willie's White Breast," "She Had a Roving Eye," and other laments from the Old Sod. The doll-like June Walker would listen, with Miss Gilmore, and Alice Duer Miller, Harpo Marx, and the peg-legged hero of Broadway and the Argonne, Laurence Stallings.

Woollcott, swept off his own not-too-solid pins by the wonders of *What Price Glory?* cried out, "I'm willing to bet five hundred dollars that *What Price Glory?* will be playing to infatuated audiences one hundred years from now!"

"I'll take your bet," said Benchley, "if you'll promise to be buried with the money in your teeth, so I can get at it easily."

Another Broadway hero was on hand—Jimmy Gleason, playing the prize-fight manager in *Is Zat So?* The Higher Criticism was dipping its toes in the comic strips and other unexpected hiding places of Art. Tributes to Jack Dempsey, Rube Goldberg, Milt Gross and Joe Jackson (the bicycle tramp of vaudeville) appeared under the bylines of aesthetes. Master Woollcott himself gave constant space to the genius of his friend Harpo. Perhaps it was easier to seem an aristocrat when you went slumming. But it may have been something else.

There was another one in the center of the room with admirers thick around him—the Negro Paul Robeson. The singer and ex-football star was in high social demand in the Woollcottian areas. Singlehanded, he enable everyone to feel free of bigotry and Jim Crowism. Robeson was the only Negro to be seen in this center of liberalism—but one was enough to make the point.

There are hundreds of parties as glamorous to be attended today. And more celebrities drink, chatter and carry on today than were ever dreamed of by Woollcott and Ross.

But there is a difference. Today the celebrities come from everywhere—out of the movies, television, radio, politics—and out of a mysterious hatchery invented by the columnists of the town. This is a type of celebrity of whom nothing is known except their visibility.

On that February evening they came only out of the theatre,

and its attendant world of letters. When you sat in a corner looking at Alec's guests, you looked at the only "greatness" that mattered.

There is just one thing in common between today's and yesterday's celebrity parties—their importance is chiefly in the eyes of people who can't get in. Social fame is usually a matter of convincing others that it exists. The uninvited make the feast.

Among the Woollcottians the bedazzling of the uninvited was made easy by the fact that nearly all of Alec's captains conducted gossip columns in the press and magazines. F.P.A., Broun, Ross, Frank Sullivan, Miss Parker, Corey Ford and Woollcott himself wrote about each other swooningly.

They kept the public informed on how much they won at cards and croquet, whom they loved, what new parlor games they fancied, and how their tea parties crackled with epigrams.

Though most of the talent of the day (in fact, nearly all of it) was missing from their salons, this Algonquin school of wags offered itself as the artistic vortex of the town. Among the missing at its tables were Thomas Wolfe, Sandburg, O'Neill, Sherwood Anderson, Willa Cather, Mencken, Nathan, Hemingway, George Luks, George Bellows, Edith Wharton, Edna Millay, George Grosz, Elinor Wylie, Vertès, Sinclair Lewis, Wyndham Lewis, Hergesheimer, Irvin Cobb, et cetera.

The artist was wise who was absent. For a young novelist or playwright with his roots not yet down, to sit in such a clique of know-it-alls was to get the art frightened out of him. A pickpocket keeping company with a pack of boastful cops might feel similarly hesitant toward the practice of his profession.

Any writer who makes critics his cronies is almost certain to quit writing. MacArthur had more critic pals than any other writer in town. He didn't quit, but he went in for long hesitations.

Back to our party.

"Hello, Helen," said a voice.

Somebody had finally spoken to her, as at Miss McMein's studio. It was the same Charlie MacArthur, smiling as if he were still in the barouche under the autumn leaves.

Paul Robeson stood, ready to sing "Water Boy," and Alec was going about denouncing everybody who wouldn't fall silent.

"Let's get out of this fish trap," said Charlie.

"I'm here with David Wallace," Helen said.

"I'll not hold that against you," said Charlie. "Come on."

In the taxicab Helen wanted to talk. About the only thing she had said on their first meeting was, "I'm in the telephone book." And a lot good that had done.

"I'm rehearsing in Bernard Shaw's *Caesar and Cleopatra*," said Helen. "We're opening at the new Guild Theatre. I'm playing Cleopatra."

"I wish I could play the asp," said Charlie.

While studying the odd remark, Helen was suddenly seized and kissed. So much for the illusion she had had that this one was different from all those seducers who hung around actresses like game hunters. According to Brownie and other sources, this is what they all did—grabbed you without knowing you, and wrestled for kisses (and worse) even in taxicabs.

Helen turned her head away on the seducer's second try for a kiss. She kept her head twisted out of range so that she was practically looking out of the rear window of the cab, all the way to Gramercy Park. (They lived in an apartment now where you could drive nails in the wall.)

Outside the cab, Helen looked intently at her taxicab assailant. He was holding her hand and smiling abstractedly as if nothing had happened. Evidently kissing girls in a public taxi was routine business for Charlie MacArthur. Helen wanted to explain to him that no man had ever kissed her before, except on stage, but decided against mentioning it.

Still holding her hand, Charlie asked, "What's your phone number?"

"It's in the telephone book," said Helen, and smiled despite the crick in her neck. "Would you like to come see me in the play?"

"Love to," said Charlie. "I'll be there."

He was back in the taxi waving good-by, and riding off. Helen tried to wave gaily back at the cab but her hand stopped. A loneliness was in her heart.

A Balcony in Verona

EVERY night before the play started, the young Siren of the Nile would stick her eye to the peephole in the house curtain and remain motionless for several minutes. Helen Westley, royal lady-in-waiting, came in the Empress' side one evening.

"It's not right for a young star to do," said Miss Westley.

"What isn't?" asked Miss Hayes.

"To count the house before every performance," said Miss Westley. "It looks awfully mercenary."

"I'm not counting the house," said Miss Hayes, in a voice both lofty and querulous. "I'm just checking if someone's in the audience."

"Does he come every night?" Miss Westley smiled. "That's very nice."

"He hasn't been here at all—yet," Helen answered.

"Good God!" said Miss Westley. "And you've been looking through that hole every night for two months!"

Helen nodded.

"That's insane!" Miss Westley said. "We didn't do that in my day. In my day one called the fellow and kept after him till he showed up."

"I can't do that," said Miss Hayes. And Cleopatra returned to her dressing room.

For the next two hours, the darkened audience saw and heard only an Egyptian queen, as conceived by G. Bernard Shaw. This whimsical, voluptuous daughter of the Pharaohs was carrying no torch for any Charlie MacArthur. And there's a thing that distinguishes acting from the other arts. Poets, painters, musicians, in the throes of creation, can whistle at their work and woolgather. The novelist can have a love affair (his own) in the middle of a chapter—and art marches on.

But on the stage, no. The actress who writes only on air, whose performance is like a puff of smoke or a little fire that the final curtain puts out, must operate with the intensity of a hypnotist and a cavalry charge. If she is a fine actress, she is also an architect and a historian and many other things. She builds Egypt for you out of a papier-mâché rock and a yellow floor cloth. She walks and gestures like the past. Things vaguely remembered from the reading of them become alive as a St. Patrick's Day parade. The ghost of Time walks in the flesh again. There is also the matter of characterization. The fine actress, having created temples and deserts, proceeds to live in them. She must do this so thoroughly that even the stage manager in the wings will forget for moments his duties as monitor of make-believe.

As for the audience, it will sit like spellbound children looking through the proscenium window at a Cleopatra more real than its dentists. It will live in Egypt instead of Washington Heights, and it will make the exodus at 11 P.M. with a sigh of regret unknown to the Israelites.

Helen did all these things for one hour and fifty-five minutes. And Mr. MacArthur was no more part of the proceedings than if he had never been born, and never come to sit in her heart like a brushfire. In the last five minutes, art suffered a small setback. The great Julius Ceasar spoke to the childlike but love-hungry queen: "—bid me farewell; and I will send you a man . . . not lean in the arms and cold in the heart; not hiding a bald head under his conqueror's laurels; not stooped with the weight of the world on his shoulders; but brisk and fresh, strong and young, hoping in the morning, fighting in the day, and revelling in the evening. Will you take such an one in exchange for Caesar?"

To this Cleopatra replied (stage direction, "Palpitating"), "His name, his name?"

And Caesar answered, "Shall it be Mark Antony?"

But that was not the name heard by the Siren of the Nile. This lapse was not entirely a blow to art. It made the tears a bit more real when she stood by the great rock waving farewell to Caesar.

The asbestos was down, the ushers were retrieving gloves and handkerchiefs from under empty seats. The audience was lost in the honking streets.

In the dressing rooms of the Guild Theatre the cast was enjoying its ten minutes of victory over the audience. Caesar, Ptolemy, Rufio, Achillas, Miss Westley and all the other finely costumed figures were full of flushed chatter, like a football team in the showers.

Cleopatra, in her black chiffon of Act Five, sat at her dressing table, thinking of that damnably absent Mark Antony with the widow's peak and the foggy eyes. It was spring backstage. The stage alley door was open and the balmy New York night intruded on Egypt and Rome still a-buzz in the corridors and on the steel staircase. Backstage is an odd world after a performance. Real and unreal occupy the same space. Equally alive are the tired-faced doorkeeper and the magic of Egypt, the honk of taxis bucking the after-theatre tides and the moody voices of the play's characters. The theatre's ghosts fade slowly while the make-ups come off.

It might not be so for businessmen, but for stage players who spend their lives outwitting reality there is seldom a sharp dividing line. Shakespeare and all his sons talk backstage as audibly as dressing-room visitors. The glaring city murmuring beyond the opened alley door has other names than New York.

There was a knock.

"Come in," said Helen.

The dressing-room door opened.

"Hello," said the visitor.

"Charlie," said Helen. "I didn't know you were out front tonight."

"I wasn't," said Charlie. "I was just passing, and thought I'd call. How are you?"

"Just fine!" said Helen firmly. And Juliet said, "My ears have not yet drunk a hundred words of thy tongue's uttering, yet I know the sound."

"How about supper?" said Charlie.

"I can't," said Helen. "I have to go home. It's a long way. I'm living in Syosset, Long Island. It's quite a nice place."

The visitor didn't answer. He was looking moodily at Cleopatra's black chiffon bodice. A young, full-blown bosom was happily visible.

"Why don't you come to Syosset with me?" said Helen. "We can have supper there." Said Juliet, "I am too fond; and therefore thou mayst think my haviour light."

Romeo wasn't talking. He was lost in contemplation of the black chiffon.

"If you can't go tonight," said Helen, "some other time."

"Tonight's fine," said Charlie.

"You can pick up some things and spend the weekend—with us," said Helen.

"I don't need anything," said Charlie.

Long after midnight, the car—driven by Helen's schoolday cohort, Halcyon Hargrove—arrived at a summer mansion in Syosset, bearing Mark Antony. Cleopatra's lip rouge was much disturbed.

Juliet said in the garden: "Pardon me, and not impute this yielding to light love . . ."

Syosset—and the Serpent

CHARLIE came to Syosset for the summer weekends. The year was 1925. Helen and her friends, Halcy and June Walker, lived in an impressive house that belonged to a rich man named Paul Hammond. Brownie was also on the premises.

Stowaway Helen of Gramercy Park was suddenly "a first-class passenger entitled to special privileges." That was Charlie's phrase for the elect of talent; the ones "who have stained-glass colors on them," he further explained.

Mr. Hammond was a bit smitten by the emerging Miss Hayes, but apparently not enough to remain on deck for any courting. He had some grouse shooting to do in Scotland. As a token of his admiration, the huntsman gave the key of his manor to Mama Brown, and left his Japanese houseman with the manse.

And how the hurdy gurdies played that summer! "Everybody" came to Syosset, and Syosset went to Mamaroneck, where Neysa McMein and her dashing husband, Jack Baragwanath, managed the revels. From Mamaroneck, everybody went to the Swope baronetcy. Games were played—croquet and ping pong attracting the more athletic. There were charades, the Murder Game and an intellectual exercise called the Word Game at which Woollcott was a bullying champion. There were pool splashing, and talk fests, and fountains of mint juleps and gin rickeys. Treasure hunts were also patronized by the city guests, who went panting through the shrubbery in search of sapphire cuff links and gold-fitted dressing cases—free to the finder.

The merry ones of the summer were Benchley, Woollcott, Alice Duer Miller and her son, Dennie, Pat Kerrigan and the Mohican-faced Ring Lardner, Cissie Schlesinger (nee Patterson, formerly the Countess Gizycki), with a small-sized steamliner to take her back and forth to her city luncheon dates. Harpo was present tooting a clarinet and winning sizable sums from his admirers at cards. Harpo was a card player feared by professional gamblers. But how expect the intelligentsia to know that side of their beamish boy?

All other entanglements melted out of the MacArthur cosmos. There were a hundred games but only one girl.

Love may be a part-time mood to many men. It fills a night and leaves no echo in the day. It dictates a few deeds, and leaves the doer untouched. Charlie was not of this tribe of half lovers. He smote his lyre seven days a week, and lugged it to work. Yet his manner and vocabulary remained as intact as if nothing new had befallen. Whatever Vesuvius bothered him inside, the outside of MacArthur remained a poker player. None who knew him (except Helen) knew that our friend was being reforged in the fires of love.

One sunny afternoon Helen, her lover, and a troupe of happy guests rode down the main street of Syosset. The Hudson automobile was as crowded and noisy as a Mack Sennett car full of Keystone Cops. The merry ones sighted a local belle passing. She was an elderly, skinny wench, but bedaubed and festooned like a menace to men. The occupants of the Hudson chuckled and made funny comments about the comic valentine of a siren parading foolishly down the street. Charlie frowned at the wags.

"If one of us was a true gentleman," he said, "he'd get out of the car and pinch her ass."

Winter came, and with it a serpent arrived in Helen's paradise. Helen had given her love and honor to a married man. There was a wife (separated) who was full of determination about keeping married to Charlie.

And there were their friends—Charlie's friends, and now hers. The friends had all the same bleak information for her. Charlie was a pillar of smoke for any girl's arms. He was a Regency Rake, a Scottish gypsy, seducing virgins as he went, they said. If you wanted to enjoy Charlie, expect nothing of him. And don't be taken in by his gallant gabble about wresting a divorce from Carol Frink.

Helen, untutored in love (not that it ever helps much), listened to this bad news with fear and confusion. A fine thing for a girl to hear who was still going to Mass on Sunday, and who had held herself proudly above the easy amours of the theatre.

To make the scene darker, there was an anti-marriage mood in the upper theatre circles in which Helen now moved. Everybody who loved anybody seemed to have a husband or wife playing banshee on the sidelines. So to hell with wedlock; let love bloom unconfined! And, speaking of confinement, there was a remarkable number of illegitimate babies befalling the stage queens. And even this was looked upon as cricket.

Doubts ached in Helen's soul (and Mrs. Brown's, too).

Of this premarital love affair I'll let my friend speak. Here are some of the letters he wrote to Helen in this time.

Letters from Charlie

HE wrote in a letter dated "Saturday morning":

"MY DARLING, DARLING!

"It's three. I've waited till you were sound asleep with a million dreams raining down on your tousled head . . . to put on paper some of the beautiful things that are romping through my mind. They die the second I try to get them through a pen . . . so light. I love to think of you asleep. If I could only be outside your door, just to listen to your breathing. I love you. I think of you somewhere among the stars—away off. I love you. If I could only have been in your dreams.

"A little while before my mother died she wrote me a birthday letter and told me about seeing a falling star before I was born—and wishing the most beautiful things for me. I didn't know how beautiful!"

In a letter dated "Tuesday," he wrote:

"DEAREST!

"When you write a letter like Sunday's, it makes me feel how lucky I am to have been born. I've never been happy before. For the first time in my life it's a luxury to live, and think about one person all the time, and . . . let go. . . . When you tell me that you're lonely for me, and that you're really living, and that I make your life vivid and you're miserable and happy too, I feel important and even necessary. I'm cram full of joy and a big noise. Don't ever quit loving me for a second. It's all I've got to go on, and if you like, I'll be holding on to your little hand from that last summer until I die."

Another, written on a "Saturday."

"Dearest,

"My every thought is for you—what will make you happy, what might make you unhappy; and not for anything in the world would I give you an instant's unhappiness. There isn't enough room for anything or anybody but you. I adore you completely.

". . . you seem to know all the things that start banjos in my bosom.

". . . But I hate this solitude of the heart. Even telephone conversations have their bad points. I hate to make you yell beautiful words over a noisy wire. You can't say a delicate thing more than twice, can you? I mean anybody. And it's got to be whispered. . . ."

"This one," said Helen, "was after an early quarrel. How vulnerable he was!"

There is no day at its masthead, and no greeting or signature—

"I'm feeling quite ratty, darling; and confounded at having done many wrong things, and said wrong things. Lord, I must have been dreadful on the nerves tonight—a little whining, if I remember. Well, I was never the boy for absolute control. . . .

"The painful part of it all is that you must be right and that won't heal very quickly. Seen from your back porch, I look rather messy; but, ah, my dear, I thought it was art.

"I'm sorry that I appealed to your sympathies. I know better than anyone else how futile that is. Love is there or it isn't, and all the king's horses can't do anything about it. I would feel less contemptible if you knew how very much I loved you. Carelessness or not, all the love I could feel or imagine went to you. It burns me up to think of its manifestations. Some of them were dirty nosed and unchecked and uncivilized, but they all came out of the same skull that thought up the finest feelings I have ever known. I'll never be careless with your memory. . . . If I could do anything, say anything to keep you from thinking hard things. It's awfully important to me, what you think. Merely as a human being the way leads somewhere from here—and Helen, little darling, I don't like the taste in my heart."

A postscript to another letter, written in red crayon, reads:
"I went to kiss the corner of this and look what happened—"
The corner of the paper is burned away. A charred edge remains—after thirty years.

Charlie went to Chicago to hurry up his divorce proceedings. Here, in remembered Arcady, he walked now in a rain of legal arrows and publicity assaults. He wired Helen in New York:
"Dearest, last night you were every lovely thing I have ever imagined—beautiful, wise and strong and so understanding. It was worth all this sorry mess to hear you say the things you did. I feel so much happier and so much more able to cope with things. Adoration isn't the word. If you send me any more wires like yesterday, the Western Union will have to hire angels for messenger boys. All my love forever—"
Another telegram came from Chicago. The Western Union office must have stared with wonder.

"MISS HELEN HAYES
"Bijou Theatre, New York, N.Y.
"Oh what a genius for the healing word. I was really sunk until I got your wire. Dearest unless you have other plans I will call you tonight at one your time and how much I love

you will have to be left to astonished historians, poets and the like.

"Charlie"

Lulu Belle opened in Philadelphia. Helen was on the road playing her favorite role, the wifely prime minister Maggie Wylie in *What Every Woman Knows*.

On an "Early Friday Morning," Charlie wrote:

"Dearest,

"This is bedlam and if I sound distracted, forgive me. All I know is that I love you and miss you and want you forever and ever and ever. I haven't slept much and I feel fuzzy and slightly incoherent and I love you. Financially, the play seems to be a wow with standing room sold out by noon every day: but, of course, there is New York to come.

"The manuscript daily gets nearer the heart's desire. None of us Belasco boys have slept much since Tuesday—me since Sunday.

"I learn from my spies that the New York *Mirror* is making a big splash today, calling the play the disgrace of the decade, etc., and aren't they foolish?

"Hull [Henry, the leading man] is acting up, shouting and playing his scenes against the back drop; and Lenore [Ulric] is wonderful about him. At the end of the third act on opening night he conveniently lost his bathrobe and stalled so long at the curtain calls that when he finally came out, panting and haggard, he took the applause and made it look as if Lenore had previously refused to let him on. Well, we'll fix that.

"The New York *World* has reported the best of the Philadelphia notices, with an explanatory paragraph saying that talk of sensationalism is unfounded. We're hitting about $25,000 a week here in a small theatre. The Wizard wants to open in Madison Square Garden, and with London next. Where would you like to live in Venice?

"Does this sound hopeful? I am tired to death and I am just staggering along with the bare ungrammatical facts. I

121

wasn't really happy until I talked to you last night and if I have seventy-five openings I'll never be so thrilled as I was at your little blue letter with the love yous in it. You're just the girl for me, Miss Hayes. Nobody ever wrote such a lovely letter, and I'm going to answer it the minute I get some sleep.

"Your lonesome Kangaroo,

"Charlie"

Lulu Belle was as big a hit in New York as it had been in Philadelphia. But Charlie didn't know that his lucky days were beginning on this opening night. His letter dated "Wednesday" went to Helen on the road:

"It was like pulling out the stitches after an operation for kidney trouble, and I must say it was comparatively painless; although God knows how I am going to describe it with your fingers in my hair and your eyelashes batting against my cheek. Anyway, there we were. General Stonewall Jackson was over on one side of the hill and the damned Yanks kept coming into the theatre all during the first act. It was the coldest house since Mrs. Insull put on 'The School for Scandal' [a Chicago event]. So many of the Otto Kahns and Mortimer Schiffs had paid their $150 to hear something hot that there was a perceptible disappointment. After the first ten minutes we hung out one of those 'Forty Degrees Cooler Inside' signs. And there was a blizzard in the street. It was a strain on Lenore to hear her old laughs soft-pedalled right along the line, but the curtain applause was encouraging. My dear thrilling child, I love you.

"Act II seemed pretty bad to me and I accidentally bit off my right thumb. The 'Doctor' was so bad, and the straight lighting and ham lines were so lacerating. Act II was the most painful stitch.

"Act III as always went splendidly. It can't possibly miss, the way it's acted and staged; and at the curtain there was a hue and cry. A few rowdies—my personal well wishers and creditors—yelled author, and the Master in regretting that Mr. Sheldon was not present explained that I could not be found. At the moment I was sitting on the gallery steps, and loving you more than I ever thought it possible to love anybody. I knew that all our baby talk about love and gondolas was coming true, right there in front of me. It would have come true anyhow; but I would have hated crashing into your Venetian boudoir like George in the last act [a penniless, despairing colored man come to claim his high-stepping true love].

"Oh, darling, you'll never know the excitement I felt talking to you last night. If I hadn't held on to myself I would really have turned into a babbling maniac in front of Ned. There was more love pent up inside me than I knew about. I felt I couldn't stand being away from you another minute. Early next week—soon as we get the royalties—I'll take the first train, my darling, my darling. And you'll never be away from me this long again. Will you?

"Act III began with me biting off two fingers. I do hate Lenore's entrance so much and the silk set parted in two or three places. Then, although she and Henry were marvelous, there was always the chance the audience would laugh out loud at the fight scene. It is so close to unbearable reactions that laughter is a relief; and all the impetus it needs is a bum silk set, or an extra bounce on one of the papier mache toilet articles that she throws, or a bull's eye on Henry's nose—especially with that show-me crowd. And would you believe it, both Lenore and Henry, feeling the slight frigidity and the strain, gave such a performance as was never seen. At any rate, I succumbed to the act for the first time and actually was swept away. So was the audience. So there is a God and a place called Venice where boys and girls can go and shove letters under each other's door and make love and pretty promises and be happy. If I can arrange it, you'll be happy all your life with never a shadow or disillusion, or anything ugly or unkind or unbeautiful. I promise.

123

"After I left Ned's, I went to Lenore's. Jimmy [Whittaker] and Halcyon and Jane, and Sidney [Blackmer] and Neysa and Jack and George Gershwin and Art Samuels and Vivian Martin, his betrothed, and a few others were there. It was dull, I thought, and yet appealing. Gershwin wanted to make an opera of 'Lulu Belle,' although that is not to be taken very seriously. All of them made up a game. The guests, at my appearance, were to pretend they thought the show was lousy; but the champagne had been flowing with the result that each, individually, tipped me off sotto voce to the scheme. It was difficult playing up after that. I adore you.

"Jane subpoenaed me to take her home and hear her grief about last summer. I flew upstairs and left word that I had been called away. Jane was a bum Toscanini for the thousand violins that were tuning up in my heart.

"I feel like going on with this letter until Friday. One thing you have done is to tap all the fountains of loving gabble that have been storing themselves deep in my heart for years and years. My writing letters is simply astounding. I love you most for what you have done to me. I'm shameless. I feel like throwing all the outlandish things right at your feet, sure that you'll love every broken marble, plugged nickel and smudgy ribbon. Do you remember the first time you asked if we were really one? God love your sweet heart and mind.

"I'm going to Ned's now—and then rush right home and call you. Spend every scrap of love you have on me, won't you? I've gone bankrupt on you. Thank God there's more coming in all the time. If you'll give me all your love, I'll double it for you in six months, like Matt does with your money."

Among the box of Charlie-letters was a faded telegram sent him by Helen from Chicago on *Lulu Belle's* opening night. It was the only one of the hundreds of messages he had saved. It read:

"CHARLES MACARTHUR

"Belasco Theatre, New York, N.Y.

"Dearest can't you feel me there close beside you in the gallery seat holding tight to your hand and hoping.

"HELEN"

On the telegram Charlie left the red penciled line—"Here's the one that made it exciting. It's from my girl."

In a Gypsy Tent

WHEN I read the foregoing letters a knowledge came to me about my friend. You can't know a man for forty years without knowing him. But you can miss a few things—like his soul, or his pain, or the underside of that glittering tortoise shell he offered with all his might.

What I see now, looking at the whole of my friend's life, is that he was like the Carl Sandburg poem about the flying fish that lives in two elements, belonging not quite in either, and suffering in both.

One summer night Charlie and I went to a Nyack carnival playing in a field near the river. As we strolled, a rain exploded in the night. We arrived, drenched, at the carnival. The rain whipped against its flapping canvas. Not a soul was visible in the blur of lights. We walked through the forlorn, rain-hallooing carnival lanes, while lightning spat and thunder boomed.

Charlie pointed a soaked arm at a sign on a tent, "Madam Shahma—Fortuneteller."

"Let's call on her," he said.

We entered the tent. Some dozen men, women and children huddled on its small ground, silent and listening to the drumming rain.

125

Madam Shahma stood up. She was a wrinkled old woman, aquiline and spangled. She wore a shining black wig.

"You want your fortune told," she said. She was giving no free refuge from the storm.

"Here's room rent," said Charlie and handed her two dollars. We chatted with the rain listeners for a time.

Madam Shahma suddenly said, "I tell your fortune," and took my hand. She amazed me for five minutes with an accurate history of my life—where I was born, where I had lived, how I earned my living, that I had been married twice and had one child at the time, a girl.

When she was finished I said, "I've got seven dollars in my pocket. They're yours if you'll tell me how you guessed or found out all those things."

She took the money and said, "Sixty years ago I started traveling. I have kept traveling all the time. I have been every place. I have told fortunes every day, everywhere. I learned. I can tell, when a man talks, in what state of America he was born. In what corner. Also his voice tells me where he has lived and traveled. You have the New York voice. But it grew up in the Middle West. You are a city man. So I guessed Chicago. You have no artist paint on your fingers. And you look like a man who never works. It is not the look of a musician. So I guessed a writer. You have money. I knew when you came in. Only a man who has money will walk in a big rain and have fun. Next—I know about men with pleasant faces who are artists—they marry often. I guessed two marriages, because you don't look unhappy. Then the one child, a daughter, it was you who told me that. Your face talked to me and told me many things."

"How about telling my fortune?" said Charlie.

Madam Shahma took his hand and looked steadily into his eyes.

"No," she said.

"Something pretty bad?" Charlie smiled.

"No," said the old gypsy woman. "I do not know you. I make a good impression on the gentlemen. I do not want to spoil it." She patted Charlie's cheek. "There is nothing to hear or see."

We put a version of the incident in the movie we made called *The Scoundrel.*

I recall the rainy night because I have a wish to play gypsy to my friend, and read his flying fish of a palm. What I see in it has to do with the problem of being an artist. It was the big problem in Charlie's life—the one he couldn't solve. It's a problem not many people have, but those who have it are born with it. The champions are marked. They arrive with the extra sound box for singing, the extra muscle for running, boxing, thinking, the extra ounce of power that makes a Balzac, Bernhardt, Dempsey, Churchill, O'Neill.

The problem is never how to acquire genius, but what to do with it. It's a sort of explosive element that'll blow up either in the world or inside you. The poet Arthur Davison Ficke wrote: "On that pilgrim's staff who betrays his art, no flower shall bloom." Worse things happen than that.

The thing that marks the artist is not that he wears a different hat, and is ready to parrot minority reports. Greenwich Village and the theatre world are full of such antisocial windjammers. The artist isn't made by a haberdasher and a left-wing editorial. He's made by the explosive in him that bears the label "Beware—Unconformity." This is true even in the theatre, where art has to make money before it can achieve existence. To write well for the theatre you must write with contempt for audience ideals, while wooing the same audience with jokes and coy conflicts—like Bernard Shaw. Or you write with a rage against life, a denial of its goodness and its prim patterns, like Eugene O'Neill. Or you protest the injustice of government and champion the poor, like Sean O'Casey and his many followers. Or you come up from the underworld of neurosis with lyric reports, like Tennessee Williams.

My friend Charlie had the label inside him "Beware—Unconformity." But he remained the flying fish, artist and no artist. He sailed through life with the gusto of seven iconoclasts. But he also believed in all the conventions he flouted. He broke laws but he never took sides against them. His loyalty was always to the virtuous teachings of his youth. He defied them, but he returned always to sup with them.

This duality in Charlie often surprised people—that he was as gentle as he was wild; that he was as much St. Augustine as Master Katzenjammer; and above all, that this most stormy seeming of mortals was as much George Babbitt as Lord Byron.

I write this about my friend because it was part of the secret self that brought on his suffering. The genius with which my friend was born had an enemy looming beside his crib. It was an enemy that roared of "guilt," "sin," and "bend the knee," and addled a child with hallelujahs and a vinegar-soaked strap.

Charlie needed a cohort against this enemy. That's why he wrote usually with a collaborator.

I've read the things he wrote by himself, some finished and published, some half finished and buried. They are better than most of his collaboration work. The words are richer, the humor fiercer. But, chiefly, the merry nihilism of his deepest self takes the bit in its teeth and runs. And this was the sin, the sacrilegious drawing on the tablecloth that must be erased.

Dr. William Telfer MacArthur and his hallelujaing deacons made a convert they never chalked up. Charlie never wiggled out of the bandages they put on his boyhood soul. Sin, sin, sacrilege, obedience, fear of punishment from somewhere by someone—these specters kept his mind, winged with words, from adventuring too far.

Luckily, there are other ways than scribbling for great talent to express itself. Charlie found all the other ways. He found the best of them—love. And many other fine ones— bright comradeship, zany adventure, and a strong arm for others. Also, he kept on writing, and damned well. So what am I in a stew about? The letters did it. They gave me a look at my friend's vulnerability and pain. During his life, you could look your head off and not see them. But there he was—a man who needed someone beside him, strong and wholly functioning, or he would be lost and doomed. A man who dared not go to himself for food, but must dine out.

Charlie knew all these things, and many more about himself. He might conform but he never hid. Hypocrisy and self-deceit were Sanskrit to him. One day in Hollywood, in his prime, he told me the pain and doom he felt.

"Should I join the Catholic Church?" he asked. "Or go get psychoanalyzed?"

The query irritated me. It didn't come from any Mac-Arthur I knew. An impostor was asking a stupid question. I put it down to a hangover.

"Lay off liquor for a month," I said, "and you'll be on top of the world again."

I remember Charlie's tired smile at my words.

"The big psychologist," he answered.

My gypsy work done, not as neatly possibly as Madam Shahma's, I'll go on with my letter about the high days and life undaunted that still marked the way of my friend.

Poverty Pie

WE spent a summer together in Woodstock, New York, where I was playing squatter in McEvoy's summer home. My bride-to-be, Rose Caylor, ran the woodland ménage.

Charlie and I talked chiefly about first wives. We both had them, hanging on tight. It was a great bond. We were scientists on the subjects of female hysteria and the workings of the marital torture rack.

On rainy days we wrote a play called *The Moonshooter*. We lost both copies after reading it to Sam Harris in his Long Island home.

My friend played, worked and helped talk the nights away.

But it was a moody Charlie, a faunlike fellow who shunned wine and women. When artist belles who flourished in the woods came after him, he waved a hand at their middles and said, "Put it away."

Charlie's heart was in the highlands. The Regency Rake was waiting for Helen.

In New York, after the summer was over, our ways parted for a time. A mystery millionaire entered Charlie's life. Rumor was that he had been urged out of London for outwitting the Crown in some vast financial doings. The millionaire feasted all New York like another Trimalchio. Orchestras played. Divas sang. Penniless Charlie was guest of honor.

Charlie's poverty was due to a miscalculation. Expecting *Lulu Belle* to go on, he had happily jumped off the Goddard payroll. Delay in the play's arrival had kept the playwright scurrying after eating money. Free lodgings were supplied by Mary Harriman Rumsey, Averell's sister. It was a house in East Fortieth Street. The sculptor Brancuşi had occupied it previously. The closets were piled with his symbolic bronzes.

Never a fellow to borrow, Charlie dined chiefly at formal parties. Five-dollar bills were vital. They paid the fare to Long Island. Here a new set of playmates awaited him for weekends. They had no relation to the arts, and were only dimly informed about Charlie's practice of them. But he needed no press notices to shine in their drinking bouts.

They were society people, and Charlie was their beau ideal, sans scripts. Among his new hosts were Tommy Hitchcock, the polo player, Phil Boyer, the amateur society boxer, Jock Whitney, still on horseback and not on a theatre angel's chair.

He dug up fare as far as Boston. Here the Braggiotti family welcomed him with gaiety, music and an unheated salon. The glamorous Braggiottis were on their uppers for the nonce. . . . And Helen was on the road.

Lulu Belle hit the town and the fare problem was over. Charlie was a reigning playwright. No one knew about the ache in his heart but Helen. He gave parties in Fortieth Street. Kolya, the Russian troubadour, sang. Gypsy Markoff played the accordion. Candles lit the table. Exotic dishes were served. Addie, the colored maid, beamed dotingly on the master.

Off to See the Wizard

"You've got to meet Belasco," Charlie said to me. "He's a great show. He whistles like a teakettle when he talks."

Charlie's stories about Belasco were a new volume of his *Arabian Nights*.

Belasco's outer office was one of the town's Eldorados for young actresses. They sat sparkle-eyed in its dusty room like polite little prizes waiting to be pulled out of the Broadway grab bag.

Occasionally the white-haired wizard with the ecclesiastic collar allowed one of them into his cloister. It had opaque glass partitions that didn't reach to the ceiling. Belasco's voice, measured and sibilant, could be heard clearly in the waiting room.

"The old boy," said Charlie, "is vain as hell about his reputation as a Lothario. He's been out of commission for some time, but he likes to keep the legend of Belasco, the seducer, green.

"When a young actress comes into the sanctum, he sits her down across the desk and stares at her till she's reduced to a half coma. Then he looses the bird calls. He doesn't move or lay a finger on the visitor. He just makes love in a loud voice so all the girls in the outer office will hear, and know that Lothario is still in the saddle.

"It's remarkable dialogue, the sort of stuff he tried to stick into *Lulu Belle*. 'You drive me mad with passion, you lovely thing! My God, those eyes! Those magnificent lips! Don't move, my darling, or I'll not be able to control myself.'

"That's the way it usually goes," said Charlie, coming out of his Belasco imitation.

We had tea with the Guvnor amid his art treasures and suits of armor.

"They're all fake," Charlie had briefed me. "He's pure plaster, inside and out. But great fresco work."

Belasco talked exactly like Charlie's imitation of him. After tea he said to me, while Charlie winked, "Let's go to my treasure chest. I'd like to give you a present, something worthy of your position in the world of letters." Charlie had informed him a few hours ago that I was a writer.

Belasco opened a floor chest. It was filled with costume jewelry, Spanish shawls bought off downtown push carts, and other obvious claptrap. He picked out reverently a long necklace that seemed to be made of hazel nuts.

"This necklace belonged to Catherine the Great of Russia," said Belasco. "I would like you to have it. Those missing jewels are where the jealous Orlov snatched it off her neck."

He re-enacted that painful moment with a powerful snatching gesture.

A few years later Charlie and I wrote the play *Twentieth Century*, based on Belasco's ornate and sibilant speech.

A Torch Abroad

STILL undivorced, and moody with frustration, Charlie sailed for Europe. It was the first of his migrations, not counting the sojourn with the Rainbow Division.

There were to be dozens of trips to all parts of the globe. Traveling became an anodyne for Charlie. He was at ease when in motion. Strange lands drew him, and strangers. He liked trains, ships and planes as a boy likes his first bicycle.

Europe was a fine time for Charlie. He was an antilinguist, but that made little difference. International celebrities and members of the aristocracy are people of many tongues. They spoke Charlie's—and were rewarded.

On his first trip to Paris (as a civilian) Charlie went to the Beaux-Arts Ball. Only artists are admitted. To prove he was kin to Picasso, Charlie painted his torso and arms in gold paint.

Entrance to the ball is made down a grand staircase. Preceding Charlie, there appeared at its top a beautiful gal, naked under a fur coat. Opening her coat with a flourish she revealed her costume—sometimes called the Ace of Spades. At the same time the nude inquired haughtily, "Where is the cloak room?"

Beside her, the torch-carrying MacArthur spoke. "I didn't bring my hanger."

The mood of virtue persisted. Charlie flung roses riotously to put his Helen out of mind, but he embraced no substitute.

At a dinner given by Marie Harriman for the Grand Duchess Marie and her brother, the Grand Duke Dimitri (of Russia), Charlie was seated next to the ousted noblewoman. As the meal went along, Grand Duke Dimitri began glowering at Charlie, to whom the Grand Duchess was listening with a lighted eye. His Highness did not approve of his sister's democratic leanings.

There were several blobs of hollandaise sauce on Charlie's shirt front.

"You have some spots on your shirt," said His Highness critically.

Looking at the Grand Duke's medals, Charlie answered: "I, too, am wearing my decorations."

"Possibly from the night before last," His Highness replied.

"Garçon!" Charlie ordered sternly. "The Grand Duke's hat and kiddy car."

His Highness rose, clicked his heels and strode out in a huff.

"My brother is too 'aughty," the Grand Duchess beamed on the admirable character at her side. "You are good to have done this to him."

In a taxi an hour later, Charlie sighed at the royal head resting tenderly on his shoulder.

"Forgive me for not responding to your loveliness and charm," said Charlie, "but I am impotent."

"And so young," sighed the Duchess.

"Yes," said Charlie. "It's a tragedy—at times like this."

Several years later Grand Duchess Marie, now in New York, called up the MacArthurs to invite them to a dinner party.

"Helen can't come," said Charlie. "She's pregnant and almost ready to hatch."

"Ah," the Duchess sighed, "naughty Charlie."

There was a similar unsatisfactory incident in the night train from Antibes to Paris. Grace Moore had insisted Charlie accompany her and lighten the journey. She was to audition the next day for Mary Garden and the French opera, and didn't want to be tense and sing badly.

It was a rainy night. The diva started disrobing.

"Take off that sailor suit," she said to Charlie, "it looks silly on a train."

"Not till you've sung me a song," said Charlie

"What do you want to hear?" Miss Moore, always the musician first, asked.

"The first act of *Louise*," said Charlie.

And thus the rainy night to Paris went away. Charlie kept Grace singing one aria after another until the sandman stepped in. I am reminded of Amelia Bingham introducing one of her vaudeville impersonations—"Lady Godiva rode naked through the streets of London but, however, retained her virtue."

Bonus from the Past

BACK from his pensive fling, Charlie moved into the Rumsey house once more. We met in the street one day and decided to write a play about Chicago newspaper days. We did the writing chiefly in my Beekman Place home, where there was a stack of pencils and paper, and a parchesi board.

Charlie had a child's eagerness for games, particularly ones in which you spin a pointer on a card. He graduated finally to backgammon. We played games for twenty years. It was his habit to lose, complain violently of cheating, and never pay. When the deficit reached a hundred thousand dollars, Charlie would put a five-dollar bill on the table and say, "Tear up that crooked score, and we'll start playing for cash."

We used Charlie's lodgings, also, for work on *The Front Page*. There were a few Brancuşi oddities still visible on the shelves. Charlie stuck them into a closet with the rest of the art work, "so they won't distract us."

It was a true MacArthur gesture of straining at a gnat— for never was there a man surrounded by more distractions than my friend. There were nightly parties, platoons of hail fellows on the phone, and a hundred happy friendships to keep going.

There was also Helen, in New York now and playing in *Coquette* under the banner of Broadway's leading Svengali, Jed Harris. The seven-year battle for divorce from Carol, that had actually taken Charlie's last kopeck to win, was won. Charlie and Helen were making plans for their wedding. The planning was interrupted by quarrels that reduced the prospective groom to a hearse driver.

Yet none of the distractions mattered. Charlie worked like a house afire. We were both writing of people we had loved, and of an employment that had been like none other was ever to be. Also, of a city we both called Avalon.

There were no bandages on Charlie's soul for this job. The explosive went off. I remember of the collaboration chiefly the fact that I have never known since in anyone the inventiveness and certainty, the burst of creation, Charlie brought to *The Front Page*.

Our procedure was established on the first day. It continued, unchanged, through twenty years of play and movie writing. I sat with a pencil, paper and a lap board. Charlie walked, lay on a couch, looked out of a window, drew mustaches on magazine cover girls, and prowled around in some fourth dimension. Out of him, during these activities, came popping dialogue and plot turns. A single quality was in them. They were always true. It was always a character who spoke, not a line born of another line.

The most important thing in our collaboration, however, was not the plot turns and dialogue we made up. It was our faith in each other's judgment. I'd throw a speech into the pot that seemed perfect to me. I'd chuckle dotingly as I offered it. Charlie would shake his head—and the speech would vanish. I believed in his headshake. He believed in mine, too.

We had many headaches writing scripts. But they were never the headaches of argument. How different from Hollywood! And what different work came out! In Hollywood—but I'll come to that (again).

When *The Front Page* was finished, Charlie and I walked to the Algonquin for lunch.

"Which of our names will come first in the billing?" said Charlie.

"I don't know," I said.

"Let's flip a coin," said Charlie. "Winner comes first. I'll flip it so there'll be no cheating."

"Call it," I said.

"Heads," said Charlie, and flipped a nickel.

The coin said tails.

Undaunted Days

HE was grasshopper thin. He purred when he spoke. His skinny jaw jutted. His eyes were dark and slightly upturned as if listening to some tender inner music. He had the grin of a sorcerer. He was not an unkindly man. His voice usually held a note of pity for the listener. He was genuinely sorry the listener was less brilliant than he. Yet he never boasted. He used the pronoun "I" seldom. The pronoun he featured was "you." What you were, what you weren't, what you needed, how you could improve.

This was Jed Harris. Good old Jed, when he was young! I've been exposed to a raft of High Cockalorums in the entertainment world. Jed was the best of them. His joy over a good scene was as creative an emotion as went into its writing. What he loved became his. He took no credit for doing it—much. He merely snatched it up, like a doormat thief, and ran to the theatre with it; and brought it to life.

For many years Jed's play producing was as exciting as marine landings. There were casualties, but always victories. During his great Broadway decade, Jed's personal relations fascinated the intelligentsia, vying for its attention with backgammon and anagrams. His friendships were rooted in dynamite. They exploded daily. The town was loud with the moan of the Harris wounded. Writers, directors, actors, actresses, hostesses and sweethearts (all once his disciples)—ended up snarling at a man who had somehow hamstrung them. The truth may have been quite the opposite. It was Jed who ended up hamstrung—while most of his "victims" continued to ride high in the theatre.

This is a law as old as the stage. Of all the geniuses who serve the theatre the quickest forgotten is the Great Producer. Along with the Great Director, he vanishes almost the day his publicity ceases. Jed was twice as dominant a figure in the theatre as Elia Kazan plus Josh Logan. The theatre belongs to the playwright and actor and actress. The producer-director side of it owns the press megaphone. It also raises the money for the production and gives out the jobs. And it has another vital function—the exercise of common sense. Playwrights have little, performers almost none. Confusion verging on idocy marks their relation to the public. There is now and then a writer who can cast and direct; and occasionally an actor who can "manage." But 95 per cent of them, if left to put a play on, would make hash of it—and wind up in jail. Nevertheless, the stage is theirs.

A dozen great directors are worth less than half a good playwright. And a gross of great producers doesn't equal one star. Yet, as I write this, it seems to me a little unfair that limbo should lie so near for the theatrical obstetricians who pull a play out of a hat, sometimes. You can treat yourself to this luxury feeling—afterward. You don't feel that way when you're in their hands—coming out.

In the days when Jed was the town's head Earthshaker (a title given him by Dick Maney) MacArthur almost knocked his block off.

Charlie was sitting at his typewriter in Fortieth Street re-writing a speech in act three of *The Front Page*. Jed came in. He entered a room as noiselessly as smoke. Unaware of our visitor, Charlie kept on typing. Jed looked pensively over his shoulder at the words appearing.

"That's no good," said Jed, and yanked the copy paper out of the typewriter. It was the only time I ever heard Charlie roar with rage. Jed dashed for the door. I held Charlie's arm from behind. Carnage was averted.

We put the incident in the play. Hildy sits at a typewriter, trying to bat out a lead. Walter (Burns) says, "Wait a minute, Hildy." (The pentecostal fire upon him) "I got an inspiration. Now take this down, just as I say it." (He pulls the page out of Hildy's typewriter.) Hildy (Leaping): "Someday you're going to do that, Walter, and I'm gonna belt you on the jaw—you God damn know-it-all!" Walter (Chanting): "Here's your lead—the Chicago *Examiner* again rode to the rescue of the city in her darkest hour, etc. etc."

Thus the sorrows of life become the joys of art.

A year or so later Charlie received a letter from Jed. It was on quite another subject. It was in the Earthshaker's best scatological vein. "Disillusioned" with Charlie, Jed let go a furioso of "shits," "bastards," "stinkers" at his clay-footed playwright. Charlie sent the letter on to me in Hollywood. Across its top he wrote, "Shelley is loose again."

Jed took *The Front Page* to Atlantic City for a summer tryout. With him went his Court of Inferiors. This included not only the cast and two playwrights, but a flock of train-bearers—Woollcott, Connelly, Harpo, Kaufman, Tony Minor, Dick Maney, Harold Ross, Whittaker Ray and a small harem that was kept out of sight.

There was one vital figure missing. This was the Negro actor who was to play the part of Alderman Willoughby. The Alderman was dear to us. We had expended effort on him. He entered the pressroom several times during the play. We had written Alderman Willoughby "from life," and had taken care not to make him comic. It was the politics he represented that were comic.

Next to Lee Tracy and Osgood Perkins, the actor who had rehearsed the Alderman was our favorite. When he disappeared (as actors will), Charlie, Dick Maney and I scurried through Harlem on his trail. We learned finally that our boy was incommunicado, kicking the gong. We spent a sad day writing the Alderman out of the script, and went on to Atlantic City. There would never be any Alderman Willoughby.

What a cast Jed had hired!

Watching them rehearse, Charlie said, "I give in. The son-ofabitch is a genius."

What we had written came out of exactly the right faces and the right voices. You would have thought you were in Chicago, 1917, looking at the real beauties of the Criminal Courts pressroom. Lee Tracy was our friend Hildy Johnson (plus Charlie and me, who were also Hildy Johnsons) as if all three of us were on the stage together. There was never a better actor for a part than Lee Tracy for Hildy. For one thing, it was hard to believe he was an actor at all.

"Howey would give him a job on sight," said Charlie.

Osgood Perkins was a Jed victory. Charlie had bridled at his casting. So had I, to a lesser degree. It was Charlie who knew Walter Howey, his every gesture and intonation. Oggie had none of them. He was no more Howey than Tiny Tim.

Yet Howey appeared on the stage; not his gestures and intonations, but his soul. Even the original, sitting in the audience, swore the actor had copied every one of his mannerisms. There was no resemblance. Howey added that we had exposed his inner life for the laughter of the world, and he was going to have us shot. But he loved Charlie, and forgave us both.

We apologized to Jed about our stupidity in the Perkins debate, and thanked our director, George Kaufman. Dorothy Stickney, Frances Fuller, Claude Cooper, Frank Conlan and all the rest were equally perfect. It's a rare thing for a playwright to see his work intimately revealed. It is usually performed by in-laws.

While the actors prepared for the opening, we played games in the Marlborough-Blenheim Hotel. Harpo played the piano and I fiddled and Charlie blew the clarinet. The room emptied. Woollcott took on the field at cribbage and wiped everybody out. Charlie howled for his money back, contending that Woollcott had used marked cards.

We had a luncheon game. Each of the nine eaters took turns making up a dish named for its filthy ingredients. I'll offer no examples. Connelly was the loser. He took sick and had to leave the table, and pay the check.

It was a hot summer. Jed called Charlie, Kaufman and me to his suite for a conference. We arrived and found Jed sitting naked in a chair. His hairy and coleopterous nudity stuck in our eye for an hour. George was the most irked. We went on with the conference, however, as if our producer were vested in his usual royal purple.

As we were leaving, George, passing the naked Jed, said casually, "Your fly's open."

The most important figure that entered our ken in Atlantic City was Dick Maney. He was Jed's press agent. We had no interest in his professional activities, which were, at the time, diluted by liquor. What was fetching about Dick was that he was a man of language. Epithets rolled out of him as out of a thesaurus. He swayed mid priceless metaphors. An Irish cry of disdain was in his smallest comment. We wrote him later into *Twentieth Century*, calling him Owen O'Malley. We never paid him the money we promised him for this theft of his soul, because he was always richer than we were.

Success in the theatre is difficult to describe. It is chiefly an absence of pain. The thousand devils of disaster are on leave. Present are only a few smiling friends, and the box-office statement. There is, also, an inner glow, depending on how keen for playwrighting you are. I began writing books. A book would be always for me the fine symbol of achievement.

For Charlie it was a play. He loved the theatre as a man loves his country. He had the bigger glow in Atlantic City.

When *The Front Page* opened in New York, Charlie became a "Chicagoan" again. He was casual, idle—smiling at a world full of entertainment. He was pleased that he had helped provide some of it. He rode his bandwagon as modestly as if it were a trolley car. Success seemed only to increase his carelessness toward it.

He uttered only one ambitious statement in this time. He said, "*The Moonshooter* is a better play than *The Front Page.* You've got to find it."

"I didn't lose it," I said. "You did."

"I never lost anything," said Charlie firmly.

We were confused about the matter. It had been a loud night in Long Island when we had read the play to Sam Harris. We had settled down at 3 A.M. on a Broadway curbing in front of an all-night drugstore. Harold Ross sat between us. We talked for an hour, trying to convince him that his scheme for a magazine to be called *The New Yorker* was a bounderish and hopeless venture. How the hell could a man who looked like a resident of the Ozarks and talked like a saloon brawler set himself up as pilot of a sophisticated, elegant periodical? It was bounderism of the worst sort. We reduced Harold's snorts of laughter to a glower of doubt. Nevertheless, he staggered off to found *The New Yorker.*

An event mightier than *The Front Page* took place in

Charlie's life around this time. He and Helen were married.

"We want to get married secretly without any newspaper fuss," said Charlie to me. "I want you to find some taciturn judge who'll perform a private ceremony in his chambers. And I mean private."

The assignment depressed me. I knew that a confused Charlie was thinking of me as functioning reporter. In his happiness, he possibly thought we were both in Chicago. I knew no judges in New York and called on Tommy (T. R.) Smith for help. Tommy was the cultural side of the Liveright publishing firm that printed my books. He was a man about town, with a ribboned pince-nez and a cocktail glass usually in his hand. He gave parties for Lesbians and was full of sophisticated lore.

Tommy arranged for the judge.

"Be sure it's private," I cautioned him.

Helen and Charlie arrived at Judge Oberhofer's chambers. They had some difficulty getting in. The room was blocked with reporters and photographers. The ceremony was delayed because some of the reporters my taciturn judge had summoned had not yet arrived. I was as surprised as MacArthur, but he was angrier.

"You were always a lousy reporter," Charlie said, and then grinned sourly for the popping cameras.

One of the pictures appeared on the front page of the *Daily News*. Its caption read, "Bridegroom or Bigamist?" But the bout was over.

After the ceremony, Helen and Charlie came to my Beekman Place apartment, where Rose had prepared lobster *diable* for a wedding supper. Woollcott came with them. Ross got wind of the important event and arrived, uninvited. He was given a plate at our hallway dining table.

Youth, fame, a dreamed-of marriage, money rolling in, good health, and a hundred colorful friends suing for his presence, and happiness all around—these were in Charlie's world now. It was the top of the Ferris wheel. He had the air of a man to whom no day is unwelcome or distressing.

A Child Who Was Wanted

OF my friend's moods and activities as a father, there is not more to tell than that a new love came into his life, and remained there. Fathers of girls are much alike. They grin, dote and feel a trifle mysterious—as a source of life. Their bosoms swell with a sort of knighthood; they have a little lady to defend and protect.

These fatherly clichés appeared in my friend with the birth of his daughter, Mary, on February 15, 1930. He popped into the nursery with unusable gifts, sang his small repertoire of songs to the smiling infant. When she took to talking, he boasted of her sayings as if a new Confucius were in the playroom. He had the same pointless tales to tell of her childhood activities that all fathers tell as if they were reciting from a new *Iliad*.

The only thing somewhat different about Charlie as a father was that he never outgrew his first welcome of his child. During all her years into young womanhood, he spoke of her with an unchanged sense of her newness. She remained a gift that had arrived on a snow-heaped winter night.

He was, also, an unusual parent in some ways. He never assumed the role of Supreme Court Justice, which is an oddity in the father of a maturing girl. He seemed aloof from what are called the duties of fatherhood, yet he seemed also to walk, work and travel with Mary's hand in his.

He offered no edited version of himself for *jeune fille* consumption. As he talked in the world, so he talked in his home. When Mary was attending the Nyack High School, she invited her teacher home for dinner. Pops agreed to give up his Saturday-evening diversion and be present at "the grisly meal." Shortly before the educator's arrival, young Mary threw her arms around her father and said, "Pop, don't be funny tonight." She explained plaintively that she loved his jokes and stories, but that "the world" was different. Charlie agreed.

Charlie's daughter had been exposed to his Chicago language since cradle days. At Dwight School the little girls of the fourth grade decided to play "Kick the Can." They told Mary she was "It." Mary, not knowing the game, leaned over and waited for its painful innings to start. She came home saying it had been very embarrassing.

Charlie's aloofness as a parent was, actually, a matter for outside eyes. From Mary's toddling days through her life, he followed her growth with happy attention, helped Helen to guide her from school to school, galloped off with her across the world.

Several times in his life my friend boasted to me in the halting way of a man not used to airing his interior that his daughter, Mary, was unique among children.

"She tells me all the things that confuse her," he said. "And asks me for advice. Not as if I were her father, but somebody she can trust. We talk about everything."

The "success" of the MacArthurs as parents was written pleasantly from year to year in the bright face of their daughter. She grew up a child gaily in love with her folks. Through all her tutelage at Dwight, Nyack, Rosemary Hall, Miss Hewitt's Classes and the American Academy of Dramatic Art, Mary beamed on her parents as people of wonder and charm, and endless love.

Growing up under Charlie's nose was the latest MacArthur, brought into the house as an infant. Called Jamie first and later Jim, this arrival grew into a sturdy boy, clattered around the garden and the river bank, was to be seen in flashes, thereafter, running, climbing and consorting with oddly sweatered colleagues.

Charlie and Helen were full of love and pride toward this MacArthur. When Jim was entering his teens his pop began to note a quality in the strong lad none had expected. Talent entered his moods and doings; and a likeness to Charlie grew in the boy. It was no likeness of feature or gesture, but of mood. Charlie's reticence, his nonobtrusive look at his fellows appeared in duplicate in Jim.

Charlie, who had what we used to call a "snake's ear" for the signals of talent, noted first its presence near him.

"Jim's different," he said. "He's heading for someplace. I can't figure out what particular kind of noise he's going to make. But it's obvious there's going to be a racket."

This was when Jim was fourteen, and not even Jim had inkling that a new movie star, James MacArthur, was hatching.

In Charlie's letters from the varied fronts in World War II, Mary and Jim remained objectives more vital than the Allied aims. The letters were to Helen in 1943, '44 and '45. Here are excerpts:

"We spent the morning of the Day with General Patton. He reminds me a great deal of Jamie. . . . Here—with a kiss for Mary, even though I haven't heard from her, and a whack on the behind for Jamie."

". . . I'm worried about your cutting into your rest. . . . Don't forget the children need you, too—and spending the day with them will be good for you. Please think it over."

". . . I don't know what to tell you about Mary's movie career. I really don't. I think, underneath all that concern by her teachers, that they are really babying her, the way you'd baby a fond, rich relative. I get that impression from that 'interesting case' tone in all their voices when I express my concern. I mention all this in the thought that a movie might spark her into some more definite pattern of life, but I'm passing the buck at the same time. We may have a lazy daughter, but she's so lovable. As for her day dreams, Shakespeare seemed to think that day dreams were the pleasantest things in life. Mine are, because they're all about you. . . ."

". . . I've been trying to get you all day to reassure you about Mary. . . . Our child is well and happy, somewhat worried about examinations today, but breathless and excited as ever. She said she hadn't learned to read properly, so that it takes her three times as long to read a book than the other girls. I was mean enough to remind her of how we used to heckle her to read. She was nice enough not to mind it. I'll call her tomorrow and forward the news of what happened today at Phillipi. I'm going to make a stab at getting to Toronto. . . . If I don't make it I'll take Mary to lunch in N.Y. She put Jo on the phone and when I told them my Gestapo had told me how they had corrupted the school with their drawings, both laughed like hoodlums."

"DARLING,

"By the time you get this I'll probably have spoken to you and told you all about the party, but here goes, anyhow: I had a hell of a time getting to New York on Saturday. It was one of those times when transportation was promised all day, with nothing taking off for one reason or another. . . . So I didn't get to the hotel until long after ten. The girls were waiting in the lobby. I took them to the River Club, where I dropped my bag, and then to the 'Stork.' En route Anne told me that Mary had said: 'It may take him till three in the morning, but Pop will be here, because he said he would.' Which made up for the long trip in by way of bus, subway and elevated train. I'd been worrying all the way. They had a wonderful time. They were photographed from all angles, danced with Billy Reardon, saw the stars, met a lot of them, received gifts of Prince de Bourbon perfume, had a lighted birthday cake and clung to their perches until past three."

From London during World War II:
". . . Tell Mary I bumped into her old producer, Gabe Pascal, wrapped in gypsy scarves and leaning heavily on a great stick. He yelled: 'Where is my star?' . . . All my love to all of you. There is no one here so pretty and gay as either one of my darling girls. I miss you all with everything I've got."

There was a letter from his office in Washington. It concerned the problem of Jamie, who had not yet learned he had been adopted in infancy. The lieutenant colonel, busy with the study of cholera germs and other lethal possibilities for winning the war, was fearful that Jamie would be hurt on learning of his status. He wrote to Helen while still a major:

"DARLING,

"I keep thinking the word 'adoption' may be popping up any day and catch us unprepared, so I stuck it in the enclosed 'promotion orders.' It may strike his fancy and lead into a discussion."

(The subject was five years of age at the time.)

The enclosure read:

WAR DEPARTMENT
SERVICES OF SUPPLY
OFFICE CHIEF CHEMICAL WARFARE SERVICE
WASHINGTON, D.C.

March 24, 1943

FROM: CHARLES MACARTHUR, Major, U.S.A.
TO: HELEN HAYES MACARTHUR
SUBJECT: PROMOTION OF CORPORAL JAMES MACARTHUR

1. It has come to the attention of the undersigned that, since Corporal James Gordon MacArthur adopted the army as a career, his conduct has been consistent with the highest standards of military behavior and deserving of promotion.

2. Helen Hayes MacArthur, in the absence of his Commanding Officer, is therefore and hereby empowered to promote the said James Gordon MacArthur to the grade of Master Sergeant.

3. A pair of Master Sergeant's chevrons are enclosed.

> CHARLES MACARTHUR
> Major, U.S.A.
> Special Assistant to the Chief,
> Chemical Warfare Service

Family Life

I CONFER again with Helen in the MacArthur house down the street in Nyack. Our subject—Charlie.

Having written about Helen Hayes of the twenties, I look at the midcentury edition. The face that was flowerlike is strong and handsome. It is a survivor's face, but a child still looks out of the blue eyes. She seems more historian than woman; she keeps the archives of a vanished world. As O'Neill says, "The past is the present and the future." Except to the artist. The artist works on us as if there were no yesterdays.

I ask Helen no questions. She talks slowly and carefully of Charlie as if some of his reticence had survived in her. In this Nyack parlor Charlie is as vivid as a locomotive headlight. She recalls their trip to Europe twenty years ago.

One of Charlie's favorites was on the ship, young Baronet Bobby Throckmorton, whose family had been stepping high in England since the Crusades. Bobby and Lady Venetia Montagu, the aviating Jewess, were among the pick of Charlie's Britons. It was Lady Montagu who invited Charlie to dinner—"to meet the best-kept woman in London." He came on the wrong evening and dined, confusedly, with Winston Churchill, a half dozen other statesmen, and their wives.

Young Throckmorton admired Charlie as an example of how to live. You laughed and had fun, and trouble was a beggar you dismissed with a dime.

Charlie was pleased to find another pal on board. This was Major Beaufort, an English ex-warrior with a shoe-brush mustache and an arrogant eye.

"We were a cozy little group on the first night out," said Helen.

148

She had just closed in one of her acting triumphs, *Victoria Regina,* and was tired from its long run. She looked forward to Charlie beside her in a deck chair, telling stories and reciting from the poets.

On the second afternoon, Major Beaufort joined the MacArthur party in the lounge for cocktails. He was stark naked.

"Sorry to be late," the major bowed to Helen. "I couldn't find a proper tie."

Outnumbered by a gang of American seamen, the nude Britisher was carried off to the ship's hospital. Here, in an effort to scuttle the S.S. *Manhattan,* he broke the plumbing in the bathroom and flooded the deck.

Thereafter the prisoner sent hourly notes to the captain demanding to know the course and position of the ship, and questioning the ability of any Yankee to run a ship.

The loss of the major's society left Charlie at loose ends for a day. But he drummed up other diversions.

Two days later a scandal hit both sides of the Atlantic. Mr. Avery Brundage, chaperoning our athletes on the *Manhattan* to the Olympic games, announced that the beautiful Eleanor Holm, world's champion backstroke swimmer, had been dropped from the American team. The fie-fo-fumming blue-nose Brundage declared her guilty of breaking training by participating in a drinking session with a fellow-passenger, Charles MacArthur.

Never did a bit of ocean-going wassail receive such publicity. The entire civilized world was set agog. Had the S.S. *Manhattan* hit an iceberg and gone down, she would have received no more newspaper space.

Charlie woke up the next morning unaware of the to-do he and the backstroke champion had kicked up by taking a drop too much. His movements were slow and moody. He lit a cigarette and looked at his famous missus. She was packing a trunk.

"What's the rush?" asked Charlie. "We don't get to Southampton for several days."

"I'm not going to Southampton," said the star of *Victoria*

Regina. "I'm getting off in Ireland. At a place called Cóbh."

"What are you doing that for?" Charlie was concerned. "Are you seasick?"

"Because I can't stand to be on the same boat with you and your friend Miss Holm. They've thrown her off the Olympic team for getting drunk with you."

"They shouldn't have done that," said Charlie. "She's a great woman."

"A great woman, is she!" said Helen. "Then what does that make the rest of us—just sober, stick-in-the-mud no-bodies!"

"She's not only a great woman, but a fine one," Charlie replied. "And I'm going to look up Mr. Brundage and kick the hell out of him, after I've had a bite."

A pity Charlie didn't. But the home fires required full attention. Helen didn't get off the boat in Ireland.

"How awful it would have been if I had," she said twenty years later. "I'd have missed the happiest trip Charlie and I ever took. Yes, we were happy again in a day. It was always easy to forgive Charlie. We were supposed to meet the Gilbert Millers in Baden-Baden but Charlie said no. He wanted us to travel alone. Besides, he had a feeling something was going to happen in Europe. He said we ought to have a look at it before it exploded. He always had these sort of gypsy instincts about world events, and he was nearly always right."

They drove through the Burgundy country, stopping at inns and castles. The Frenchmen wore short black coats and looked like illustrations of a vanishing era. Charlie's goal was the ancient walled city of Carcassonne, on the River Aude.

"When we got to Carcassonne," said Helen, "I tottered into bed. I'd had a bilious attack from all the wines we'd been sampling through Burgundy. And while I lay in bed Charlie came hurrying in every hour or so with new reports of the wondrous battlements of Carcassonne. He talked about the Romans and the Visigoths, the Arabs and Pippin the Short, and the Crusaders and the Black Prince. They'd all fought on the walls of Carcassonne."

Helen recovered and they walked the historic land.

"He had stories and poems about every bit of the scenery," said Helen. "It was like walking with Peire Vidal, or some long-ago minstrel. He'd say, 'Over yon hill the soldiers of Simon de Montfort met the archers of Raymond Roger.'"

They visited the village of Huillicourt. It was the village in which Private MacArthur had been billeted during part of the war against the Kaiser. As he walked the village streets again, peasants and shopkeepers recognized him and called his name, "Charlot, Charlot."

Charlie introduced Helen to the "foster parents" who had adopted him as their Huillicourt son. They sat in the inn and the villagers crowded around the MacArthur table. Helen listened to stories of the fun Charlie had brought to Huillicourt during the booming of the big guns.

They went to Domrémy-la-Pucelle and Charlie's tales switched from Battery F to the Maid Joan.

"The one reward Joan of Arc asked for from the kingdom she had saved," said Charlie, "was that the village of Domrémy should be exempt from taxation." He added indignantly, "You'll find hundreds of statues of Joan of Arc all over France—but the inhabitants of Domrémy are still paying taxes."

"When Charlie first asked me to marry him," Helen recalled, "he said, 'You'll sometimes be discontented but I promise you you'll never be bored.' I wasn't."

In his white-painted, turreted Nyack home on the Hudson, Charlie worked and wrote and was full of projects. Yet he seemed always like a man on a vacation. He played tennis, baseball and ice hockey in Peterson's frozen shipyard basin. He walked on the bottom of his pool in a diver's helmet. He played backgammon, and went canoeing and sailboating, and he fished for crabs and river eels. He walked in his garden and stared long at its flowers and shrubs. Camera in hand, he chased Helen from bedroom to bedroom. He was out to bag nudes. He had his own darkroom in the basement and spent weeks developing artistic snapshots. We were rival photographers. At the end of two years Charlie was several nudes up on me.

Charlie wrote on an electric typewriter in a cubbyhole off his basement barroom. The secret of his "studio" was that it looked as bleak as the corner of a newspaper local room.

Electrical gadgets were a passion with my friend. He was curiously lured by science, of which he had no knowledge. But he liked to peer through a telescope and stare into a microscope. He did this for hours at a time, to what end he never said.

He kept the icebox stocked with tins of inedible shark's-fin soup, octopus steaks and salads made out of ancient Chinese bird nests. He played Spanish records. Gypsy music held nostalgia for him.

On the shelf over his bed were all the volumes of Baedeker. He read himself to sleep with information about Byzantium and Baghdad and the lost cities of the Sahara. The artist Herman Rosse had designed the room for him. It was a room of gray wood paneling. One of Charlie's projects was to have the names of all the battles of Napoleon carved on his bed—with a space left for the last one.

On weekends the MacArthur ménage became crowded with theatre people and cronies from far places—and Charlie talked. His tales further peopled Nyack with his dozen worlds.

Among the guests were women in open pursuit of him who came boldly to sigh under Helen's nose. You couldn't scold him for this any more than you could scold a trout for luring the fishermen's flies.

Charlie toured Rockland County with Helen and the children at his side. Here, too, he knew the tale of "yon hill," of the Liberty Boys who had peppered away at the Redcoats from behind the crumbled stone fences.

He and Helen bought some acreage on the outskirts of

Nyack, where they planned to grow crops and let the land support them. Although he loved every tree and swampy creek of his rural domain, the crops were fitful, and the MacArthurs had to sustain themselves by other means.

Charlie read constantly—and secretly, for he did most of his reading in the bathroom, as he used to do when his sin-chasing father had placed all secular literature under taboo. So preoccupied was Charlie with the charm of his home and the love of his family that when you came on him sitting idle at his ship's-wheel garden table you felt you were interrupting an important activity.

One winter's day the hilly streets leading into Nyack's Broadway were covered with snow. Lederer, MacArthur and I bought a sled at Dropkin's sports store. When it was MacArthur's turn to lie on his belly and go scooting down the hill, he steered the sled into the curbing and rolled off after a few yards. We denounced him for this cowardly action. Charlie grinned. He said nothing about his boyhood Nyack memories that, catching him again on a sled, had risen out of his soul to harass and frighten him.

Reverend William Telfer MacArthur arrived one summer day in Nyack to deliver a Sunday sermon in the Tabernacle on the hill, where missionaries and ministers were still being trained. The Reverend rode to his pulpit in Charlie's chauffeur-driven limousine. In the entourage were a number of MacArthurs, including brother Alfred, rueful and sarcastic plutocrat, and their sister, Helen Bishop, gray haired, youthful faced and handsome as a movie queen.

The Reverend MacArthur was dressed in fine new black clothes with expensive boots and a gates-ajar collar. He was as stylish looking as an archbishop. His sons saw to it that he remained the sharpest-looking, best-fed evangelist in the country.

Dr. MacArthur addressed the economically harassed student body of the Tabernacle on the subject of how to live. "Think not," he said, "of unimportant, earthly problems—such as how to get along and make both ends meet. I never think of such unspiritual problems. I think only of the Lord. I have faith that He will provide for me. And He does. He feeds me as the ravens once fed Elijah."

"Do you remember the great decalcomania renaissance?" Helen smiled. "Those wonderful transfer pictures?"

It was summertime. Across the Hudson each morning dawn lit the towns of Tarrytown and Ossining with an elfin glow. A green and sunny day came up the river bank. The Hudson sparkled, sailboats moved like white tepees over the water, and the birds sang in the high trees. Mary was home from school, and riding about on a donkey. Jamie was cutting up in the play pen. Helen was reading play scripts and remembering Burgundy and Carcassonne and Pippin the Short—and smiling on her minstrel, now in bathrobe and slippers and busy as a beaver with his transfer pictures, a sponge and a pot of warm water. He worked intently, covering the walls, doors and marble mantelpieces with decalcomania clusters of flowers, buds, bugs and butterflies. By the end of the summer MacArthur's Victorian house looked as if it had been tattooed.

Hollywood
and
Movies

The Jute Mills

In Rome, you do as the Romans. The point is, if you don't fancy Romans, why go there? Why go to work in Hollywood if you think movies are mainly trash, and the bosses who turn them out chiefly muttonheads?

A fair question. I'll answer for both of us. Charlie and I worked together in Hollywood on many scripts. We had the same opinions, although we expressed them differently. I was for broadcasting mine. Charlie said, "Complaints are only a sign you've been hurt. Keep the wounds out of sight."

We argued this point from our earliest meetings. Once, in a speakeasy, Dorothy Parker quoted Hemingway's line that "courage is grace under pressure." I dissented. Charlie agreed. "That's posing for others," I said. Charlie said, "It's posing for yourself."

A number of things used to lead a good writer to Hollywood—when it was Eldorado and not a ghost town. (It'll be a tourist spot like Tombstone, Arizona, before the century's done.) I'll make an honest list of these things.

First, the money. It was easy money. You didn't gamble for it as in the theatre. Or break your back digging for it as in the field of prose. It was money in large sums. Twenty-five- and fifty-thousand-dollar chunks of it fell into your pockets in no time.

You got it sometimes for good work, more often for bad. But there was a law in the studios—hire only the best. As a result, the writer who had written well in some other medium was paid the most. His task was *not* to write as well for the movies. His large salary was a bribe.

The boss liked a superior writer to turn out his kindergarten truck—for a number of reasons, some of them mystic. It was a foolish waste of money, like hiring a cabinetmaker to put up a picket fence. But there was a certain pleasure in it for the boss. The higher the class of talent he could tell what to do and how to do it, the more giddily cultured he could feel himself. A good four-fifths of Hollywood's bosses were money-grabbing nitwits whom movie-making enabled to masquerade as Intellects and Creative Spirits. The boss who hired Dostoevski to write like Horatio Alger somehow became Feodor's superior.

Not all the talent of a good writer was discarded. A part of it could be used for a script—a dime's worth. And there was an occasional script you could work on with all the stops out. But that wasn't why you came to Hollywood— to do the masterpiece. You came as a pencil for hire, at sums heretofore unheard of for pencils. You brought no plots, dreams or high intentions. If you wrote a good movie it was because you were lucky enough to get on the payroll of a classy boss. Classy or not, the boss called the shots and you did as bid. You were a sort of literary errand boy with an oil magnate's income.

Next to the lure of easy money was the promise of a plush Bohemian vacation. Witty and superior folk abounded. The town was loud with wild hearts and the poetry of success. The wit, superiority, wildness had no place in a movie script. But there was happy room for them in the cafés, drawing rooms and swimming pools.

"You write stinking scripts," said Charlie, "but you meet the people you like to be in a room with."

The other matters that took you to Hollywood had nothing to do with the movies. They had to do with flaws in yourself—flaws of laziness, fear, greed. Being a good writer is no feather bed. Writing is almost as lonely a craft as flagpole sitting (and is becoming almost as passé). You write behind a closed door, and fun is your enemy.

Also, the writer intent on "doing his best" has to expose that best to critical blasts that mow him down, two times out of three. And if he wants to keep serving his art, he and his lacerations must lead a sort of hall-bedroom existence.

A writer who goes over a fifteen-thousand-dollar yearly budget has to serve other than Art. The figure may be a little high for the poet, but who considers the poets? Plato long ago threw them out of any ideal republic.

The movies solved such matters. There were no critics to mow him down. The writer of a movie is practically anonymous. The press agents employed by the producers, directors and stars see to that. In the roster of who made the movie, his name is lost among the tailors, hairdressers, sound mixers and other talents that toiled toward its creation. It's a pleasant anonymity.

Writing a good movie brings a writer about as much fame as steering a bicycle. It gets him, however, more jobs. If his movie is bad it will attract only a critical tut-tut for him. The producer, director and stars are the geniuses who get the hosannas when it's a hit. Theirs are also the heads that are mounted on spears when it's a flop.

The movie writer is stranger to these ups and downs. A man could even brag about being a bad script writer. It was a sign he was possibly a genius who couldn't bend to lowly tasks. Neither Charlie nor I was of this kind, but we met them.

I've written it was easy money—and that's a misstatement, if you examine the deed. Writing cheaply, writing falsely, writing with "less" than you have, is a painful thing. To betray belief is to feel sinful, guilty—and taste bad. Nor is movie writing easier than good writing. It's just as hard to make a toilet seat as it is a castle window. But the view is different.

Charlie's problem in Hollywood was greater than mine. His love of the theatre included anything that required actors. And he had no second speed for writing. He had to write with all he was or not at all. The gift of faking dialogue and pumping up Valentine plots was small in him.

To bring a sense of perfection to Hollywood is to go bagging tigers with a fly swatter. Charlie would rewrite a scene ten times, improving it each time with a phrase, a piece of business, a flash of wit or a more human sound. Likely or not, such scenes were cut out of the script by the boss. Why such sabotage? Because the boss who "edited" and okayed the script had no way of knowing one scene was better written than another. He had never been a writer, or reader; never even earned his keep as a critic.

A boss said to Charlie, "I know less about writing than you do. But so does the audience. My tastes are exactly those of the audience. What I didn't like, the audience won't like."

It was the credo that finally landed Hollywood in the dust bin. But when movies were the only toy on the market, it was the Eleventh Commandment—"Write down."

Once I saw Charlie's boss cut out the first fine sixty pages of his script *I Take This Woman* and turn it from a civilized comedy into a Darkest-Metro soap opera. The boss was Bernie Hyman, successor to Irving Thalberg as producing lord of M.G.M.

Bernie was a "darling" man, gentle spoken, and with a puppy's eagerness for life. He was devoted to Charlie, imitated as best he could his mannerisms, and annexed him as a traveling companion on trips to Europe and Africa. Yet all this admiration never stayed his boss' hand—the hand, in Hollywood, that knows not what the other is doing, or what it itself is up to.

In his story conferences with other writers Bernie would say, "Let's make the hero a MacArthur." And he would beam creatively on the room.

"Let's make the hero a MacArthur" was, in fact, one of Hollywood's more artistic mottoes for many years. I heard it in scores of conferences. It meant let's have a graceful and unpredictable hero, full of off-beat rejoinders; a sort of winsome onlooker at life, no matter how hysterical the plot.

Clark Gable, Spencer Tracy, Cary Grant, George Sanders, Robert Taylor and a dozen others, including Jimmy Durante, "played MacArthur." The trade-mark of the character was that if somebody fired a gun he didn't look up, and if a woman was madly in love with him he amused her by sliding down a banister.

(I recall Dotty Parker's remark about a movie actress who said she had been hurt "sliding down a banister." "Perhaps it was a barrister," said Miss Parker.)

I used to say to Charlie, "Why the hell try so hard? All they want is snappy dialogue and snappy scenes."

Charlie could write badly, but not on purpose. He was also sensitive to criticism, from bosses as well as critics. If his work didn't please the boss, Charlie went into a nose dive. He had valor and tenacity, but he was a man of small defiance.

He knew as well as I that the boss was, rather often, a dreary fellow, incapable of criticizing a waffle. He knew, too, that such criticism was usually the mutter of incompetence, in a position to make its mutterings heard. But it didn't matter. Charlie darkened at its sound.

There are no letters of protest from MacArthur on this gloomy topic. But there was one from F. Scott Fitzgerald, written a few weeks before his "crack-up."

Scotty had toiled on a movie script for four months in the studio. He handed it in proudly to his boss. Like many of his kind, the boss, who had never written anything, had not even sold a he-and-she joke to a newspaper, fancied himself a writer. He redictated the Fitzgerald script in two days, using four stenographers. He changed all the dialogue.

Scotty's letter to this man read, in part, "How could you do this to me? If there's anything I know it's the sound of how my generation has spoken. I've listened to its dialogue for twenty years. I've done little else with my life than listen to it speak—How can you throw me away in this fashion?"

Signature—and crack-up.

A Gavotte with Critics

THE boss could drive you crazy, but it was a drubbing you took. It was not a knock-out punch such as the critics threw. There are some writers who can take a critical belt on the jaw and stay erect and intact. You need for such non-response a soul dormant as a frozen caterpillar. Charlie and I both pretended to have such interiors. Our pretense stood up everywhere except in our homes, with the blinds down.

It doesn't help to know the critics, or to have an honest disdain of their talent. Dr. Samuel Johnson wrote, "Criticism is a study by which men grow important and formidable at very small expense."

Knowing this, the doctor, nevertheless, bellowed half his days away in cries of critic-induced pain. In our time Eugene O'Neill was driven out of the theatre by the journalistic jumping jacks. Woollcott wrote, "O'Neill began the peopling of his stage with characters he himself did not know much about, hardly undertaking, in the succession from *The Great God Brown* onwards, the writing of plays which called (and called in vain) for the touch of one who was both poet and prophet. In the lamentable *Dynamo* and in *Strange Interlude* (that *Abie's Irish Rose* of the pseudo-intelligentsia) he had finally taken on a kind of bombazine pretentiousness."

Alec, the frothy but potent man on the aisle, was one of many. O'Neill made his answer his way. He wandered off, hid away, and continued to write. And he made certain that no play of his would be exposed to New York critics while he was alive.

MacArthur was no O'Neill, although the talent he brought to New York was wide and handsome. And a fear of critics had much to do with his many years of silence as a playwright.

On the way to the opening of his comedy *Johnny on the Spot*, Charlie came out of the Algonquin Hotel elevator holding a morning newspaper in front of his chest. Its wild headline concerning the Japanese assault on the Philippines read, "Strafe MacArthur."

Critic George Jean Nathan was in the lobby. Charlie walked past critic Nathan with his placard and a grin. The next morning the critics strafed. Charlie stood beside Helen in the kitchen as she scrambled eggs for breakfast. The bad notices were on the floor.

"He suddenly put his head against mine," said Helen, "and wept."

People of Fine Odor

THE honors Hollywood has for the writer are as dubious as tissue-paper cuff links. Hollywood's function is to serve the Public Taste, not to burn, bite, or ecstasize it. This is the unlucrative function of Art, and Art—major or minor—is to Hollywood the Scythian wastes of bankruptcy.

The mental vacuum known as Public Taste is man's one permanent gift to nature. Serving it will make you (for a time) prosperous and influential. This is a considerable step up for the peddlers, salesmen, gamblers and rough-and-ready sports who launched Hollywood some fifty years ago. They own it today—sound stages, backlogs and front-yard oil wells. They wear their purple no worse than other sharpies who have located the public fundament and saluted it tirelessly. For writers, such salute puts no purple on them.

But, travail and crack-up to one side, there was fun in Hollywood. The sun shone. The dinner parties looked like stage sets. International beauties sat in candle-lit café nooks, holding hands with undersized magnates. Novelists, poets and playwrights staggered bibulously in and out of swimming pools. Floperoo actors and actresses from New York, ex-waitresses, elevator girls, light o' loves, high school graduates with the right-size boobies, all met their Good Fairy and were given seats on the royal bandwagon. And out of the hotel suites, brothels and casinos came a noise of life undaunted such as had not been heard since the Forty-niners drank themselves to death looking for nuggets.

MacArthur entered the new Eldorado with a casual step. Hollywood itself looked like a row of one-storied candy stores. There were a few estates, thick with butlers; a few ornate hotels minus house dicks; and a half dozen claptrap-looking refugee camps called the studios. Except for the sun, the cockscomb palm trees and the beaming sky, it wasn't much of a place to look at. But Charlie's favorite humans were already in possession. Benchley, Fitzgerald and Larry Stallings were welkin-ringing in the Garden of Allah (a hotel). Fowler and Jack Barrymore were hawking violets on the street corners. Bea Lillie, the deadpan Titania, with an elfin lilt to her wisecracking, was there. So were the moonlit Tilly Losch, graceful as pipe smoke, and Sandra Rambeau, the Illinois telephone operator with a maharaja's scalp in her belt. On view, also, were the bright talents, Lillian Gish, Marlene Dietrich, Lila Lee, Patsy Ruth Miller, Joan Crawford, Jack Gilbert, Bill Haines, Jimmy Durante. Jo Swerling was there (with more money than he could give away); and Donald Ogden Stewart, one of the authentic sons of Mark Twain; Dr. Sam Hirshfeld, the balm-bringer; all the Marx Brothers; and Sam Hoffenstein, the Broadway lark with his acid madrigals; and Herman Mankiewicz, the Tong warrior.

Samuel Goldwyn, Louis B. Mayer, the Warner Brothers, the Schenck Brothers, Adolph Zukor, Harry Cohn, Irving Thalberg, Carl Laemmle, Jesse Lasky, B. P. Shulberg and their *mishpoochas* were conducting a Semitic renaissance, sans rabbis and Talmud. The fact that they were flinging at the world the ancient Greek credo that deluding the mind of the public with tommyrot was better medicine than torturing it with truth (Plato) cut no ice about who was running the renaissance—Greeks or Hebrews. And the first wave of geniuses from Broadway, London, Paris and Berlin was already on hand issuing dinner invitations (black tie), collecting weekly bags of gold and denouncing Hollywood, much as in these pages. For when we started we were all much alike. It was my misfortune to remain unchanged.

And the MacArthur reputation was there, ahead of him, spread by his friends. It was a legend that stepped casually from the Santa Fe *Chief* into the Los Angeles depot.

"I'll tell you the kind of fellow he is," said Herman Mankiewicz to a coterie of bigwigs. Herman himself was a legend then. His wit lashed the new Eldorado, his derisive salvos at Hollywood geniuses kept them writhing and blushing and laughing. A greater phenomenon than Herman's wit was the fact that his victims employed him, at large sums, to write movies he despised for bosses he ridiculed.

"In New York one night," said the always nostalgic Herman, "MacArthur and I were sitting in a stage box at the opening of an Earl Carroll *Vanities*. We had been drinking—drink for drink, nobody loafing. The chorus girls suddenly appeared on the stage dressed as musketeers, nude to the crotch, and carrying weapons. They went into an ooh-la-la fencing dance, crossing swords and doing high kicks. Carried away by the glamour and gallantry of this spectacle, MacArthur leaned out of our box and applauded like an idiot. He kept applauding till he fell out of the box and landed on the stage, where he bowed several times, with ass to the audience, and tottered into the wings. If such a thing had happened to me, all you would have heard the next day was, 'Manky was drunk as a beast last night and fell out of a theatre box—and he is ruining his life.' Well, about MacArthur they said, 'Did you hear about Charlie playing D'Artagnan last night?'"

Barrymore

CHARLIE's friendship with Jack Barrymore began in his early New York days. Barrymore was one of Ned Sheldon's errant cronies, a man as much in need of guidance as of applause. The bed-anchored Ned continued to look after the zigzagging actor. Charlie was Ned's wazir in this emprise.

Curbing and piloting the Barrymore was a job for Tantalus. Charlie discharged it chiefly by bringing back rosy reports of their boy's activities. He kept any bad news from Ned until it exploded in headlines.

Watching Charlie the Samaritan at work on Barrymore, you were put to it to figure who was saving whom, from what?

"It's Christmas Eve," Sheldon said to MacArthur, "and I hear Jack and his new bride are in town. It would be nice if they spent the evening together."

"I'll go find him," said Charlie, whose own bride was far off on the road in a play.

He found Barrymore in an unlikely saloon, knowing that his quarry fancied unlikely spots.

"Let's get out of here," said Charlie.

"My soul is an old sock hanging from a gas jet," Barrymore replied.

"You'll leave barefooted, then," said Charlie.

"As you wish," said Barrymore.

It was a snowy night. Charlie guided Jack through the deserted snowbanks of Christmas Eve to the "21" Club, on Fifty-second Street. Here a moving scene greeted them. Jack Kriendler and Charlie Berns, the club's impresarios, had induced a Salvation Army band to play and sing its hymns in the foyer. The adjoining bar was lined with teary-eyed drinkers.

"She's a beauty," said Barrymore.

"Which one?" said MacArthur.

"The soprano with the gray eyes," said Barrymore.

The Salvation Army captain, John Martin (to become manager of the Algonquin Hotel), objected to his hymn singer being wined and wooed under his nose. Captain Martin was removed to the gentlemen's room and warned against further intrusion.

Barrymore, MacArthur and the soprano, with her tambourine, sat at a private table. Wine flowed, anecdotes sparkled. The soprano grew giddy, and sang a hymn, "Brighten the Corner Where You Are." It was one of Charlie's favorites. He joined in the chorus. Jack improvised a bass. Then the soprano wept. Her head fell forward on the table.

"We have committed a sin," said Charlie.

"Of omission only," said Jack.

"Arise," said the graduate of the Wilson Memorial Academy, "and show your respect for a worker in the vineyard."

Charlie stood up and emptied his pockets of money. He dropped forty dollars in the tambourine. Barrymore followed suit with another wad of bills. The weeping soprano raised her head from the table and hiccuped, "Thank you, gentlemen."

Barrymore hiccuped back, "Merry Christmas."

"To all lost souls," said MacArthur.

With a farewell pinch of the vineyard worker's bottom, Charlie and his charge moved toward the deserted snowbanks outside.

A few years later MacArthur and Gene Fowler organized a permanent Barrymore Rescue Mission in Hollywood. Thomas Mitchell, the learned and indestructible actor, and artist John Decker were among the members. The banjo-voiced Roland Young was another Thespian aide. The Rescue Mission induced Barrymore to retire to a chicken ranch in the desert.

"You'll sober up in a week," said Charlie, "and in two

weeks you can return and take your rightful place as king of this sand dune."

"I am at your command," said the rueful Barrymore.

Charlie and Gene drove their friend into the desert and unloaded him on a chicken farmer. There was no drop of liquor on the place, and no vehicle of any sort. The farmer relied on friends for transport. He was given his instructions. He would be paid at the end of the two weeks if he was able to retain his famous guest on the premises until his friends came to remove him. The farmer saw no difficulty. Barrymore had not a penny in his pockets, and the nearest habitation was ten miles over hot sand.

Barrymore sat down humbly amid the Leghorns.

Two days later MacArthur received a desperate call from the exile, charges reversed.

"I'm sober, sunburned and healthy as a swine," said Barrymore, "and willing to continue in this desert Bastille. But, by God, man, you can't deprive me of my manhood in this fashion."

"What fashion is that?" MacArthur asked.

"There's no woman in this foul waste," said Jack. "Do you want me despoiling the desert sands like Onan?"

"We'll see what we can do about the situation," said MacArthur. "Sit tight."

The Rescue Mission conferred and decided to invest another seventy-five dollars in a female for the isolated actor, with a rented car attached.

"We'll have to pick one who can drive a car," said MacArthur.

"Women are very talented," said Fowler.

The desired type was found, with the aid of the full membership. She was given her instructions.

"Mr. Barrymore is a convincing talker," said MacArthur. "You mustn't let him talk you into driving him back to Hollywood. Remember, he hasn't got a dime and you won't be paid for your services unless you return tomorrow night, alone."

"Is Mr. Barrymore sick?" the starlet inquired.

"Mr. Barrymore is not ill," said Fowler, "but he needs another ten days or more in the desert, to bake out his soul."

The lady Samaritan rode off gallantly in the dawn. She arrived at noon at Barrymore's chicken roost.

"Come here, my beauty." Jack rolled a lewd eye at her from behind the chicken-wire fence. She came forward, a co-operative smile on her lips.

"I hate to do this to you, my darling," said Jack, "but I am in the power of two blue noses with warped Christian minds. I can surmise the damnable instructions they have given you."

With these words, Barrymore punched the bewildered girl on the chin and dropped her amid his feathered friends. He dashed for the rented car, leaped Mercutio-fashion to the driver's seat, and was off for Hollywood and freedom.

"The first we knew of the ingrate's behavior," said MacArthur, "was his picture in the morning *Examiner*. It had been taken in a Hollywood night club. It showed Jacko sitting, wine glass in hand, leering drunkenly at a blues singer."

Charlie's fondness for the prince of actors increased with his Jacko's misfortunes and misdeeds. He rallied to the Barrymore side during a dozen disasters. With Fowler and Mitchell and Decker, he helped resuscitate, dust off, and replume the demon-driven genius again and again.

"There's too much talent in Barrymore," Charlie said of him. "His head's a library of poetry. He wants too big a bellyful of living before he dies."

They understood each other.

Of the many deathbed spectacles he prized, MacArthur held Barrymore's among the highest. Shepherded by Fowler and Decker, the greatest man of our stage rode finally in his last ambulance. On a similar occasion, rushed *in extremis* to the hospital, Barrymore had risen from the stretcher and ordered the ambulance halted.

"Where in God's name are you taking me?" he had demanded.

"To the hospital," said Fowler. "You've been unconscious for hours."

"I was resting," said Barrymore. "Let's get out of this foolish buggy."

The happy friends had helped Barrymore back into the streets of the living.

There was no about-face this time.

Barrymore lay dying in the hospital. Fowler stood guard at the sickroom door. Cranks, publicity hunters and all sorts of weirdies sought entrance for a look at the expiring Hamlet and Ahab. One of them was a medical quack, loudly offering a therapy of his own invention. Fowler collared him and kicked him down the stairs, calling out to the bruised medico, "Physician, heal thyself."

It was a sad but active death chamber in which our prince of actors lay. Food and drink had been forbidden him. He was fed intravenously. Thirst and hunger brought protesting bellows from his bed.

One night a nurse brought in a priest. Fowler had hired the nurses with a wary eye for his friend's devotion to the female. The nurse who ushered in the Father was a plump, homely wench of middle years. The priest spoke gently to the dying man.

"Is there anything you wish to tell me?" he asked.

"Father," said Barrymore. "I have carnal thoughts."

The Father looked in surprise at the wasted man in the bed.

"About whom?" he asked.

Barrymore raised his head with difficulty and rolled his eyes toward the homely woman who was his nurse.

"Her," he said.

The woman blushed and smiled and the priest smiled with her at Barrymore's last gallantry.

Carnival Faces

AMONG the new friends around MacArthur from his first Hollywood days were Irving Thalberg, Bernie Hyman, Nunnally Johnson, George Jessel, Sam Goldwyn, Jack Gilbert, Myron and David Selznick, Norma Shearer, Joan Crawford and one we called for many years "the other Charlie"—Charles Lederer. There were others, scores of them, for the Pied Piper of Quincy Number 9 was still in high.

As in Chicago and New York, MacArthur overflowed into various strata of the town. The wistful bawdiness of Aldous Huxley's books pleased Charlie, as did their tall, myopic author.

The town was full of ex-geniuses that stuck out of the mist like dead limbs. Huxley's was among the few talents unblighted by the Hollywood smog.

"Aldous will never become a movie writer," said Charlie. "Being a philosopher he naturally knows less than the front office of Metro or Paramount. Besides, as an Englishman he can't write about love without getting erotic."

Irving Thalberg was a fine boss for MacArthur. The soft-eyed, skimpy-limbed genius of Metro saw quickly into Charlie's talent. Unlike his assistant, Bernie Hyman, Irving's delight in the new Metro employee included a respect for his carefully created sentences.

There was a certainty in Thalberg to which Charlie responded as he had to Howey's. There was another quality, as incredible in Hollywood as feathers on an eel, to which Charlie also salaamed. This was Irving's modesty.

Although Thalberg worked on the plots of some forty movies a year, cast them, edited them and guided them, scene by scene, to the cameras, he never put his name on the screen as a participant. There was no "Thalberg Presents," or "Produced by Irving Thalberg," or "A Thalberg Production." All these and more credits are stuck to this day on the film by producers who have had no more to do with a picture than pass the hat for its funds. As production chief of Metro, any multiple billings Thalberg might have chosen were his. He chose none. Till his death, this leading Hollywood creator of movies remained to the public the little man who wasn't there.

About this, Charlie said, "Entertainment is his God. He's satisfied to serve Him without billing, like a priest at an altar, or a rabbi under the Scrolls."

There was no pain for my friend in writing movies for Thalberg.

Thalberg's reticence as a movie maker was an irritant to his fellow Pharaohs. These were gentlemen given to marching through the world with drums banging and calliopes tooting their wonders.

I wrote about President Woodrow Wilson in conference with our European allies at Versailles that he was like a virgin trapped in a brothel, calling sturdily for a glass of lemonade. There was about Thalberg a similar out-of-placeness.

"He's too good to last," Charlie said in Irving's heyday. "The lamb doesn't lie down with the lion for long."

The institution, M.G.M., that Thalberg had built to greatness, rewarded him for his efforts by reshuffling its stock issue, thus wresting voting power from him, and demoting him to a Mayer and Schenck underling. This was done while Thalberg was vacationing in Europe with MacArthur.

"Ten years of sixteen-hours-a-day work had tired him," said Charlie. "He didn't know how to rest, or play, or even breathe without a script in his hands."

On his return from his health-building vacation to which the studio had handsomely blown him, Irving Thalberg learned he had been dethroned in his absence. He caught cold, went to bed, and died.

This was the time of Charlie's disillusionment. Not long

afterward, he played a joke on the studio. He was having his car regassed at a Beverly Hills gas station. The young man filling the tank was good looking and spoke with a British accent.

"How much are you getting a week?" Charlie asked.

The young Britisher answered, "Forty dollars."

"Hop in," said Charlie. "I've got a better job for you."

A few hours later, Charlie introduced the well-known English novelist "Kenneth Woollcott" to studio chief Bernie Hyman. It was the good-looking gas-station attendant. The young man had never written a line of anything in his life. "Kenneth is one of the most brilliant and successful young novelists in England," said Charlie, "and has also written a couple of comedies for the theatre that have been hailed as worthy of Bernard Shaw. He's against doing any movie writing because he insists there's no room for any honest creative talent in them. But I've persuaded him to listen to you, Bernie. Maybe you can talk him out of his snobbism."

Bernie did. He succeeded after an hour in persuading young Kenneth, the gas-station attendant, to sign a year's contract as a Metro writer at a thousand dollars a week.

Kenneth Woollcott flourished as a Metro writer for the full year, writing nothing and, coached by MacArthur, making the properly superior faces in conference. Neither Bernie nor any of the dozen directors and producers with whom he "conferred" ever found out that Kenneth was a fake, incapable of composing a postal card.

At the end of the year, Charlie wrote a letter which his protégé signed. It was addressed to L. B. Mayer, Grand Pooh-Bah of Metro since Thalberg's death.

"DEAR MR. MAYER,

"I wish to thank you for the privilege of working this year under your wise and talented leadership. I can assure you I have never had more pleasure as a writer.

"I think if you will check your studio log you will find that I am the only writer who did not cost the studio a shilling this year beyond his wage. This being the case, would you consider awarding me a bonus for this unique record? I leave the sum to you.

"Sincerely,
"Kenneth Woollcott"

The bonus was niggardly withheld.

The greatness that was Metro is down the drain. Its captains and its kings have tottered into limbo. Charlie's joke is part of its legendary wonders—wonders that were half mirage and half bad writing.

Castle on a Hill

Looking into the life of my dead friend, I find myself only glancing where I should stare. There was a bright light of permanence that lit the lived hours. I turn away from where this light was as from something I don't want to know—too well. When a man dies this light is gone from all his days. He seems to have lived in a twilight. Remembered, he becomes half shadow. The insistence of his voice and gesture subsides. He died, and continues constantly dying. If you would know how vaguely you will be remembered by your most loving ones after you're gone, try to remember yourself. You will be surprised that your self-fondness can evoke so little. The past has already grown its sod.

As I write about my friend, my heart aches for the sceneries and actions of our youth. But my mind will only glance backward, unless I urge it, as now. The mind has a healthy distaste for exhumation.

I come to a wooden castle on a hill in Hollywood, perched above a hundred pumping oil wells. Here, Leland Hayward, Charlie and I lived for six months. There were two hundred and fifty turkeys on the grounds. The landlord, Colonel

Youngworth, high in the Masonic order, was a turkey breeder. There was a big mosaic fountain on the front terrace. The drawing room, large enough for a baseball diamond, was two steps down from the entrance hall. Its furniture had been bought over the telephone. No eye could have assembled such an unfriendly clutter of couches, chairs, carpets, floor lamps, tables, vases and, God help us, oil paintings.

The room was also full of people. My memory is that it was never empty. Figures toppled over in sleep as the dawn mist blanketed the hill. They grew silent, but remained present. Who could have thought that most of these figures, all so lusty and sure-footed, could age and die? Or that they could even age? They wore their youth with such certainty that it seemed as permanent as the ground on which they stood. In this big room, parties, drinking bouts, fist fights, love affairs, debates and bragging made a racket as loud, I'll bet you, as ever was around King Arthur's Round Table.

I mention King Arthur's Round Table not because we were modern knights engaged in anything valorous, but because we were special people. We could prove it by our salaries, our press notices and our wit. We drank more, swore louder, sinned oftener and expected bigger things of ourselves than was the drawing-room norm, even in Hollywood.

Instead of bird-dogging the memory of my friend as he tumbles through Europe, Asia and Africa, as he snoops in the Taj Mahal, puffs his way up pyramids, dines by mistake with Winston Churchill, beats up Ernest Hemingway in a fist fight on the Riviera, plays spy in the Balkans, and flies in fifty airplanes over every arc of the earth; instead of that, I'll pin him down in this baseball diamond of a salon and see if I can turn its lights on again. What more important is there in a man's life than the fact that he was alive? On the Youngworth Ranch, Charlie was as alive as a buffalo herd.

Leland was our agent and Charlie and I blamed him for our predicament. This was what we called living off the fat of the land in Hollywood. It was an absurd indictment.

Leland, our agent for five years, had never gotten us a job.

"He stands like a stone wall between us and employment," Charlie said. "The only way we can ever make any money is to outwit him."

We had done just that in the following manner, a few months before. Riding in the elevator of the Hotel Pierre in New York, Charlie and I found ourselves in the ascending company of Sam Goldwyn. The yellow, billiard-ball head, the nutcracker jaws, the flossy tailoring, high-priced cologne, yodeling voice and barricaded eyes that were Sam Goldwyn greeted us en masse.

"You are my two favorite authors," said Goldwyn. "I have a tremendous respect for your abilities. I really have. You can ask Frances [his wife]. I want to engage you to write the next motion picture I am going to produce starring Ronald Colman. I intend to make it the finest thing I have done."

"No movies, thanks," said Charlie.

"We're finishing a play," I said.

We were on Act Three of *Twentieth Century*.

Ignoring these interruptions, Goldwyn continued, "Here is ten thousand dollars for you boys. And, I say this in absolute sincerity, you should get another hundred and twenty-five thousand dollars for the kind of scenario you are going to write for me."

Out of this double talk Charlie and I heard only the pregnant phrase, "another hundred and twenty-five thousand dollars." Thus we landed on the Hollywood hill in our tur-key-surrounded *palazzo*.

There was a printing press in the cellar on which we printed our dinner menus. We never counted the bedrooms. We maintained an around-the-clock telephone contact with the Eastern seaboard. Two chefs in ballooning white hats cooked for us. Four other males cleaned and dusted and stole all of Charlie's Charvet shirts. Suspicion fell naturally on Leland, who spent the evenings roaring he was not a thief. At the end of ten days we were stony again, with creditors charging up our mountain as if under the banner of Rough Rider Teddy Roosevelt.

"Go call on Goldwyn," Charlie said to Leland, "and get some of that hundred and twenty-five thousand dollars we've got coming."

Leland returned for dinner with a check signed by Goldwyn and marked "Paid in full" on the back. It was for a thousand dollars.

"You're pretty smart, you two!" Leland shouted before we could comment. He had a gift for shouting his way out of his failings as an agent. "That deal you and Sam shook hands on is a participation deal! You get paid by your palsy walsy Sam out of the goddamn profits, if any. Mr. Goldwyn threw this chicken feed in as a gift. And believe me, I talked myself into a nervous breakdown to get it out of him."

"I've been offered a job at Metro by Thalberg," said Charlie moodily.

"Great!" his agent-on-the-ball cried. "It's exactly what I had in mind for you. Metro is perfect! I'll settle the deal tomorrow, first thing in the morning."

"It's settled," said Charlie.

"For God's sake, I'm your agent, Charlie!" Leland started shouting again. "You can't work behind my back like that!"

"You're a goddamn shirt thief," Charlie answered, "and if you don't give me back my two dress shirts with the cuff links in them, I'm going to sell your whole college-boy wardrobe to the Salvation Army."

"God Almighty!" Leland screamed. "It's like living in a cave with a maniac!"

He went off to be soothed by his bride, the beautiful Lola, who had unexpectedly joined our ménage.

Charlie reported at Metro for work. I hired two stenographers and dictated the script we owed Goldwyn for his skimpy ten grand. The job took twelve hours. We had made up the plot on the train. There was a sanctuary hotel in Africa from which no felon could be extradited. Our hostelry was filled with European nobility wanted by the law for crimes of all sorts. The lowest title among our miscreants was a countess. The rest went on up from that to dukes and princes. We figured Goldwyn, who was becoming a man of the world, would like that.

Charlie listened to my dictation for a half hour, and went for a swim.

"I can't stand bad writing," he said.

But, luckily, Goldwyn could. Leland brought him the scenario, rolled up and tied with a blue ribbon. A few days later we received a fan letter from Arthur Hornblow, Jr., Sam's creative major-domo.

"After reading your magnificent script, Mr. Goldwyn and I both wish to go on record with the statement that if 'The Unholy Garden' isn't the finest motion picture Samuel Goldwyn has ever produced, the fault will be entirely ours. You have done your part superbly."

The Unholy Garden was produced exactly as written, and was one of the worst flops ever turned out by a studio. I found employment the next day—and the bootleggers were happy again.

Drinking Bout

It was a foggy night on Turkey Hill. Our *palazzo* was going full tilt. George Antheil played the piano. He was the *Ballet Mécanique* genius fresh from the concert stages of Europe. He played the piano as if it were an anvil. He favored his own compositions, which at that time sounded like elaborate and deafening musical jokes.

But we knew there was genius in them because of the assailant at the piano. Full of a gallon of Spanish wine, ignored by the assembly as if he were a rock driller that went with the estate, Georgie played on with the strength of Vulcan. He was boyish faced, round eyed, pink skinned, Negro lipped, short and inexhaustible. As he played, he complicated matters by singing in a voodoo falsetto.

Two lovely girls sat on the large window seat. They were audience, not for Antheil but for a crap game on the floor nearby. One of the girls was a pretty actress, Nora Gregor. Later she was Princess Von Starhemberg of Austria. But this night she still belonged to the arts.

The other girl was the movie star Jean Harlow. Miss Harlow was the reigning blonde in the movie capital. She was a bubble bath of a woman of whom the press agents sang that she left a row of asterisks when she moved.

"I spent three hours with the new cold cream Paul brought me," said Miss Harlow during a treble passage by Antheil. "It is very softening for the posterior. Is that the correct word, Paul?"

Paul Bern, a soft-voiced, scholarly man of middle years, answered it was.

"Jean and I are going to get married in a few weeks," he said. He didn't add that he was going to stand naked in front of a mirror soon after their bridal night and shoot himself dead. And who could have imagined that Jean, too, and all her erupting glands, would soon be moldering underground? Perhaps MacArthur. He had a nose for witchcraft. He smelled trouble for his friend Paul Bern.

"No use trying to disillusion him," Charlie said smilingly at the infatuated scholar. "He's out of earshot."

We had a house guest, John Lee Mahin. Charlie and I had imported him from Rockland County, New York, and put him on a salary of $250 a week and keep. We looked forward to Johnny, who was a clever lad, doing our movie writing for us, or at least part of it, and thus allowing us to finish our play. But our ghost writer, overcome by the wonders of Hollywood, got drunk the night of his arrival and remained unproductive for the ten weeks of his contract. Released from our bondage, Johnny became a fertile scenarist.

In another sector of the salon there were three other girls clustered around Jack Gilbert. He had called Madam Frances' fancy brothel and ordered them sent over. "I get to feeling lonely," the great star and ex-boyfriend of Greta Garbo sighed. "That's a lonely mountain out there."

The whores were young, grateful and silent.

Charlie's nose for witchcraft sniffed the cold air over Gilbert.

"He's got a hex on him," said Charlie. "Don't kid him."

Gilbert was found dead in his bed a few months later.

The crap game occupied the talents of a half-dozen men. The youngest, despite his mandolin-shaped bald head, was Charlie Lederer. MacArthur had instated him at our table. Lederer was a dynamic idler and youthful scorner of our civilization. He struck back on a number of fronts. Charlie and I were exempt from his Fu Manchu plots against society. Among the dice contestants were Harpo and Ernst Lubitsch, who was being instructed in the rules of play (by Lederer) as he went along. Death stood close to the black-haired directorial wizard from Berlin, but there was no detecting it this night.

The principal business of the night was transpiring at one end of our salon. Here, MacArthur presided as host. Three aides were at his elbow to open the bottles and apportion the ice. Around him were drinkers of Pantagruel merit. House guest Johnny drank only champagne, but out of a quart saucepan. Howard Hawks, lean as a banjo string, was looking fondly on his second bottle of Scotch. It was difficult to tell when our great director was drunk. Drunk or sober, he was equally silent, nodding and smiling.

Myron Selznick, of the wildcat heart and gentleman purr, was helping himself to some mysterious brew his chauffeur had delivered earlier in the evening. Here was another beside whom stood the uninvited One—but there was no Reaper's shadow on him now.

"I'm drinking no bootlegger slops that you fellows think is liquor," said Myron. "Gives you insomnia."

The two drinkers out front were MacArthur and Dashiell Hammett. They had taken the lead early in the evening and held on to it without signs of strain. They were drinking Scotch. I was drinking tequila.

The talk was loud, and still in its early stages—the horrors of Hollywood. If you cast pearls before swine, what happens to the swine? They turn into censors. Let there be no good word for any boss. Myron was ready to smite any boss lovers. That was the trouble with the goddamn town—its ass-kissing slaves. We understood the situation. The slave liked to sing the wonders of his master's soul (or behind). It lessened the sting of his own servitude.

Leland was cached away upstairs in debate with his lovely Lola. He appeared at midnight in bare feet and pajamas and tried to make himself heard.

"I'm part host of this goddamn party!" he shouted. "And I want you bastards to go home. My wife's upstairs and she can hear every filthy word that's spoken in this cesspool."

Leland had a point there. Though our *palazzo* was as grand looking as the Alhambra it was built like a chicken coop, with paper-thin walls and doors that came off their hinges if you banged them.

At 3 A.M. Leland made another appearance.

"Aren't you bums ever going to get out of here, for God's sake?" he shouted. "This is worse than living in some goddamn Harlem whorehouse!"

He paused and added, with sudden worry for his clients, "You fellas are just going to kill yourselves drinking this bootlegger puke."

He remained, as one who enters a tent during Diavolo's drum roll. The party had climbed a high perch. Oath, laughter, insult and anecdote sounded above Georgie's lunatic piano. Myron bellowed on the phone for another six bottles. Hawks sat staring at his third emptied Scotch bottle like a fascinated sparrow. House guest Johnny sang a song about the University of Princeton. Dash Hammett remembered a gun duel in San Francisco with a marijuana smoker. Gilbert was sobbing in the three hired laps. There were some strangers who had been lured up the mountain by the sounds of revelry. One of them had brought a cornet and was annoying Antheil by blowing "Taps" in his ear. The pianist removed a pistol from his coat pocket.

"I shoot people who interfere with my music," he stated. "Quiet, everybody!" The cornet stopped. Georgie returned to his concert work.

It is in this hour I remember my friend MacArthur alive and gleaming, drunken and on his feet, talking like a tale teller from Baghdad. His foggy eyes happy, as if they looked on an inner audience, he talked on alone. Scotch, gin, wine and rum had snuffed out all the other vocal candles. Georgie was asleep on the piano keys. The mystic audience sprawled amid a city dump of empty bottles, snored and gurgled, as Charlie talked of his favorite cadaver, the Ragged Stranger. How alive it was, this memory! Drink was like a time machine on which Charlie revisited the past.

He swayed and frowned at his mystic audience.

"You're a fine pack of poops," he said. "I'm telling you a story, you impolite bastards—about the Ragged Stranger who lay on the bar, shrinking at the rate of an inch a week."

He stopped and filled his glass again. He drank alone. The empty glass slipped from his fingers. It broke on the floor.

"They're getting the range," said Charlie.

A questing look came to his eyes, as if dreams were suddenly in him. He was off in silence to somewhere on his time machine.

I heard a noise on the terrace and wandered out with Leland to look. Charlie was standing on the rim of the mosaic fountain. He had a long stick in his hand and was stirring the basin water with it. The basin was stocked with Colonel Youngworth's goldfish.

"Wake up, ye sinners," Charlie cried to the foggy night, almost gone, "arise ye sinners and hear me," he urged the sleeping goldfish. There was no mockery in his voice. A glow was on his face.

"Corinthians, thirteen," he announced, as his father used to. " 'Though I speak with the tongues of men and of angels,

182

and have not charity, I am become as sounding brass, or a tinkling cymbal.

" 'And though I have the gift of prophecy, and understand all mysteries, and all knowledge; and though I have all faith, so that I could remove mountains, and have not charity, I am nothing.' Hear me—nothing!"

The roar of his voice was still in the foggy night as Paul of Tarsus joined his congregation.

Leland and I fished him out of the water.

"After my last shirt, eh?" said Charlie, noticing Leland on his left. Identifying me on his other side, he grinned. "A friend can have anything I've got."

We entered the *palazzo*. Several doors were off their hinges. Figures lay slumbering on couches and on the floor. It was silent, and all the lights were on.

A Movie Secret

It was a summer day in 1934. Charlie and I were in Nyack, trying out a new diving helmet in the pool.

"Mr. Leland Hayward is on the phone," a voice called through the pleasant morning.

I returned to the pool with Leland's news.

"He says there's a fellow who wants to give us a million dollars to make movies in Astoria, Long Island," I told Charlie. "He wants us to have lunch with this fellow tomorrow."

"Nothing doing," said Charlie.

It seemed a logical answer. Our friend Leland was already rolling up fortunes—and would go on to wallow in millions—but he was, to us, an unconvincing business type. He was a tall, boyish-faced man with a crew cut and a slight paunch.

He slanted backward when he stood, and had an explosive way of talking that made him sound as if he were covering up on something. Half the fun of having Leland as your agent was that there were so many things you could denounce him about; and that he was seemingly invulnerable to the heartiest of attacks. He was to go to the hospital a number of times with almost fatal attacks of ulcers, but we didn't foresee that.

Among the flaws that fascinated his clients was the fact that agent Hayward seldom knew which of us was working on what. He had an aversion toward reading our scripts.

Dragged to a movie a client had written or directed, Leland would writhe and sneer in his seat. His coolest verdict was, "Terrible." Where other Hollywood aficionados were cooing, "Wonderful, marvelous," Leland offered usually the counterpart of "Godawful crap."

Leland's disdain for movies earned him quickly the respect of the movie makers—particularly the front-office bosses who did the buying. They felt that a man so full of sneer for their product must be peddling a superior kind of wares. This wasn't true. All that Leland peddled was a superiority complex—and the same old plots.

Another of our agent's flaws that for some reason pleased Charlie and me was his inaccessibility. We preferred an invisible agent to one constantly in our hair. There were some drawbacks to his will-o'-the-wisp habits as our representative. When we wanted something, getting Leland on the phone was as difficult as contacting a bank robber on the run. Not that Leland was robbing any banks, but, on the other hand, no one ever knew what he *was* doing, or even in what city he was. Part of this came from his practicing to be an aviator and getting lost for days in deserts where he had been forced down. Also, his romantic problems kept him ducking in and out of New York and Hollywood, without advance notice.

We liked Leland, however, for his basic qualities—his disdain for movies and his larkish attitudes toward the movie Pharaohs. He said to me once in my hotel room in Beverly Hills, "I've got a deal for you with Zanuck at Twentieth. You've never worked there before. I figure we ought to be able to take them for three or four hundred thousand before they get wise to us."

My wife, a listener, threw a vase at his head.

It was Leland's call that summer morning that launched Charlie and me as independent movie makers. We were the first writers "in the industry" to branch out as directors and producers, simultaneously.

The summer's end found us in a row of offices previously occupied by Adolph Zukor, Jesse Lasky, Walter Wanger and other cinema potentates. We were to do four movies. Our first script, *Crime Without Passion*, was ready for shooting. We had assembled a staff headed by Lee Garmes, Hollywood's best cameraman. With him were Arthur Rosson and Harold Godsoe. There was also a brooding fellow named Vorkapich whom we had hired through a misunderstanding. We had thought he was a movie cutter. It developed he was a montage expert. Not wanting to waste Vorky's talents and paychecks, Charlie and I wrote a montage prologue for our movie. Vorky put together four handsome minutes of Furies flying through the canyons of New York.

Neither Charlie nor I had ever spent an hour on a movie set. We knew nothing of casts, budgets, schedules, booms, gobos, unions, scenery, cutting, lighting. Worse, we had barely seen a dozen movies in our lives. Finding ourselves with all this unknowingness in sole and lofty charge of bringing movies into existence, we were, however, not for a moment abashed.

We were aware of the great Secret about movies. It was a secret which a thousand directors and a thousand producers and their thousand press agents had buried deep from the world's ken. But not from us. We knew it well.

This secret was the fact that 90 per cent of the success of a movie (or of its failure) lay in the writing of its script. Producer, director and stars could add less to a movie script than they could to a stage play.

I make it less because acting counts less in the movies than in the theatre. The difference on the screen between a first-rate performer and a panting neophyte with bulging casabas is not especially in favor of the first rater. One of the reasons is that movie audiences bring a Peeping Tom complex to the cinema. Perhaps it's the gigantism of the male and female photographs that inspires the enthusiasm for their Secondary Sex Characteristics. Our American preference for skyscrapers over cathedrals is possibly reflected in our excitement over a VistaVision breast, three feet in diameter.

To return to the Secret, we knew that any improvement at all to the writer's script by director and producer was an unlikely matter. Out of some sixty scripts I have written (good and bad), a half dozen of them seemed to me to have been "improved," or at least not mangled, on their way to the screen.

This high mortality rate was not because of stupidity or incompetence—although these often figured. It was due mainly to the fact that three, five or nine people having the power to alter a script are certain to distort it and bleed it to death.

There is a type of movie exempt from the Secret—the historical spectacle or the movie in which the wonders of nature are active. Of such a movie the script is only 10 per cent of its existence. The clash of extras in togas or tin hats, the blowing up of ships, bridges, volcanoes, the setting fire to forests, the landing on Mars, the continuous decimation of the American Red Indian and the constant fall of the Roman Empire—these require the special talents of director and producer.

The writers of such movies usually fall under the spell of their prop-crazed makers and subscribe to the aesthetic that dialogue, plot turn and characterization are of feeble import where so many charging chariots and toppling temples are involved.

As for putting the kind of script we usually wrote on the screen, Charlie and I felt, despite inexperience, we were ahead of most of our Hollywood colleagues. We wouldn't have to figure out ways to shine as directors at the expense of dialogue and story.

It has been the habit of great Hollywood directors to distort a script so that it would seem a director and not a playwright was telling the tale. To this end, a small, straightforward drama often gets lengthened into a three-hour epic by the addition of fist fights, moody walks, extensive facemaking in close-ups (without any authors' words to deflect from directorial genius), and by explosive mob scenes, panoramas showing the littleness of man and the bigness of the director. Behind these thousands of feet of "director film," symphony orchestras fiddle away like mad. In the good old days, when movie fans were content to gape at a movie as if it were an animated magic-lantern slide, this brought in the crowds.

It still does, as witness the success of Mike Todd's *Around the World in Eighty Days*, and Cecil B. DeMille's *The Ten Commandments*. But these are magic-lantern slides without pretensions. They can be enjoyed by the same eye that likes to glue itself to a kaleidoscope. A frank, uncomplicated appeal to the childishness of Americans is still good for vast grosses.

Art and Hi-jinks

NONE of the actors we hired for *Crime Without Passion* had ever before played in a movie. Our leading lady, the seventeen-year-old exotic actress Margo, had, in fact, never opened her mouth in public. She was a moody sort of dancer. The beauty, Whitney Bourne, was, as far as we knew, an heiress and nothing else. Claude Rains was a stage actor who had never faced a camera. Add to this the fact that Charlie and I had never directed anybody or produced anything (except scripts) and you have the full picture of Astoria as an Amateur Hour.

Our knowledgeable movie maker, Lee Garmes, insisted on "testing" our players. Charlie and I argued against it as wasteful and pointless—but we lost. After the silent tests Lee said, "Claude Rains can't play a lover. He's got no neck, for heaven's sake." Of Margo, our good Lee said with a sigh, "She has an interesting face, but her head comes to a point. Are you sure she can talk?"

We were sure of Margo—and of everything—because we thought the script a good job. Claude played a lover very well, except for the fact that his feet bothered him. They swelled under the movie lights. As a result, he played most of his love scenes with his bare feet cooling in a basin of medicated water. We "cut" at the waist, eliminating Claude's troubled feet.

Crime Without Passion turned out well. So did *The Scoundrel,* in which Noel Coward, Julie Haydon, Stanley Ridges, Alec Woollcott, Alice Duer Miller and other nonmovie players appeared. *The Scoundrel* won an Oscar from the Hollywood Academy.

Directing *The Scoundrel* and *Crime* consisted of putting our scripts on the screen as we had written them. The actors did what the written stage directions said they should do, and recited our lines with a minimum of coaching. They were people of intelligence and knew the meaning of their speeches as well as we did.

Acting is the only one of the arts run by amateurs, for what else is a director but an amateur actor? Except, possibly, an amateur writer.

Crime Without Passion cost a hundred and eighty thousand to make; *The Scoundrel,* a hundred ninety thousand. We used up less than eighty thousand feet of film on each picture. A half million feet is normal for a Hollywood feature picture.

Time is the most expensive item in picture making. We saved time by cutting the usual number of camera setups in half. Directors, lusting to put their stamp on a picture, will change camera angles on every sentence or two of dialogue. Each such change requires from one to three hours of relighting. Another time waster is reshooting a scene thirty to a hundred times. This wanton business is identified as a passion for perfection. I have known a number of directors addicted to "reshooting." Most of them were sadistic fellows who found pleasure in browbeating actors, rattling them, undermining them. By doing this to his actors, the director can loom godlike on his set.

There are other "painstaking" directors with less psychopathic objectives. These fellows go in for their fifty takes on a scene in the hope of stumbling on some contortion or posture that will take the scene away from actor and playwright and make it "a director's scene."

Another cost cut Charlie and I made was in music. We went to Richard Rodgers' home, taking along our music man, the veteran Frank Tours. Frank had been an orchestra leader for the Ziegfeld shows.

Dick Rodgers had a large collection of Beethoven records. He played them for us, and Charlie and I prodded Tours when we heard passages we liked. Ludwig's music with a few fixings went into our sound tracks, saving us the cost of composing and orchestrating.

Later we employed Oscar Levant, but some mixup in the bookkeeping system resulted in Oscar's not receiving his salary for several weeks. He lost faith in us and quit. We regretted his going. The composer was small in Oscar but his wit was large, and it was always a delight to hear his piano playing and watch his hands moving on the keyboard like an electric fan.

George Antheil took over our composer post. George received his pay and wrote a fine score for our picture *Once in a Blue Moon*. This movie was a flop, despite its lovely music and its galaxy of gay players—Savo, Balieff, Gypsy Markoff, Cissie Loftus, wrestling champion Sandor Szabo, Bobby Breen, a Cossack choir—and wonderful scenery and trick effects.

The truth was that Charlie and I had "gone Hollywood" in making *Blue Moon*. We had forgotten the Secret. Our script for *Once in a Blue Moon* was a dud.

My memory of our Astoria movie making doesn't include any glow of success or burn of failure. It is a memory of a two-year party that kept going seven days a week. We did nothing to show off, or get our names in the paper. Among our economies as producers was the dispensing with a publicity department. We employed no press agents to rush tidbits of our doings to the newspapers. We preferred to enjoy our party privately—in our own eyes.

When we started in Astoria, Charlie and I decided we would never change a script once we were shooting it, and never make passes at any girls in our employ. With emergency conferences and studio romances, the two greatest handicaps to movie making, out of the way, we had plenty of time for honest work and honest merriment.

What were the jokes we played, or laughed at? There were the thirty-foot banners on our office walls reading, "Better than Metro Isn't Good Enough," "Cut to the Chase," and "Let the Audience in on Your Secret." There were the five life-size photos of female nudes pasted on the doors of our office. This was a psychological device for confusing businessmen and promoters who were constantly trying to hook us into shady schemes.

There was our secretary, ex-Chicagoan and international littérateur Allan Ross Macdougall. Dougie's labors were simple but they required character. Charlie and I had agreed when we started that we would neither write nor read any letters during our reign as Astoria's moguls. We stuck to this, except for one time. Dougie's functions were to answer our phone and say we were not in, to anyone except our wives, to enter the office at 4 P.M. and dump the daily pile of unopened mail into the fire, and brew us tea.

We regretted our one lapse into letter writing. The *Exhibitors' Herald*, a leading movie trade magazine, printed a letter from a theatre owner in Iron Mountain, Michigan. The letter complained about *The Scoundrel* being bad for the box office, and annoying to the citizens of Iron Mountain besides.

Charlie and I spent a day answering Iron Mountain. We pretended in our letter that its citizens lived in trees, played with coconuts, told time with sticks and were otherwise wanting in American initiative. The next month's issue of the *Exhibitors' Herald* contained Iron Mountain's reply to our "devastating" onslaught. Wrote this Anatole France of an

Exhibitor: "Messers Hecht and MacArthur, I have received your letter, framed it and hung it in the lobby of my theatre, where it is attracting a great deal more attention than did your motion picture."

There was a new member of our firm whom we put behind the desk of our largest office, with the title of producer. This was Bippo, one of the three pinheads on exhibition at Coney Island. Poor Bippo's head lolled and he drooled a bit, but he was always happy to listen to visitors come with plots, inventions and promotion schemes to sell.

One of our pleasantest events in Astoria was the hour—or two—of luncheon. Charlie had solved our eating problem by having the "21" Club as our caterer. Every noon three taxicabs carrying waiters and lunches for twenty-five pulled up at the studio.

There were constant games, musicales, yarn-swapping marathons and athletic contests at this time. I recall one summer afternoon in autumn. Charlie and I had organized a baseball team called "The Writers." We challenged a team who called themselves "College Athletes." This team consisted of the leading young bar flies of "21." Tommy Shevlin, Jr., of Yale fame, was its captain.

The game was played in Nyack in the ball park of Oom the Omnipotent, maestro of a local cult. Oom was an ex-New Jersey barber, a homely, modest man who never wore a tie, and who made a fortune peddling Hindu philosophy to rich and lonely old ladies.

Our team had on it Ed Sullivan, Bugs Baer, Robert Sherwood, Billy Rose, Denny Miller, Harold Ross, Harpo Marx. Charlie played first base. I pitched. We all wore sailor suits. Alice Duer Miller umpired. Boris Morros had stolen the Paramount Theatre band and whisked it out to Nyack. It paraded through the town followed by Oom's five oriental elephants and four busloads of mink-coated chorus girls from the Paradise Club and other night spots. A fifth bus held Master Jack Kriendler, his Yale, Princeton and Harvard boys, and enough liquor to flood the Yankee Stadium.

Shevlin, Jr., swung at the first pitch and connected. The ball exploded and young Shevlin vanished in a thick cloud of talcum powder. Thus we sowed doubt in the opposition—when it went to swing again.

These are all pointless details. I've put them down devotedly as an alchemist might write out his formula for making gold.

More Charlie Letters

HERE is a report of a MacArthur prowl through the world. They are letters he wrote Helen while touring Europe and Africa with Bernie Hyman and his wife, Lou.

"DEAREST,

"We have been rolling quietly through continuous mist with less people aboard than have ever fared the seas before, sixty or so. One died yesterday—of boredom, I think. Bernie and Lou are very quiet. They sleep all the time. I spend my leisure hours with John Gunther, a newspaper friend of mine, and a very nice woman named Rosso, whose husband is the Italian Ambassador to Russia.

"I've done quite a bit of work, along the lines I spoke of. It greatly improves the movie which will be done in no time now. Every day we decide where we are going—every day it is some other place. The last vote was Naples, Athens (with a few Grecian isles thrown in), and Egypt.

"I adore you and wish you were along. We have the three luxury cabins and mine is ever so empty. I dream of you a lot—"

The next letter to Helen is on the stationery of Hotel Grande Bretagne in Athens.

"MY DARLING,

"There are no words for this heavenly place. Just outside my window hangs the Parthenon, rose grey in the sunlight and

192

mystic white under the moon. There is nothing like it in the world. Athens itself is just another town, although this is a magnificent hotel. It is balmy and blue outside, the sun always shines, the people are nondescript, but picturesque enough, and some work is getting done (due largely to Bernie's discovery that we can't get to permanent quarters in Cairo for five days more). Outside of Vesuvius, we have had no adventures, unless the Acropolis is one. It's queer how personal it is, how quickly you forget Pompeii, just seen the other day.

"In Sorrento—what we didn't cover from Saturday to Monday in Italy! In Sorrento I brought you a set of sixteenth century dolls—terra cotta figurines used in the Christmas festivals of the day—all dressed in tattered brocades. I thought the little gallery might replace the shells in the front hall if you like the idea.

"There is one Herald Angel among them that is too large. I thought it might fly about Mary's room as the patron saint of her other dolls. I bought her a Tarantella costume in green and yellow and myself a Roman striped silk stocking cap. With it on I was immediately acclaimed an old Sorrentonian and given the key to the wonderful hotel there.

"Last night we took in some Greek night life—the Femina, a horrible approach to well, say Grade D Budapest, minus pretty girls and with a dreadfully harsh overhead lighting. We were joined by the assistant American Consul, who was depressed and wanted us to do a movie exposing the consular service."

(The next paragraph concerns one of Charlie's deepest and most curious ambitions. It was to get the full detailed story of Gavrilo Princip, whose assassination of Archduke Francis Ferdinand in Sarajevo started the First World War.)

"Did I tell you that on the boat I hob-nobbed extensively with a Dr. and Madame Pavelich of Belgrade who want me to visit them on route home for the purpose of meeting Gavrilo Princip's brother? All that is needed is one week's notice—for Sarajevo in a nutshell. I'm certainly going—

"I think of you every day a lot and wish we had an itinerary, so that you could have written me. I'll be thinking of you at seven o'clock next Tuesday morning when I will be packing for Egypt and you will be taking the bows for Monday night's performance of 'Victoria' in Toronto. And I'll be thinking of you all the way to Cairo, where I hope there will be a cable. All my love—"

Again, from Athens a few weeks later, Charlie wrote:

"Darling, darling!

"I'm off to Belgrade and Sarajevo, having just escaped going to Jerusalem with Bernie.

"Egypt was wonderful, especially Luxor. It is more expensive than New York and I never saw so many flies and sick-eyed natives. But Karnak and the Valley of the Kings! La, la! Especially the Valley—so unearthly, so still and mysterious you might be on the moon.

"We went out in the Arabian desert, taking a wild-eyed dervish who claimed he could charm snakes from whatever place I chose to select. I picked out a desolate stretch of sand dunes and the holy man immediately went to work, running about like a demented partridge, crying from the Koran and beating the sands with a long stick. Presently he stopped, sniffed and yelled: 'I smell snake! Sand adder!'

"At which he stopped, flung off his outer garments and in the name of Allah commanded the snake to come out and give himself to the son of the Great Suliman, King of all the Snakes. And from right under my feet twisted an ugly little adder, horned and hissing, and reluctantly crawled to the howling dervish whose eyes were rolled up to the back of his head. How that snake hated to come out but he did and so did two or three others.

"The bold man bagged them—I carried the bag to prevent any sleight of hand—and we went into another part of the desert. Again he was off, crying the ninety and nine names of Allah and beating the hot sands. Out came an asp, then a vile looking ground viper that hissed like escaping steam, and finally a cobra nearly six feet long.

"The cobra put up the best show, striking out and spitting poison at us for five minutes, at least. He was terrifying, sitting up with his hood out, but Suliman's tenor wails did him in at last and he moved a little nearer, and actually laid his head in Suliman's hand. I didn't believe it until Suliman made him do it three times. The professor then stuffed him into the bag and offered to sell me his skin. It seems that the snakes fight it out and are generally all dead by the time they reach Cairo. While the negotiations were going on (I didn't buy) a sand adder got out and bit Suly in the thumb. That's death in five minutes, but Suly only pushed him back and stood rigid, wailing Mohammedan sounds. He began to sweat like mad and soon announced that he was fine. He had rubbed his bloody thumb in the sand. He was worried, though, and I found out later that his only rival in snake calling couldn't make his magic work on an adder last year and keeled over as pretty as a picture.

"I got some pictures of the old boy, some in color.

"Well, this has been a lot about snakes when I wanted to tell you all over again how very much I love you and miss you, and Mary—and how glad I am that every mile from now on is homeward. It has all been wonderful but Nyack is more wonderful still, and you excel the pyramids—or do I mean Cleopatra? That's when I met you. I've remembered it so often here, my first Victorian shock (a wonderfully pleasant one) at your breasts budding behind a mosquito netting costume so wantonly.

"Your
"CHARLIE"

The next letter to Helen was from the Grand Hotel Hungaria in Budapest.

"I arrived in Belgrade a week ago (via Lufthansa) from Athens. I told you I knew a member of the government. I had wired him that I might see him on Tuesday, just before leaving Alex. He concluded that I was coming by air and met me with more fanfaronade than Billy Rose usually gets.

"Lunches and dinners followed for two or three days, but

the matter of Sarajevo was charmingly hushed. Because it again raises the question of who started the war. It seems to be a ticklish topic here and I was an E. Phillips Oppenheim character because of it. I began to feel that semi-official personages sent to see that I saw everything in Belgrade—there is nothing there but hospitality—were really seeing that I saw nothing of Sarajevo. At last I announced that I was going to Budapest and engaged the local Lindbergh to fly me down.

"The trip was wonderful, over the most awesome mountains I have ever seen for an hour and fifteen beautiful minutes. At last the town: curled like a white porcupine (it has 110 minarets) deep in a magnificent valley.

"We got out and instantly were in the Levant—Cairo is the Wild West by comparison—girls and women skittering along in striped bloomers and full black veils, thin for the pretty ones, thick and mysterious for the older belles, howling dervishes, bazaars, almost as the Turks left it years ago. They held it 500 years.

"It was the end of Ramadan and the Moslems were whooping it up—singing girls, dancers, etc. and delighted customers giving each special number an especial 'bravo' by smashing their glasses against the sides of their heads. One man I saw was whacking with a beer glass by mistake. Five times he banged his skull with it and missed each time—that is, it didn't break. On the sixth try he knocked himself out, while the café burst into applause. There were fist fights, fights with bottles and knives. It was all wonderful.

"I met a lot of people (through the aid of neutral Belgrade newspaper correspondents) including Princip's brother, and took a lot of pictures. The story is even better than I first thought. For instance, the inscription that dying, and with an arm rotted off, he carved in his underground cell:

" 'Our ghosts shall walk through Vienna, through the great palace, frightening Kings.' Or that's my free translation of it. . . ."

The Lure of Sarajevo

THE never-quite-understood tale of Bosnia's doomed young patriots was almost forgotten when MacArthur came on it. But he was drawn into this ghost story with all the violence of a living cause.

The assassination of the Austrian Archduke Ferdinand by a group of four teen-age Bosnians was the deed that launched the First World War (and an era of war not yet done). Bosnia is now a part of Yugoslavia. It has been part of a dozen states and empires since it was known as Illyria under Roman rule—there has never quite been a Bosnia. No sooner did a Bosnian climb to a throne than Turks, Serbians, Austrians, Russians, Hungarians and other Balkan powers came in and put an end to its independence. But curiously, in this football of a country, the cry for independence never quit. From the time it was grabbed by the Turks in 1463 and its king beheaded on a hill, through its conquest by Serbians and Austrians in our century, Bosnia carried on an underground revolution for freedom. It was sometimes the revolution of a handful, and often it was a revolution uncertain of its enemy—there were so many of them.

In 1914 the underground had been reduced to a group of schoolboys and -girls. They were innocent of politics. The deed that set off our global wars was without political objectives. It was a deed of vengeance. Their little dream of "freedom" struck down a new "tyrant" come again to silence them.

Bosnia did not "rise up" with the deed. There was never to be a free Bosnia—and in 1914 no such political objective existed. There were only a few young ones dedicated to the death of a tyrant who happened to be Ferdinand, pawn of the power-dreaming Kaiser Wilhelm..

The assassination of Ferdinand was a murder *in vacuo*. It

was a symbolic rather than political action. It was meant only to show to a little audience of Bosnians that the cry of freedom still survived in the ten-times-conquered Bosnian soul.

That it was to topple the world was not in the dreams of the teen-agers who did the killing.

MacArthur was strangely lured by this Bosnian deed. He outwitted his Balkan friends and went to Sarajevo. Here he toiled day and night, as he used to for Howey. He dug up the complete factual and emotional story of Gavrilo Princip's killing of the Archduke Ferdinand.

Months later, in Charleston, South Carolina, he met up with Orson Welles, then on some explosive project of his own.

"For two weeks," said Orson, "Charlie talked of nothing but Gavrilo Princip and his killing of the Archduke. I told him I thought it was magnificent material for a play and a movie, and that I'd be happy to be involved in both projects."

When he returned to Nyack from Charleston, Charlie wrote out his Sarajevo story. He put the plot treatment in the form of a letter beginning, "Dear Orson." It was never mailed. Nor was Helen, in the house with him, aware that Charlie had ever written it.

Orson was out of it, and so was everyone else. Charlie never submitted his finished Sarajevo treatment to any producer. He said to me once, "There's a great play in Gabriel Princip of Sarajevo." I asked him what it was like. He wandered off on another topic.

The story of Gavrilo Princip remained buried in Charlie's file till his own death.

I mention this because there is a secret in Charlie's Sarajevo script; there was a reason for his writing it that had nothing to do with movies or history.

The Great Sarajevo Story

"DEAR ORSON,

"Here is the story of Gavrilo Princip, interpolated with some notions of my own.

"The first such notion was that his mountain mother (who bore him standing up, in the best Bosnian tradition) had named him Gabriel because she thought she was giving birth to Gabriel of the Heavenly Hosts. Gabriel's horn couldn't have brought more havoc than his namesake's shot that started the World War with its 10,000,000 killed, even if you happen to think the World War stopped in 1918, instead of spreading on into China, Spain, and who knows yet where else.

"I asked his brother in Sarajevo last year if Gabriel's mother might not have had some such thought. I'm sorry to report that while he said that her religious views approached fanaticism, he had never heard that theory before. He was named Gabriel because he was born on the day sacred to the Bonny Bugler on High, a fact which later postponed his death by establishing that he could not have been 21 when he assassinated the Archduke.

"Between his birth and that event stand a great many people and things, as follows:

"His boyhood in the Bosnian mountains was as simple and severe as Lincoln's. He was shy. He had little to do with his eight brothers and sisters. He read everything he could lay hands on. He harangued the villagers like a boy Jesus, the while a great plan formed in his head—to rid his country of the Austrian tyranny.

"At fifteen, encouraged by his mother, he set out on foot for the capital, Sarajevo, to carve out his destiny.

II

"The romance of Gabriel and Dragitsa was more like Dante and Beatrice.

"He met her at a mountain picnic, a picturesque celebration in memory of the battle of Kossovo, five hundred years before, when the Turks first conquered the Bosnians. (Like all the daffy Slavs, the Bosnians only seem to remember defeat.) Every year since the Turks had beaten them in the 15th century, the townspeople poured up to the mountains in the night to watch the sunrise, while they chanted ballads of revenge. The girls gathered red poppies, called Flowers of Vengeance, and gave them to the boys to wear. Then they danced and sang, and I suppose, got stewed. The Turks were gone now, but the ancient ceremony of revenge went double for their successors, the Austrians.

"Dragitsa gave a flower to Gabriel. He was sixteen then. He told her what he meant to do—rid his country of the Austrian tyrant, the Archduke Ferdinand. She said he would be a great hero, greater even than his idol, Bogdan, the ancient hero of Bosnia. Gabriel's shyness vanished. He fell in love.

"Watching the two was Gabriel's best friend, Danilo Ilitch.

"Danilo was the leader of a secret revolutionary society of which Gabriel was a member. He was older than Gabriel, intellectual, and a bit of a Svengali. At heart—when the time came—he was a coward.

"In the middle of the music and dancing, Danilo drew Gabriel aside. He reminded him that he had sworn to do one thing only—to kill a Hapsburg—and told him that love of country and love of woman didn't mix. Gabriel stoically agreed.

"Though he saw Dragitsa often, though they loved each other, he kept his feelings in the sternest check. It was not until a few seconds before he shot the Archduke that they kissed for the first time.

III

"Other members of Gabriel's secret society who were active in the assassination are as follows:

"Danilo, the poet-leader, the only son of a widowed mother who suspected the plot and lived in daily terror of the consequences. She saw him hanged.

"NEDIELKO CHABRINOVITCH, the son of a police spy, who joined the movement to make up for his father's treachery to Bosnia.

"TRIFKO GRABEZH, another sixteen-year-old, late expelled from Sarajevo for striking an Austrian schoolteacher.

"These four musketeers were the principals, although a dozen minor characters crop up in the course of the story.

"At their secret meetings, the silhouette of the Archduke was drawn in chalk on barn doors, etc., and the youngsters practiced shooting at the image. They were rated according to their skill at hitting the vital parts. Gabriel was often first. His bullet usually found the heart.

"For two years the lads discussed the great plan. None having money enough to go to Vienna, it was decided to murder the Archduke the instant he set foot in Bosnia. All took oaths to this effect at the hero Bogdan's grave.

"While their scheme was cooking, Kaiser Wilhelm was busy playing on his mad friend Ferdinand to invade Serbia and knock over Bosnia. The Kaiser worked on Ferdinand's wife, the Duchess Sophie.

"Sophie had been an actress. Not being of royal blood, she was regarded as his concubine rather than wife, despite the marriage ceremony. The Kaiser told Sophie that if Ferdinand became king of Bosnia, her children would be kings some day, instead of illegitimate offspring of an ex-actress and a Hapsburg. Ferdinand had promoted Sophie from actress to lady-in-waiting. That was as far as an Archduke could go.

"In 1914 the Kaiser promised to bring his whiskered buddy, Admiral von Tirpitz, to Sophie's summer palace near the Bosnian frontier, ostensibly to see Sophie's famous rose gardens. In reality, they would map out a campaign and set a day for the Balkan war.

"The Kaiser and von Tirpitz arrived, looked at the roses, and decided that Ferdinand should commence military maneuvers near Sarajevo on June 28. Knowing Bosnia's touchiness, the Kaiser counted on something happening that could be made a pretext for war.

IV

"At this time Gabriel, in Belgrade, received a clipping from a fellow conspirator in Sarajevo. The clipping related the Archduke's proposed maneuvers near Sarajevo.

"He was coming there at last. Gabriel and his two friends swore to one another he would never leave alive. They wrote to the fourth musketeer, Danilo, to be ready.

V

"The Hapsburg-hating Black Hand, which ran through the Balkans, heard a whisper of the plot. Just as the boys were despairing of getting weapons, a member approached the police spy's son, Chabrinovitch, in a Belgrade café and said the arms were theirs for the asking.

"The three were taken by the stranger to the secret headquarters of the Black Hand. There they met the terrifying head of the organization, Tsiganovitch. He looked them over shrewdly, talked to Gabriel—decided they were sincere. He promised them bombs and revolvers.

"But there was a condition.

"With the bombs and revolvers went a flask of prussic acid for each conspirator, to be taken immediately after his attempt to kill the Archduke, whether he was successful or not. Each had to swear that he would take the poison. Tsiganovitch explained that it was to protect the rest, as the Austrians would undoubtedly torture the truth out of any survivor.

"The boys had never thought of suicide and were horrified. Gabriel alone agreed, instantly. The others took the oath after him.

"They wrote Danilo the plot was going to come off, and asked him to recruit three more conspirators. They explained, also, about the prussic acid.

VI

"The item about the prussic acid made Danilo sick with fright, but he wrote back with pretended enthusiasm, outlining the details of the assassination.

"The plan was to station seven assassins in the Archduke's

triumphal line of march, each laddie with his weapon and flask of prussic acid. Danilo went about getting the recruits, purposely selecting the weakest in the hope the plan would miscarry.

VII

"At Sophie's summer home, the Kaiser, von Tirpitz, the Archduke and Duchess wandered among the roses, talking of thrones and war.

"On deserted hillsides near Belgrade, Gabriel and his friends practiced with bombs and revolvers, waiting for the time when they could slip over the closely watched border with their load of death.

"They learned that the Archduke was making his entry into Sarajevo on the Day of Vengeance, their Fourth of July. It was also Grabezh' birthday—his nineteenth.

" 'Well,' said Tsiganovitch, hearing this. 'You will have been born, and you will have died on the same glorious day.'

VIII

"The conspirators re-entered Bosnia by the underground route used by smugglers, refugees, etc. It was a long and desperate trek, crowded with thrills and hardship. Rivers had to be waded, forests traversed at night. To have been stopped once was certain death. Once when they were lost they got a guide at the point of a gun.

"After endless escapes, the boys reached Tulza, some forty or fifty miles from Sarajevo, hid the bombs and revolvers there in the barn of a sympathizer. Dirty and dishevelled they made their way onward. Finally, Gabriel arrived at Danilo's house.

"Danilo's fears had almost left him as days passed without news. He was beginning to feel the plot had failed. When Gabriel staggered in, caked with mud, but with no bombs, he was overjoyed. His high spirits vanished, however, when he learned that the bombs were in Tulza, and that he himself, as the one conspirator not under suspicion, would have to go and fetch them. He began to stall. But Gabriel was now leader of the four. He demanded that Danilo go—told him outright that only his getting the bombs would protect them from his betrayal.

"Danilo promised to go, but he was terrified. When he had received the arms and poison at the hideaway he tried to abandon the bombs in a little junction station on the way back to Sarajevo.

"For an hour the station cat lay sleeping on the box that held the fate of Europe.

"During this hour Danilo started for Switzerland, but felt himself drawn back by Gabriel's iron will. He turned, and brought the bombs to his home in Sarajevo.

"Danilo hid the bombs under his bed and went out to look for Gabriel. He found Gabriel at Bogdan's grave.

"While he was out, Danilo's mother found the box of bombs under the bed. She knew what they were for, and that her son must die for his part in the plot. She fell across the box in a faint.

"In the days that followed, every time that Danilo's mother, with her peasant thoroughness, swept beneath the bed, she wept anew.

"In another bed, Ferdinand tossed and dreamt of his Bosnian throne.

IX

"The plans were laid, the conspirators rehearsed, the Day of Vengeance nearly at hand.

"On the eve of Sarajevo, Ferdinand, his court and army were just outside of town at Ilidza Springs, preparing to enter the capital, hoping for the disorder that would be the pretext for war.

"The conspirators had hidden the bombs at Semes' café, near the bridgehead in town. All of them liked Semes and it was decided to clear him of any conspiracy. So tonight they staged a row over the bill. After a convincing scuffle, Semes kicked them all out.

"A few hours to go. Danilo and Grabezh, together with two schoolboys and a Turk who had been introduced into the plot, spent what they thought would be their last night on earth in the cafés with their girls. There was some drinking.

"Gabriel had gone to the suburb of Ilidza Springs to get a look at the Archduke, to be certain that he would know his man on the morrow. After a close look he went to the cemetery and slept on the grave of his hero for the last time.

"Morning. Danilo posted the conspirators in the proposed line of march. Each was given his bomb or revolver and flask of prussic acid.

"Feeling that the new recruits, two of them schoolboys, would do nothing, Danilo and Gabriel posted them first in the line. Gabriel chose the bridge the Archduke must pass.

"The long parade began, led by two open cars. The first contained Ferdinand and Sophie and the hated military governor of Bosnia. It wound its way through a press of defiant school children, a sea of Turkish fezzes and veiled women. At all the cafés in the line of march, orchestras came to the sidewalks and played treasonable Bosnian airs.

"The Archduke was irritated and launched a tirade at the Governor. They were approaching the bridge now.

"They passed the first conspirator, poised with his bomb. As Gabriel had foreseen, he was too terrified to throw it.

"On past the two schoolboys, whose knees began to buckle. They, too, were afraid. One ran away.

"A few feet from the bridge, Chabrinovitch was standing, white as death. The Archduke saw him and cried out. Chabrinovitch, the suspected son of the spy, threw his bomb. It sailed over the Archduke's head and exploded among the spectators on the further side of the car, killing several.

"There was panic. Chabrinovitch hurled himself through the stunned spectators and jumped over the little parapet into the river. Soldiers and policemen leaped the parapet after Chabrinovitch, landing on top of him in the shallow stream as he tried to swallow the prussic acid. He was beaten into insensibility.

"The Archduke was the coolest in the ensuing riot. He cried an order to his chauffeur and the car plunged through the crowd, Ferdinand holding Sophie close. She was his one concern from the moment of the explosion. He tried to calm her as the car raced on, telling her the dogs had missed.

"Gabriel and Grabezh had heard the explosion and thought the bomb had found its mark. While they pushed through the crowd to throw theirs, too, the royal car shot past. The boys looked after it in a daze. Their chance was gone.

"The Archduke pulled up at the town hall, where a reception was waiting. He tore into the Governor and local dignitaries for the criminal attack, and warned that his troops would march tomorrow.

"In the midst of his tirade he was told his favorite aide had been wounded by the bomb. Leaving the town hall, he drove to the hospital to see him.

"And here is the strangest part of the whole story: To reach the hospital the Archduke's car should have taken the road that ran parallel to the river. Instead, the German driver, stupidly adhering to instructions for the original line of march, made a right turn into the town from the bridge-head.

"The angry Archduke screamed that he was a blockhead. The driver braked the 1914 concrete mixer to a halt in the middle of a milling crowd of panic-stricken flower girls, peasants, etc., just a few feet away from Semes' café, in which Gabriel was bitterly bewailing his lost chance to rid his country of its oppressor. Semes was giving him coffee and trying to dissuade him from suicide.

"And then the door opened and his loved Dragitsa came in with the basket of Flowers of Vengeance she had been giving to the young Bosnian patriots outside.

She brought the news that the Archduke's car was stalled outside the door.

"Gabriel rushed out, pistol in hand. Dragitsa thrust a Flower of Vengeance in his coat. He kissed her quickly good-by—their first and last kiss—and was in the street.

"The Archduke was still tirading against the slow-witted chauffeur. The Governor stood on the running board of the car, clearing the crowd with his sword. And Gabriel was twenty feet away.

"The Archduke had risen in the car. Gabriel fired into his heart. Sophie sprang up as Gabriel fired again—this time at the Governor. But she had risen in the line of fire and the second bullet found her heart, too. Her arms still around Ferdinand, they collapsed together on the seat of the car.

"Never dreaming that she had been hit, Ferdinand kissed her and moaned: 'Sophie, Sophie, live for our children.' And she supposed she had died to save him. So the romance between the actress Sophie and the Archduke was over. (The social gulf between them widened still further in death. Ferdinand had the burial of a king. Sophie's casket followed after, on it a pair of gloves, a symbol of a lady-in-waiting.)

"After the shots, there was wild confusion. Soldiers and police rushed at Gabriel, who was trying to swallow the prussic acid. Bosnians, including Dragitsa, tried to rescue him in vain.

"So many people were hitting him and holding his arms that the poison went streaming down his face. His ribs were broken from the kicks.

"A soldier kicked him in the stomach and the bomb fell from his belt. Gendarmes and the crowd scattered as Gabriel kicked it into their midst. It exploded without much damage, giving Gabriel a chance to recover his revolver, and with his last remaining strength, to put it to his head. But this, too, failed as someone rushed in and knocked the weapon away. He was beaten into unconsciousness and taken away.

x

"Gabriel was chained to a post in the Sarajevo barracks and tortured for the names of his companions. They tied him from a beam so that his toes barely touched the floor. He refused to say a word. The plot was his—and his alone.

"Search was started for his known friends.

"It remained for their old leader Danilo to spill the beans. Confronted with the prospect of torture he told everything, even the route of the underground. The Austrians seized everyone implicated—many of them were innocent—and hangings were held by the dozen.

"The boys would have been hanged, too, but the Austrian high command felt it politically necessary to stage a trial that would establish Bosnia as the organizer of the plot, and thus justify the Austrian invasion. The trial was held.

"Danilo was sentenced to hang, but was cruelly kept alive for a year before his execution.

"Gabriel, Chabrinovitch and Grabezh—all being under twenty—were sentenced to twenty years' imprisonment. The Austrians openly predicted all would die in jail. All did, within four years, of tuberculosis contracted in the wet dungeons of military prisons, chained to the walls, and overrun with rats. Gabriel was the last to die.

"There was much drama in the last three years of his life. Through a system of tapping, he learned, even in solitary, the tremendous consequences of his act. Every day the oppressors of his country had a new nation to fight, Serbia, Montenegro, Russia, England, Italy and France, and, finally, America.

"Often his jailor came to his dungeon to jeer news of Allied defeats. But his spirit remained unbroken. Chained to a wall, knee deep in slime, he could still hear the guns, and knew that his country was being freed—that his great aim had been won.

"His arm rotted off with tuberculosis. A friendly Slav amputated it. His only anesthesia was the whispered news of Allied victories.

"They chained him up again when his arm began to heal. He managed to cut these words on the wall of his dungeon with the empty shackle:

" 'Our spirits will haunt the palaces of the Earth, terrifying kings.'

"But nothing could live in that dungeon. And one night in April, 1918, a little more than six months before the war came to an end, he died.

"They buried him as they had buried Bogdan—scraping the nameless grave level with the prison yard. But when the war was won there was a search. His body was identified by the missing arm, and now rests beside the others in a common marble tomb—the most impressive monument in the Balkans.

"Early in the war, statues of Ferdinand and Sophie were erected at the little bridgehead at which they were slain. When Gabriel's body came home, these were pulled down, and his name raised there instead.

"THE END"

L'ENVOI

Tell me, Charlie, who was "the boy Jesus," Gavrilo Princip? And who were his three musketeers who formed a brotherhood of vengeance to slay the tyrant who was depriving them of liberty?

And who was the tyrant, Archduke Ferdinand, who "tiraded" and "tiraded," and was slain in the midst of a last tirade?

Another War

MEN of all sorts whose age had earned them an easy chair threw themselves into the second war against the Germans. Most of them were impassioned disciples of democracy, and eager to knock out the new German philosophy of winner take all.

This idea of a People's State in which the people have no rights—a sort of paradise for winning politicians only—stirred as much fury in our republic as it does today regarding Russia. It was an easy war for a humanist to take sides in, it being essentially a war on behalf of good manners. The torture and mass murders practiced by the Germans might strengthen a political state, but they lessened the human soul.

Charlie's attitude toward the war from its start was that of a soldier, however, and not an idle philosopher. He never fumed against the Germans, but he couldn't rest until he had joined the army that was going to pulverize them.

Before the U.S. joined the war, Charlie and I worked together on propaganda pageants.

Fun to Be Free, in Madison Square Garden, was one of them. We wrote it. Billy Rose put it on. It made a big pro-war bang. We were in the front propaganda lines.

This was a satisfying enough position for patriots hitting fifty. But for Charlie, propaganda was a side-line exercise. The virtues of democracy and the sins of the Nazis were in his head. But the battle of ideas was less for him, still, than the thrill of action.

MacArthur was too old and in no physical condition to serve as a private soldier. He swallowed his pride (and his memories of youth) and accepted the commission of major.

"I had to," he apologized, "to get into the war."

A major couldn't go about deriding officers and playing jokes with lusty young men. But there was other fun. He could travel more, see more, and liquor was of easier access.

Charlie scooted around the world as if he had entered a steeplechase. He was courier, escort and military observer. General Porter, of the U.S. Chemical War Service, was his Walter Howey.

Charlie's "happiness" as an officer in the war is in the letters he wrote home to Helen and Mary. They are the letters of a man on a spree. There's no mention in them of his trips to the hospital as an ulcer patient, or of the physical collapses that followed drinking bouts in Europe and in Africa. Correspondents and fellow officers brought back wide-eyed reports of the major's (later colonel's) high-di-ho on the battlefronts. They brought back stories, also, of his remarkable stamina and high morale. A battlefront with MacArthur on it was a cheerful place.

The fact that his prowess as a drinker became a military anecdote annoyed Charlie. Mankiewicz had it that Charlie was the Chemical War Service's chief weapon. They were going to fly over Berlin, said Manky, holding Charlie head-down by the heels, and let him breathe on the city.

There was a morsel of truth in Herman's slander. Charlie hitchhiked on several air raids over Berlin. He dropped empty whiskey bottles on the capital.

Throughout the war, however, he scowled at any reference to his ill health or drinking. His only complaint in his letters is of what he called "the whispering campaign" against him. He wrote, righteously, that it was getting almost as big as the whispering campaign against Roosevelt. His sense of guilt toward his drinking was as strong as if he were still under the eyes of the deacons in the Missionary Academy in Nyack.

Although he consumed a river of Scotch in his life, nothing could wrest from him the admission that he was a drinking man.

Charlie's letters from the front complete the story begun on the Mexican border in 1914 with Colonel Foreman's Dog and Pony Show. War was a place for wild frolic, and a happy vacation from inner problems. The noise of battle was soothing to inner tensions. And it was the place where his old pal Death wore his most glamorous suit.

No bullets hit Charlie, but he came out of the war with a grin and battered elderly insides.

Charlie Letters

He wrote to Helen from Claridge's in London.

"Darling,

"As the letter head suggests, we've been roughing it so far. There has been an alert and for the last half hour I've been hanging from the window looking into a soft moonlit sky and wishing you were here. Evidently no bombs are going to fall and I feel like a louse for even looking for excitement. Up above are blinker lights from friendly aircraft while taxis wheel like sedate beetles down below. I've had a wonderful time with a lot of people—Juliet Duff, Bea [Lillie]. I introduced her to Clark Gable and I think something ignited. I've seen Buzz Meredith, Johnnie McClain, Rupert Bellville (with whom I flew to Berlin years ago). Who else do you want to hear about? I've seen Adele Astaire, Edie Baker, millions of generals, Adolphe Menjou, who is in top form, and tomorrow I hope to see Jean Throckmorton and Venetia Montagu. Then, as far as I'm concerned, we can pass on to our next station. This place is like '21' with Mack Kriendler buzzing about. I've also run into Sam Spewack, Ben Goetz and even John Marquand within fifteen minutes the other day. Beazie [Bea] is wonderful, and the pride of my sex is Clark, who continues on the long daylight raids despite pressure and is quite larkish about it—nothing about himself—all he wants to talk about is what the waist gunner in 'The Witch's Tit' said to the pilot as they passed over some really terrific anti-aircraft fire the other day. He yelled over the inter phone: 'Put your wheels down, Colonel. We can land on this stuff.' What morale!

"Bea said only one thing about Bobby [her son]. She took me aside at a party and whispered, 'I don't talk about it, but I know he's gone. Mother thinks he isn't, so keep her happy.' Who else have I seen? Pat Wallace (Edgar's daughter, remember?) and millions besides. I'd trade them all for one look at you. I miss my chickabiddies and it makes me happy to think that every mile from now on will bring me nearer—or at least every day will. I'm sorry to be having so much fun. There's some serious stuff I haven't missed that I can tell you about when I get home.

"There goes the all clear, as we used to say about the dinner bell. Good night, darling. Kiss Mary and Jamie and give my love to Ned.

"CHARLIE"

The following was written on the stationery of "Headquarters, European Theatre of Operations, United States Army":

"Darlings,

"This is the first chance I've had to sit down in four days. Gen. Porter takes his wars seriously. We've been running around like coach dogs and everything is very exciting. We had a rather lousy trip over, having to put in here and there because of weather. And then something went wrong with the heating system on the plane, with the result that we arrived somewhat parboiled. We're not in town much and yet I've managed to see quite a few people for ten-minute intervals. Bea is wonderful. So is Bobby and Jean and Ernest [Byfield]. The other Ernest [Hemingway] bumped into something during a recent blackout and is badly off indeed. Only his beard saved his life, I'm told. . . . I've also seen very briefly Charlie Baskerville, Adele Astaire, Edie Baker, Jere Knight, Alfred and Lynn [Lunt], Bob Sherwood and others, all of whom sent their love. . . . I miss you all with everything I've got.

"Love, love, love,
"Charlie"

A communiqué from battle reads:

"September 1st

"Darling,

"We've come from Greenland's icy mountains to India's coral strands, in the words of the old hymn, and the end is not yet. I can't tell you where we are, of course, but I think the censor won't mind my saying that en route here we paused for gas near the Taj Mahal and dropped over for a visit. It's an exquisite thing, quite worthy of the legend (which you will find in my guide book on India). The priests howled prayers that echoed forever from the lovely dome, then blessed us and bestowed a love flower, which I enclose. Treat it with care. It cost five rupees, along with the sandals I had to wear over my shoes. Despite war, India comes up to expectations, all jasmine and poverty, purple and rags, with the scent of sandalwood everywhere. They're nearing the end of the monsoon and warm rain falls most of the day, but flowers bloom everywhere, even from behind the ears of little children. Pony

213

carts spank along, stopping only for the sacred Brahma cows, and turbans glow with all the colors of the rainbow. The air is heavy and sweet and damp, with insects by the trillions, cigarettes, clothing, food all slightly mildewed, but who the hell cares? They tell me it's wonderful in a month or two. . . .

"I'm going at a terrific clip, countries like Egypt and Persia and Iraq flying beneath us like so many railway ties, but it may be slower from now on. . . . I am very well, and if I thought you were all happy, I'd be happy, too. I played poker last night with a bunch of fliers and two chaplains and lost about $25 worth of rupees. I saw Quentin Reynolds, Jack Belden, H. R. Knickerbocker, John Steinbeck, Reynolds Packer, a little enemy action, and my last quart of Scotch go into St. Clair McKelway, and expect soon to say hello to your old pal and well wisher, Brooks Atkinson. Any messages? I'm wearing shorts and long stockings, looking damned British. Once more, all the love this soggy paper can hold.

"CHARLIE"

Charlie's letter about the Invasion reads:

"DARLING,

"This is the first time I've been able to sit down and write you, and even now I can't say much. So much will have to wait until we get home. The invasion was even more exciting than it read. For a few days before it was a little like that other battle of the century, when Tunney met Dempsey for the second time in Chicago. More and more important people kept drifting in, the kind who at home know the right scalpers. The only big shot missing was Swope. In the period when they clamped down on the mail, Porter and I were motoring hundreds of miles a day, inspecting the mortar crews who were locked up along the Coast. Some of them had been cooped up for days waiting for the kickoff. They were all in good heart. All England was in bloom, great banks of rhododendron, some of it red as any rose, lilacs, lupin in every shade and miles of wood, teaming with tanks, cannon, landing barges and the like, and more men than you thought were in the world. They moved like ants. Before the Main Event and while mail was still taboo, we had a day with Jean and Bobby in their week-end place in Surrey. It was very pleasant and all spoke lovingly of you. I whacked my head several times on their 15th Century door frames. The next time I go there I'm taking my tin hat. We spent the morning of The Day with General Patton. The day following I was at Whyte's Club with Rupert Bellville. One hoity toity member stalked in and demanded his mid-day paper. Told there was no newspaper, he began to remonstrate, then reflected and said: 'Ah, of course! The racing at Newmarket!' Other members gathered patriotically about the news bulletins as they were posted on the board, then edged over one by one to follow the racing returns. The editorials in the next day's papers explained this attitude, saying that the Invasion was too big, too deep for any Wordsworthian tears. We've visited a lot of air bases and spent a very pleasant afternoon with Jimmy Doolittle. I'm in the best of health and spirits. Life is very exciting and I love you."

Odyssey

This letter to Helen was written in the Carlton Hotel, Washington, in December, 1943.

"Angel,

"It's 5:30 a.m. and I've given up the idea of sleep so I might as well be writing you a letter. I've been alternately reading bad plays and thinking pleasantly of you and wishing you were here in my arms. I've been remembering so many things from our buggy ride to Fraunces Tavern on down the years— all my boobish love antics return to entertain me. I run upstairs in East 40th Street with you in my arms (I believe I could do it still without getting too much out of breath) and I see you coming down Madison Avenue in a little gray suit with a green orchid I sent you on your shoulder or wearing that awful Empire dress I brought you from Paris or that pretty postillion coat or standing on the dock when the Belgenland hove to when you told the newspaper boys we were engaged and I got slapped with Miss Frink's summons at the baggage pile. And the first time I ever kissed you in a cab and how you lied ever after when you said you didn't lean toward me first. And sitting up with you in Childs and going over the brow of yon hills in France and the fight about Molnar's picture and the swing at Syosset and the open fire at Otto Kahn's. And the Victrola I bought you for your birthday and the way your stomach felt at the Santa Barbara Biltmore when the embryo Mary was only a few weeks old, and how I rubbed your stomach later with cocoa butter and got my face slapped for further familiarities and how I nearly abandoned you on the street (or said I would abandon you) when you told me the waterbag might burst on the way to the hospital. And how I used to chase you around with a Leica whenever I caught you with your clothes off, and the time you posed with hat and fan. 536 Madison, with you frightening me stiff by telling me you were going to stay the night. The bed at 15 Park we were never going to sell. The time you got tight and gambled and were so gay at Barney Glazer's, and picking out the hat for Madelon Claudet and my horror the first time I went back and saw an old belle of mine in a bustle after a performance of Victoria. And my boobish names for. . . . And now I'll go to work. Don't worry about me. I hope I always have this particular form of insomnia. Thank you for a very pleasant night, my dearest, only love.

"All this is so little of my happiness,

"CHARLIE"

Mary

In September, 1949, Charlie was in the Lenox Hill Hospital in New York. His recurrent ulcer troubles were being treated. Helen and Mary were playing together in the tryout of a play, *Good Housekeeping*. Mary caught a cold in Westport and felt tired. Helen sent her home to Nyack. Feeling worse a few days later, Mary joined her father in the Lenox Hill Hospital. *Good Housekeeping* and Helen went on to play in Bucks County.

Two days later Charlie called Helen and told her he thought Mary was seriously sick. Helen closed the show and came to New York.

Polio symptoms appeared. Mary was put in an iron lung.

Charlie and Helen sat watching her for two days. She looked at Charlie and said, "Help me, Pops." On the third day Mary died.

She was buried on the Nyack Hill. A year after her burial Charlie had an inscription chiseled on her gravestone:

Here beneath this stone doth lie
As much beauty as could die.

The Fire That Wouldn't Go Out

Troubles came to Charlie in his fifties, troubles that didn't leave with the morning. One of the troubles was age—the aging that takes us slowly off the main roads. Age was a surprise to Charlie. Growing old to him was like losing a leg.

Most of us grow old without too much protest. We stop dreaming, we expect less and less. We cut ourselves down to fit our smaller years—and people's smaller opinions of us. They've heard our stories, and there's no mystery left to us. We've become what we were going to be, and there's nothing more to watch for. The new ones are on hand. Most of us accept all these insults with a biologic shrug. We're ready for the white hair, et cetera. Age, then, is no disease for us but a sort of mild boredom from which we eventually die.

At fifty and fifty-five, Charlie looked on age exactly as he had when he was twenty. It was not for him.

Age wasn't the only trouble; it was the one on top, the one you could see. Were I writing fiction I would catalogue all the dark urges in such a character—as I have sometimes done. But of reality I know as little as the doctors who attend it in its troubles. Looking at Charlie's last years I can only generalize—the smiling spectator became a horseshoe on an anvil.

All the things we are come to the Halloween of middle age. The ghosts of childhood attend and hobble around us on their crucifixes. The guilts we've kept in the closet come out, swinging nooses at us. And there's a Pierrot who does *entrechats* while tears run down a face that was once ours. It's quite a party. When it gets too noisy, you send for the doctor or buy another drink.

In his last years Charlie had doctors attending him, and he drank. The doctors were new. In fact, liquor since his youth had been his only doctor.

In his younger time when his dolors and mysteries became too annoying he used to hit them on the head with a bottle. And he would wake in the morning smiling like a man rid of a toothache. He drank, also, because there was fun in liquor. It was fuel for the mystic time machine in which Charlie liked to travel. Liquor was medicine and magic—in the beginning. But it was medicine only for the soul; it wasn't that for the tissues.

Charlie's old friends began to ask, What's happened to

Charlie? Some asked it with concern, some with a sneer. People find a foolish satisfaction in seeing their betters take a tumble.

Except that Charlie didn't come tumbling down. A man of courage never deserts himself. My friend had courage. What happened to Charlie was that he was a sick man pretending he was well. This stubbornness confused the medicos who came to cure him. He refused to look on either disease or drinking as a matter of importance. They had been unimportant in his youth, and he would give them no other standing. Like Job's faith in God, Charlie's devotion to youth stayed intact in his wilderness.

It was a considerable wilderness, but it was no new locale for Charlie. He had always lived in it—with the aid of his medicine, his strength and his wit. When he aged, the first two of these aids failed him.

In his last year Charlie holed up, much of the time, in his New York East River apartment. He had bought the place, and an apartment above it, before his marriage to Helen. Here the young MacArthur and the young Helen gave their New York parties, and here they camped merrily when Nyack was snowed in. After Mary died, the MacArthurs gave up the second apartment.

The sick man on the East River was taken again and again to the hospital. Various doctors began various treatments for a variety of diseases. The treatments were seldom concluded. As soon as Charlie was able to put his pants on by himself, he was out of the hospital, joking and unregenerate. He scorned the medicos as an innocent man might scorn the police for false arrest. He scorned the manners, tones and identity of the invalid. He preferred to remain in others' eyes "that bad boy Charlie" rather than become that dying man MacArthur.

During his score of illnesses and his stubborn indifference to them, Charlie kept his eyes glued on the world his feet had left—the world that went on without him. He kept track of all the events, and of the people in them—most of whom he knew. It was amazing the people Charlie knew, the people he had feasted, worked and adventured with. They were in all the countries.

Occasionally, Charlie emerged and flew the seas again. He dropped in on old faraway haunts. He sat grinning and half stricken at café tables, and cronies joined him, and the talk was of "Do you remember when . . . ?"

One of his last travels was as chaperon for Mary and two of her *jeune fille* schoolmates. He escorted them on a grand tour of Europe. He was deep in his own wilderness in this time. He tried to drink himself out of it. He made an odd chaperon, but a successful one. Mary remained devotedly at his side, and her friends with her. And they saw Charlie's Europe—all the battlements and barrooms.

New faces came around Charlie in his fifties, chiefly young ones. They had never known the MacArthur of the glittering days. But in his East River apartment, this Charlie was still to be heard and seen. He told his exuberant tales again. But he told them now chiefly for his own ears. The past imprisoned him. It was as alive for him as a skyrocket display.

It was in his words that life had always had for him its real home. The words were still in his noggin. There was no age on them. They were sharp, nimble and full of odd cunning. They offered unexpected wisdom and kept the story of life undaunted going.

He talked on, and wrote. With his fingers swollen to the size of bananas, with ulcers and kidney poisons bedeviling him, and with the Halloween mysteries clamoring in his guts, Charlie kept at his appointed task of writing. He wrote under any and all handicaps.

He worked alone, and with various collaborators. Among these were Nunnally Johnson, Ludwig Bemelmans, Anita Loos and I.

Nunnally was one of Charlie's favorites—a sort of Benchley with a Georgia drawl. They shared a distaste for the shams and pomp of adulthood—and were loyal knights of the bottle.

"I saw Charlie from time to time back in the twenties," said Nunnally, "but it wasn't until 1939 that he and I began to hang around together. We left a party to go to a saloon, where you don't have to wait for the host to give you another drink, and in the course of a couple of days we decided to work on a play of his suggestion. It was about Jack Barrymore and his daughter, Diana. We based it on Charlie's story about the time Barrymore, after fifteen years of never remembering he had a daughter, decided to look into her welfare.

"This anecdote resulted in the longest and most fruitless collaboration in the history of American letters. Charlie and I wrote and rewrote and consulted, mainly in saloons, for a year or so, until my money gave out and I had to return to Hollywood. But it was worth all the waste of time and health to come to know him as well as I did."

Until the day he went to the hospital to die, Charlie worked on his last play. He worked slowly. His fingers drooped on the typewriter keys. But he kept on. If he couldn't run, he walked; if he couldn't walk, he crawled. And if he couldn't crawl, he tapped out messages, like his hero, Gavrilo Princip.

I like to remember of my friend in this time his indifference to affliction, his lighthouse grin of youth. Collapse was on him, yet how often we saw him unchanged—still a wise onlooker with a smile. How often we heard the bright words of life from this friend of life.

The thing about Charlie's last years that made them different from Barrymore's—and King Lear's—was the woman he had taken to him in the happy summer of Syosset. Her fame was world-wide, now. Causes, politics and the arts bombarded Helen Hayes. And her heart, like Charlie's, had been cut in half by Mary's death. Helen worked on, like a carthorse pulling uphill.

But her life centered around Charlie. It never moved a thought away. His troubles never hid him from her. He was always the lover, the man of wisdom and wit, the troubadour, the chevalier—the unchanged, superior one.

To the end of his days, she held his name high in the world, and in her heart.

A Nice Day

On an April afternoon there's no better place to walk than Fifth Avenue, from Forty-fourth to the Park. Young men on their way to a rendezvous like to walk on Fifth Avenue to get in the mood. Elderly fellows going nowhere favor it for other reasons.

In 1956 I was back from six months of picture-making in London, and I walked with MacArthur up the avenue after lunch. He walked slowly and used a heavy cane. There was a shake in his leg. A black patch was over one cataracted eye. His body was bloated and his face looked gray and clawed. The one visible eye was an impostor. No smile was in it. Nevertheless, my friend was intact. The MacArthur voice was there, and the memorable vocabulary.

The sun was warm on the wide sidewalk. The plate-glass store windows were bright and speckless; their displays costly and artistic.

We were among the slower of the window shoppers. I didn't know Charlie was going to be dead in two weeks, that he was winding up his walks in the streets of the world.

We walked in silence. Schoolgirls with pony tails and big feet passed us. Ballet girls with fine calves and unpainted faces; slick, middle-aged matrons with small beauty left, but large charge accounts; carroty-haired crones in lumpy get-ups; bare-headed pansies trying to look like musicians or philosophers; and neatly dressed males who might have been financiers or office menials—all paraded by.

Charlie's one eye gave them a glance. A barouche with a smiling couple in it clopped by. He looked at that, too.

We were in front of a lingerie window. Charlie studied a frothy negligee decorated with bright streamers.

"I think I'll buy that for Helen," he said.

"It's kind of young," I said.

He had a tired grin. "Yes, I guess she's grown up."

"When are you going to have that eye operation?" I asked.

"No use rushing it," said Charlie. "See anybody in London?"

"Enemies," I said.

"Your own damn fault," said Charlie. I agreed.

"It's a nice day." Charlie stopped and leaned on his heavy cane. "I've been in and out of hospitals like a jack rabbit." I remembered his troubled years. The troubles had always seemed unreal, as if he were half pretending them. Morning would come and the troubles would be gone, as in the brave days. Morning came, and the troubles clung.

"Helen's remodeling Nyack," said Charlie. "Tearing the whole place apart. She's moving my bedroom downstairs. A goddamn waste of money."

"Why?" I asked.

He didn't answer, and the sun felt colder around me.

"I've got a kinescope of Jim's television show that you didn't see," he said. "I'd like you to look at it."

"Glad to," I said.

"Helen's involved in her usual mess of projects," Charlie said after a while. "She hasn't enough sense to say no. She'd do a tap dance in Madison Square Garden, if somebody insisted."

"What are you up to?"

"Finishing a play with Anita Loos," Charlie said. He grinned slightly. "Look at that old belle. Know who she is?" I didn't. A wrinkled, painted face, a dashing suit on wizened legs passed.

"She didn't recognize me," said Charlie.

"Are you getting tired?" I asked.

"No, I'm fine," he said. "Pretty flossy, eh—walking with a cane."

He smiled at the heavy stick.

"Helen bought it for me at the Flea Market in Paris," he said. "I couldn't refuse it."

"I met a lot of people in Paris who asked after you," I said.

Charlie nodded.

"Did I ever tell you about the time—" He stopped. He didn't want to talk about the past. It was in him like a carnival. He moved with it slowly up the avenue in silence. I noticed his large hand on the cane. The fingers were white.

"Did you call up Herbie Swope?" he asked. "He tried to help you in London, you know. He wrote a lot of letters. So did I."

"I know," I said.

His shadowed face stared at a passer-by.

"A pretty girl," he said. The pretty girl walked by without a glance for him. We crossed Fifty-seventh Street.

"I think I'll take a taxi." Charlie stopped.

We rode to his apartment at 25 East End Avenue. He was silent most of the way.

"I'm getting fat," he said, "because I have to drink that damn milk for my ulcer."

I didn't know he was lying, and that the "fat" was the bloat of poisons.

In the apartment he busied himself looking for something. He handed me a bottle of pills.

"Supposed to cheer you up," he said. "Those damn quacks and their discoveries. Keep 'em."

A wave of memories filled me. I remembered a thousand things all at once about Charlie. There was a party in this room twenty-five years ago, with dressed-up people beaming—

Charlie was poking in a clothes closet. He bent over with difficulty and picked up two film cans.

"How was the food in Paris?" he asked.

"Wonderful," I told him.

"I remember a place," he said, and stopped.

"When are you coming out to Nyack?" I asked.

"I'm staying right here," he answered firmly.

There was a bold look in his eye. I knew suddenly that this was the way a man like MacArthur said good-by—without words or comment; with his thousand and one memories locked proudly away; his voice and his phrases sharp and without hints. He was standing inside his silence as inside a mansion with many rooms.

"Here, take them along and look at them," he said. He handed me the two reels of film of Jim MacArthur's debut as an actor. "He's damn good."

That was the last I heard or saw of Charlie in the world.

Midnight Conference

MY Nyack room looks on the Hudson, now that the leaves are down and the view is clearer. A December moon makes the night shine like a knife. A New York Central train heading north sends a rumble across the three miles of spectral river.

In this room Charlie and I wrote plays and movies and spent most of our friendship. He used to lean out of the window on a summer day and whistle, and pop in with a plot turn plucked, apparently, off the maple in front. In winter he used to busy himself with the fireplace, as if he were a handyman rather than a collaborator. Occasionally he would nab a book from my shelves, but, since it was usually one I had written, I felt more flattered than robbed. He used to—

"Hello, Charlie, I was expecting you. You're late."

"I was tied up. How are you, Bennie?"

"Exhausted with this damn book about you."

HIMSELF

I figured you could use a little help.

ME

Too late. I'm on the finish.

HIMSELF

You're out of your head. Twenty more years. Are you going to stick them in a barrel?

225

ME

You surprise me, Angus. You used to be indifferent to publicity.

HIMSELF

People change.

ME

I know; I took a look in your casket.

HIMSELF

You won't look any prettier.

ME

Fowler says when he dies he's going to stay on the ball like a good reporter and get the story back to some editor about what goes on afterward—who's there, and all that. Care to say something on that subject?

HIMSELF

It would freeze your Israelite gizzard. I was talking to Ernie Byfield and Irving Thalberg—

ME

There are Jews up there, eh?

HIMSELF

God isn't interested in a man's religion. You ought to know that. Ernie had a story about—

ME

I'm way past Ernie. Why do you want more copy? You were always kind of modest, usually doing a back bend out of the limelight.

HIMSELF

It's different afterward. You stay warm a little while if people love you and talk about you. The wind keeps blowing and the flowers smelling awhile longer.

ME

I'll keep going.

HIMSELF

Why don't you write about Noel Coward—the time he almost drowned in the tank when we were shooting *The Scoundrel?* Because he was too artistic to let us use a dummy of him as a dead man in the water.

ME

I never cared too much for Coward. Vaudeville patter with an English accent. And a superiority complex that went over big with sofa-cushion menders.

HIMSELF

Always the schoolteacher, giving out marks.

ME

They gave 'em out to us, for God's sake, red hot on the shoulder.

HIMSELF

We're not in the branding business, Bennie.

ME

I've got some more stuff about critics I'd like to stick in.

HIMSELF

Not in my book. You wrote a book about yourself ten thousand pages long. I had to hire a little boy to hold it while I skimmed through it. Let's not make *that* mistake here. And let's not waste any more space on your Professor Boomler psychology. There were things—much better things—

ME

For instance?

HIMSELF

Wonderful things.

ME

The fire's going fine. You don't have to keep poking it.

HIMSELF

Coward's little day on Golgotha. When his play *Point Valaine* flopped, and the critics denounced him for having fouled the American theater, and wrecked the careers of Lynn and Alfred Lunt. And we were worried about his showing up for the day's shooting in snowbound Astoria. He was in the make-up chair, bright and chipper, when we got to the studio. He worked all day with George Jean Nathan, the worst of the hatchet men, a visitor on the set and grinning at him. He did the brightest piece of acting in the movie that day without muffing a line.

ME

Pardon me for criticizing Noel.

HIMSELF

That reminds me—what's the idea of attacking Wooll-cott? I was fond of Alec.

ME

I'm not writing a book of valentines—although I've been pretty complimentary about you.

HIMSELF

You didn't give yourself the worst of it in your own book. Remember the time we went to Mr. Hearst's masquerade party dressed up as hanged men, with ropes around our necks. And giving the girls those ankle bracelets with my favorite inscription: "Heaven is above." And the four-handed baseball game for a dollar a run when we let Billy Rose score nineteen runs in succession until he keeled over in the hot sun. And aren't you going to write about *Wuthering Heights*—how we wrote the movie in eight days on Woollcott's island in Vermont?

ME

All I remember was he was horrified at the thought of our insensitive hooligan touch ruining the world's most delicate love story. You've got to admit he was an Igorot where literature was concerned.

HIMSELF

What a bumblehead you are. Brainy Bowers—the point forgetter. We wrote ten pages of a dummy script for Alec to find when he started snooping. We dramatized a line in the book that said Heathcliff spent a year among the Indians of the New World. We wrote it in "Ugh, ugh, heap big pow-wow dialogue between Heathcliff and Chief Crooked Head." Woollcott wouldn't speak to us for three days.

ME

Leave the fire alone, will you? You'll fall in.

HIMSELF

You forget. Fire doesn't burn any more. Wind doesn't blow.

ME

What are you grinning about?

HIMSELF

I remember the whorehouse in Mexico City—the Casa Marina.

ME

Somebody told you it was the most beautiful brothel in the world.

HIMSELF

The venereal "Taj Mahal." We left Rosie at the hotel and drove out.

ME

I remember a butler in tails and white tie whom you cleverly called "Jeeves" admitted us into a huge ballroom. And you recognized the two-hundred-pound red-headed madam who greeted us as Chicago Kate.

HIMSELF

A lie. *You* recognized her.

ME

I'd seen her in a police court in her younger days. It's possible.

HIMSELF

Good footwork.

ME

You ordered wine for everybody in the place.

HIMSELF

And a nine-piece orchestra from a neighboring café. A half dozen *señores* came out of the princely bedrooms with their ladies. Your pal Chicago Kate opened a few cases of wine. And dancing and yodeling started.

ME

I remember around midnight I inquired if you had enough money on you to pay for your magnificent entertainment . . . and reminded you I was there as your guest.

HIMSELF

You daffy crook, you robbed me blind on that trip.

ME

You had the usual seven pesos on you, and I called up Rosie and asked her please to bring a thousand pesos out in a satchel, quick.

HIMSELF

What a night! A half hour later the place was raided by a platoon of *federalistas*, on account of music and liquor were forbidden in any Mexican whorehouse. I guess they figured they might discourage gypping by keeping it depressing. We were all lined up against the rear wall of the ballroom by the gun-waving *soldados* when Rosie arrived with the money. Jeeves wouldn't let her in. She started yelling, "My husband's in there! He sent for me!" This statement left Jeeves nonplused and I warned you if she got in they would cart her off with the whores to jail for a venereal examination!

ME

And you said, "Let's mosey."

HIMSELF

We walked across the room chatting to each other about the New York Giants.

ME

We were past the soldiers, four feet from the door, when you said, "Wait a minute." And you started back across the ballroom to retrieve your goddamn two-dollar hat.

HIMSELF

And the time Lederer and I went to the theatre. We sat in the front row. Helen and his girl sat behind us. Lederer hung his socks over the bass drum to dry. Then he bit the orchid off the woman sitting next to him—a suburbanite. She raised a holler. When the cops were coming down the aisle, I said to Lederer, "You might as well put your hand under her dress. You're going to be thrown out anyway." And the time Lederer and I had our dinner at "21," served from the Stork Club by Stork Club waiters.

230

ME

Let Lederer write his own memoirs. He started them twenty years ago. He wrote down the title, " 'My Thoughts,' by Charles Lederer." That's as far as he got.

HIMSELF

The hell with Lederer. This is your book. You're getting all the credit for it. I'm trying to help you out.

ME

Let's skip to World War II.

HIMSELF

What a time that was!

ME

Fun, eh?

HIMSELF

A lot of people didn't enjoy it.

ME

You did.

HIMSELF

I wrote Helen from London during the blitz I was a little ashamed about the good time I was having. India, Africa, China. And I bombarded Berlin from the air with empty liquor bottles. I chaperoned some of our scientists back from India. They were bringing home a suitcase full of cholera germs to see if they could be useful in our work . . . if we started it. There was one of our scientists who figured out how to knock off the whole Nazi Wehrmacht. He wanted to drop several million dirty postal cards on Germany with a germ culture secretly attached to each one. The Germans, while studying the artwork, which the Double Dome said would be irresistible, would contract beriberi and drop dead. There was another professor who figured out if we could get fifty spies into an enemy hotel, and they synchronized their watches and flushed fifty toilets at the same moment, it would reverse the city's water pressure—and we could poison the population through all the faucets.

There's a pause. Charlie's voice comes from the window.

HIMSELF

I was a kid here. Same old Hudson I swam across once. There was skating on it in winter. And the big maples tunneling the street in summer. Seems to me, if I were writing a book, I'd never stop. Every day's worth a chapter. Look at that night, with the wind blowing—

Index

Set in Linotype Janson
Format by Robert Cheney
Manufactured by The Haddon Craftsmen, Inc.
Published by Harper & Brothers, *New York*